THE HIDDEN HISTORY OF AMERICAN FASHION

THE HIDDEN HISTORY OF AMERICAN FASHION

Rediscovering Twentieth-Century Women Designers

Edited by Nancy Deihl

Bloomsbury Academic
An imprint of Bloomsbury Publishing Plc

B L O O M S B U R Y
LONDON · OXFORD · NEW YORK · NEW DELHI · SYDNEY

Bloomsbury Academic

An imprint of Bloomsbury Publishing Plc

50 Bedford Square
London
WC1B 3DP
UK

1385 Broadway
New York
NY 10018
USA

www.bloomsbury.com

BLOOMSBURY and the Diana logo are trademarks of Bloomsbury Publishing Plc

First published 2018

© Nancy Deihl, 2018

Individual chapters © the contributors, 2018

Nancy Deihl has asserted her right under the Copyright, Designs and Patents Act, 1988,
to be identified as Editor of this work.

Library of Congress Cataloging-in-Publication Data
A catalog record for this book is available from the Library of Congress.

ISBN: HB: 978-1-3500-0104-6
        PB: 978-1-3500-0046-9
      ePub: 978-1-3500-0048-3
      ePDF: 978-1-3500-0047-6

Cover design: Adriana Brioso
Cover image: A picture of three women during modeling for The American Look, New York in 1945.
(© Nina Leen/Time Life Pictures/Getty Images)

Typeset by Integra Software Services Pvt. Ltd.
Printed and bound in India

To find out more about our authors and books visit www.bloomsbury.com. Here you will find
extracts, author interviews, details of forthcoming events and the option to sign up for our
newsletters.

CONTENTS

LIST OF FIGURES

CONTRIBUTORS

Editor

Nancy Deihl (BA, Rutgers University; MA, New York University) is Director of the Graduate Program in Costume Studies at New York University. She is coauthor, with Daniel James Cole, of *The History of Modern Fashion* (2015: Laurence King). She writes and lectures on fashion history topics, specializing in American fashion. Recent articles and chapters have appeared in *Vestoj*, *The Conversation*, and *Charles Sheeler: Fashion, Photography, and Sculptural Form* (Jensen, K., ed., Doylestown, PA: James A. Michener Art Museum, 2017).

Contributors

Annette Becker is Assistant Director of the Texas Fashion Collection in the College of Visual Arts and Design at the University of North Texas. She holds a master's degree in Art History from the University of North Texas and bachelor's degrees in Art History and English from the University of Kansas. Her current research focuses on nineteenth- and twentieth-century American fashion, material culture, and museology.

Ann W. Braaten is Assistant Professor of Practice and Curator of the Emily Reynolds Historic Costume Collection, North Dakota State University, Fargo. She earned her PhD at the University of Minnesota in Apparel Studies and researches historical and cultural aspects of dress with a focus on women in business.

April Calahan (BA, University of Kansas; MA, Fashion Institute of Technology; Professional Certificate in Appraisal Studies, New York University) is a fashion historian, writer, and art appraiser living and working in New York City. As a Special Collections Associate at the Fashion Institute of Technology, Calahan serves as the Curator of manuscript collections and designer archives. She lectures widely on the history of fashion and is the author of *Fashion Plates: 150 Years of*

Style (2015), published by Yale University Press, and the coauthor of *Fashion and The Art of Pochoir* (2015), published by Thames & Hudson.

Daniel James Cole received his BA from the University of Washington, and his MFA from NYU Tisch School of the Arts. He is coauthor, with Nancy Deihl, of *The History of Modern Fashion* (2015). His areas of expertise include dress history since 1850, religiously motivated dress, and Malaysian and Indonesian dress and textiles. Cole presents at academic conferences internationally and has published in the annual journal of the IFFTI. His 2011 paper "Heritage and Innovation: Charles Frederick Worth, John Redfern, and The Dawn of Modern Fashion" appeared in French translation in the journal *Search Mode* by Institut Français de la Mode.

Lourdes Font (BA, Middlebury College; MA, PhD, New York University) is Associate Professor in the Department of History of Art and in the MA Program in Fashion and Textile Studies at the Fashion Institute of Technology. She has also taught at the Cooper-Hewitt National Design Museum's MA Program in the History of Decorative Arts, at Parsons School of Design, and at New York University.

Shelly Foote is retired from The National Museum of American History, Smithsonian Institution. She worked in the costume collection for many years and then served as Assistant Chair of the Division of Social History. She received her BA from Scripps College and her MA in American Studies from The George Washington University. Although best known for her work with nineteenth-century costume, the development of the Los Angeles fashion industry has always fascinated her. It is now the focus of her research.

Jennifer Farley Gordon is an independent researcher, writer, and curator. She holds a PhD in Apparel, Merchandising, and Design from Iowa State University and an MA in Fashion and Textile Studies: History, Theory, Museum Practice from the Fashion Institute of Technology. She formerly worked as Assistant Curator at The Museum at FIT in New York, where she curated or co-curated a number of exhibitions, including *RetroSpective*, *Fashion & Politics*, and *Eco-Fashion: Going Green*. She is the coauthor of *Sustainable Fashion: Past, Present, and Future*, published in 2015 by Bloomsbury.

Catherine Amoroso Leslie is Associate Professor and Graduate Studies Coordinator of The Fashion School at Kent State University, where she teaches, researches, and writes on the impact of practice and education in fashion, sewing, hand traditions, and their associated businesses, both past and present. Dr. Leslie published *Needlework through History: An Encyclopedia* (Greenwood Press) in

2007. Her long-term line of inquiry includes a biography of the pioneer sewing educator, businesswoman, and fashion expert Mary Brooks Picken (1886–1981).

Dilia López-Gydosh is Assistant Professor in the Department of Fashion and Apparel Studies and Curator of the Historic Costume and Textiles Collection at the University of Delaware, where she teaches courses in fashion history, dress and culture, collection management, and merchandising. Holding a doctorate from The Ohio State University, her scholarly work explores nineteenth- and twentieth-century fashion, and the historical and cultural aspects of Latino dress.

Adam MacPharlain is Curatorial Assistant of Fashion Arts and Textiles at the Cincinnati Art Museum. He has previously worked for the University of Kentucky Art Museum, Kentucky Historical Society, National Museum of Toys and Miniatures, and the Royal Shakespeare Company in Stratford-upon-Avon. He holds a master's degree in Museum Studies from the University of Leicester and a bachelor's degree in Apparel Design and Merchandising from Eastern Kentucky University.

Michael Mamp (BA, Central Michigan University; MA, University of Nebraska-Lincoln; PhD, Iowa State University) is Associate Professor of Fashion Merchandising and Design at Central Michigan University. His research focuses on the contributions of women and the LGBTQ community to the fashion industry of the twentieth century, and the history of the American retailer Bonwit Teller. He teaches courses including: History of Western Dress, Queer Fashion, Visual Merchandising, and 3D Printing and Fashion. Mamp also maintains a creative practice focused on the incorporation of narrative in the creation of textiles developed both by hand and with digital technology.

Sara B. Marcketti is Professor at Iowa State University. Her research expertise includes dress history, museum best practices, and the scholarship of teaching and learning. She is a coauthor with Phyllis Tortora of *Survey of Historic Costume*, 6th edition, and, with Jean L. Parsons, coauthor of *Knock-it-off! A History of Design Piracy in the U.S. Women's Ready-to-Wear Apparel Industry*, published by Texas Tech University Press.

Natalie Nudell is a historian and curator of fashion and textiles. She is an adjunct instructor teaching about the history of fashion and textiles at the Fashion Institute of Technology in New York City. Nudell wrote and produced the feature documentary *Ruth Finley's Fashion Calendar* (2018), was the co-curator and exhibition designer of "Runway Moments: New York Fashion Week," held at the 80WSE Gallery in 2014, and serves as a co-editor of the *Fashion Studies Journal*. She holds an MA in Visual Culture: Costume Studies from New York University and a BA (Hons) in History from Concordia University in Montreal, Canada.

Jean L. Parsons is Associate Professor and Curator at The University of Missouri. Her research expertise includes dress history and apparel design scholarship. She is coauthor with Jane Farrell-Beck of *20th Century Dress in the United States* and, with Sara Marcketti, coauthor of *Knock-it-off! A History of Design Piracy in the U.S. Women's Ready-to-Wear Apparel Industry*, published by Texas Tech University Press.

Jan Glier Reeder (BA, Smith College; MA, Fashion Institute of Technology) is an independent fashion historian. Until January 2016, she was Consulting Curator for the Brooklyn Museum Costume Collection at the Costume Institute, The Metropolitan Museum of Art. In this capacity she curated "American High Style: Fashioning a National Collection" on view at the Brooklyn Museum (2010), authored the accompanying publication *High Style: Masterworks from the Brooklyn Museum Costume Collection*, and coauthored the catalog for as well as co-curated the Metropolitan's 2014 exhibition "Charles James: Beyond Fashion." From 2005 to 2009, she directed a Mellon-funded project to assess the Brooklyn Museum's historic costume collection.

Hannah Schiff is an independent fashion historian. She has an MA in Visual Culture: Costume Studies from New York University. With over a decade of experience in the antique and vintage clothing industry she works as a consultant for collectors. Schiff also holds a degree in art history from Willamette University, where she was a recipient of the 2012 Lilly Project Grant and contributor to the 2011 Timeless Renaissance exhibition at the Hallie Ford Museum of Art.

Susan M. Strawn is Professor Emerita of apparel design and merchandising at Dominican University, Illinois. She earned her PhD in textiles and clothing from Iowa State University. Her research interests in dress history include the historical/cultural study of hand knitting and knitwear design.

Caroline A. Surrarrer has a BA in Fashion Merchandising from the University of Akron and MA from The Fashion School at Kent State University. An instructor at VMCAD College and the University of Akron, her thesis research focused on the life of fashion designer Libby Payne and what her career can tell us about the past, present, and future of the ready-to-wear industry.

ACKNOWLEDGMENTS

This book represents the work of a team of dedicated scholars. As general editor, I am grateful to all contributors for their commitment, trust, and good humor. It has been an honor and a pleasure to gather so much original scholarship on American fashion into one project. I also express sincere appreciation to Jessica Barker and Ya'ara Keydar at NYU for their research and editorial assistance, and to New York University's Steinhardt School and NYU's Humanities Initiative for helping to fund images. On behalf of all chapter authors, I would like to thank the museums, libraries, and individuals who provided access to records and allowed us to include photographs of sketches, objects, and other material. Special thanks as well are due to everyone at Bloomsbury: Anna Wright, who immediately evinced so much enthusiasm for this book; Hannah Crump, Pari Thomson, and Frances Arnold, all valued advisors along the way; and Amy Jordan and Manikandan Kuppan who brought it to print.

The editor, chapter authors, and publisher gratefully acknowledge the permission granted to reproduce the copyright material in this book. Every effort has been made to trace copyright holders and to obtain their permission for the use of copyright material. The publisher apologizes for any errors or omissions in the above list and would be grateful if notified of any corrections that should be incorporated in future reprints or editions of this book.

INTRODUCTION

NANCY DEIHL

Prominent names in the American fashion industry, including Ralph Lauren, Calvin Klein, Donna Karan, Marc Jacobs, and Michael Kors, have become lucrative global brands contributing to the image of American fashion as a well-developed commercial force with international influence. These esteemed American fashion talents did not spring from a barren landscape; some important forebears prepared the ground. A number of their predecessors—Mainbocher, Valentina, Charles James, Gilbert Adrian, Claire McCardell, and Norman Norell, to name a few—are known to scholars of fashion history. And others, including Bill Blass, Geoffrey Beene, and Oscar de la Renta, are familiar through licensing and diffusion lines. But throughout the 100-plus years of steady activity generated by the American fashion industry, many other designers rose to prominence, enjoyed acclaim and/or financial success, and now have been all but forgotten. Some established and served niche markets— known for a particular aesthetic or in a specific region; others worked behind the scenes, producing best-selling styles for major mainstream labels; a few moved between the fashion and entertainment industries, embodying the interlocking of those two important industries in creating and promoting fashion trends.

The Hidden History of American Fashion examines the careers of some of these little known pioneers, designers who enjoyed success in their lifetime but are not included in the canon of American fashion design. All of the designers are women; this is the first published scholarly consideration of their lives and careers. Several of these chapters began as presentations at professional conferences; authors were inspired by designers and labels they repeatedly came across during research for other projects. Often their interest was piqued by objects they encountered in museum collections. Museums across the United States include pieces by many of the designers profiled in this book that have not been exhibited or published, sometimes because information on these individuals/labels was lacking. The sixteen chapters in this book contribute background to the history of these objects and may facilitate interpretation and exhibition—important avenues for reaching the public and enlarging the prevailing narrative of fashion history. The aim of this project is to reclaim a place in history for some of the many designers who contributed to the fashion industry in their own time and therefore to the contemporary fashion system in which American designers and brands enjoy such renown.

The Hidden History of American Fashion is divided into three sections, focusing on commonalities between the designers in each section. This organizational structure underlines the fact that while the reputation of American fashion today is largely based on casual clothing, during the early and mid-twentieth century the field was much more diverse. Offerings by then-prominent American designers included custom work, fine tailoring, millinery, children's fashion, accessory design, and costume for film and theater. The first part, *Design Innovators*, consists of four chapters that profile individuals with unique design viewpoints and practices. Targeting an individualistic clientele, Jessie Franklin Turner (1881–1956) was the first American fashion designer to establish a financially successful and enduring couture business in New York. Virginia Woods Bellamy (1890–1976) developed an innovative system for producing knitted garments, and she was also a published poet. Tina Leser (1910–1986), a world traveler brought up in an artistic household, as early as the 1950s prioritized fair trade, sustainability, and a global outlook in her design and production. Sandra Garratt (b. 1951) took the idea of separates to an extreme with her minimalist Multiples and Units lines.

The second, and largest, section, *Developing an Industry*, presents the careers of designers who made important contributions to the fashion industry in terms of developing market sectors, regional reach, and the overall "democratization" of fashion in America. Pauline Fracchia (1889–1989) and Marion McCoy (1912–1960) were established wholesale designers whose careers can be charted, in part, through the patents they filed to protect their designs. A Russian immigrant, Fira Benenson (1899–1977) established herself in New York where over the course of her career she was a boutique owner, department store buyer, and in-house designer and creator of ready-to-wear. Helen Lee (1908–1991) and Suzanne Godart (1923–2002) were leaders in the legitimization of children's wear; their work set the stage for current focus on name-brand fashions for children. Based in Chicago, Nicky Ladany's (1922–2013) "Catherine Scott" label offered sophistication for the postwar suburban lifestyle. Jean Wright (1915–1967) was the designer behind the highly successful label Lilli Ann, a San Francisco suit manufacturer known for high-quality, European-inspired design. With no formal training but with an eye for details, Mollie Parnis (c. 1900–1992) produced aspirational but accessible fashion and helped shape the public image of two American First Ladies. And Elizabeth "Libby" Payne (1917–1997) worked in St. Louis, Chicago, and New York, designing for "Mrs. Main Street America" for fifty years. In addition to the chapters on designers, this section includes a chapter on Ruth Finley's *Fashion Calendar*. This important publication began in 1945 as a central organizational tool, informing industry insiders about market weeks, fashion shows, association meetings, and other events. The *Fashion Calendar* is pivotal to the history of American fashion and is also a source for information on many of the designers included.

Part three, *Hollywood, Broadway, and Seventh Avenue*, explores important crossovers between the film industry, theater, and the fashion industry through the careers of designers who worked in multiple arenas. Viola Dimmitt (1893–1978) was one of the earliest name designers in Los Angeles, and her work with Hollywood set a standard for cross-promotion of film and fashion. A native New Yorker, Kiviette (1893–1978) enjoyed success as both fashion and costume designer; her work on Broadway helped establish contemporary style as a legitimate stage aesthetic. Zelda Wynn Valdes (1905–2001), an African American designer with a celebrity client list that included Josephine Baker, Dorothy Dandridge, Eartha Kitt, and other well-known performers, worked exclusively in custom design, and at a later point in her career she was the costumer for Dance Theatre of Harlem. From her base in Paris, Vicky Tiel (b. 1943) went from producing "rich hippie" boutique styles to outfitting socialites and leading ladies.

Sometimes lacking immediate role models for their businesses, these designers adopted a variety of stratagems in order to build success. Each designer's story is different. Some trained in fashion, attending schools that included Los Angeles' Fashion Institute of Design and Merchandising, Parsons or Traphagen in New York City, or Chicago Fashion Academy. Others studied art and design—several attended the Art Students League in New York. A number of these women parlayed their "good taste" or "artistic upbringing" into a fashion career. But quite a few learned on the job. In some cases, that first job was necessitated by financial circumstances as fashion offered the possibility for self-support; this was the case for Viola Dimmitt, a young widow with a child to support. For others the identification of a need prompted the move into fashion; Tina Leser and Nicky Ladany both started their companies to produce what they couldn't find elsewhere in the market. Some women felt fashion was their destiny: Libby Payne wrote that since she could make things that people like, "why can't I sell them?," and Vicky Tiel declared while still in college that she would be a "couturier in Paris." Diligent research by chapter authors reveals the details of those jobs: responsibilities and rewards, locations and processes. The financial side of the fashion industry is part of the picture. American designers produced garments to please all segments of the fashion-buying public, with dresses priced from $22.75 for a Marion McCoy Original to $1,000 for a custom gown by Zelda Wynn Valdes and every price in between. Salary information is another point of interest. Many of these designing women were well paid in their jobs, an advantage that did not prevent them from seeking the further satisfaction of seeing their name on the label—a reward that was too often denied.

The chapters produce a picture of American fashion as a complex ecosystem. Designers and manufacturers of course played central roles, but equally crucial to its operation was input and cooperation from press, retailers, and from an immense fashion-conscious public. This collection demonstrates the diversity and breadth of the industry—correcting the popular perception of American fashion as consisting solely of casual sportswear. Viola Dimmitt's custom gowns and Jessie Franklin Turner's artistic at-home fashions, Virginia Woods Bellamy's number-knitted wardrobes, Jean Wright's peplumed suits, Sandra Garratt's modern modular separates, and Vicky Tiel's seductive evening looks—each appealed to a particular segment of the population.

The regional aspect is also highlighted. Seventh Avenue was the undisputed headquarters of American fashion for much of the twentieth century. However, Chicago, St. Louis, San Francisco, and Los Angeles were not provincial outposts but legitimate fashion centers serving huge regional markets. Libby Payne's positions at fifteen different manufacturers in Chicago and St. Louis testify to the role of local manufacturers who often enjoyed special relationships with department stores. Every city had several department stores, some local, others regional, fulfilling the diverse fashion needs of different customer bases. Since the 1970s, most local department stores have closed, corporate consolidation has stripped many of their historic identity, and many famous names—including I. Magnin, Marshall Field & Company, and Woodward & Lothrop—have disappeared altogether. Even within those that remain, department store shopping has largely lost its cachet, as house designers and "private label" are practices from the past.

There was also consistent support from the press, especially female editors and public relations executives. Eleanor Lambert, a prominent advocate of American fashion, makes an appearance in several chapters. Her enthusiasm is echoed not only across fashion magazines such as *Vogue* and *Harper's Bazaar* but also in general interest magazines and in the women's service press, as designers were also promoted in publications such as *LIFE*, *Redbook*, and *Woman's Home Companion*. The importance of *Women's Wear Daily*—a source of information for the fashion community since its debut as *Women's Wear* in 1910—cannot be overstated. It provided real-time coverage of many of the designers profiled here, and the historical archive of *WWD* was a crucial resource for chapter authors. The images reproduced in this book fortunately include a number of photographs of the designers and most are glamorous black and white studio portraits. While each designer presents her individual style, it is no surprise that they were well-groomed, polished professionals; their portraits tell us much about the fashions of the time.

This project brings together a remarkable group of scholars. All are based in the United States, at universities and museums, and their research is anchored in exemplary use of primary sources, including archives, museum collections, specialty press, and interviews with designers and other key fashion industry personalities. Through the profiles of individual designers, *The Hidden History of American Fashion* explores the interlocking forces that have shaped what is now a $300 billion industry, against the background of twentieth-century social history. The lives and careers of these individual designers, examined here for the first time, combine in a narrative that involves immigration, intellectual property, mass production and labor relations, regional identity, race relations, and the role of celebrity in American culture. It is the mission of this book to inspire further research into American fashion—there are many more stories to be rediscovered.

PART ONE

DESIGN INNOVATORS

1 JESSIE FRANKLIN TURNER: AN INTIMATE AFFAIR

JAN GLIER REEDER

Jessie Franklin Turner was the first American fashion designer to establish a financially successful and long-term couture business in New York. Before the two now-better-known couturières, Elizabeth Hawes and Valentina, began to gain recognition in the late 1920s, Turner was presiding over a thriving business that dressed American society's most distinguished women (Hawes 1938: 121).[1]

From the time she opened her first salon in 1922 until her retirement in 1942, she provided a range of luxurious leisure-based clothing suited to her clients' privileged lifestyles. Casual sports dresses for attending outdoor spectator activities such as polo matches and horse shows, day dresses for warm weather climes, beach, bathing, and bridal wear were all on offer, complementing the feminine, elegant at-home and evening gowns that were her specialty. She gained an international reputation for her beautiful tea gowns, a form of intimate attire originally meant to be worn only in the privacy of the boudoir or with intimate friends at home but in her hands became works of fashion art suitable for any occasion except the most formal public affairs. Unusual and distinctive, her clothes distinguished the women who wore them. Distilling through her own creative process the patterns, silhouettes, textures, and colors of art historical and ethnographic sources, she created styles that were contemporary yet timeless.

Jessie was born in St. Louis, Missouri, on December 10, 1881, the second child of Louise Frankman and Richard Major Turner, a painter who shared an aesthetic with the famous artist of the same name. Her mother's parents were German immigrants who settled in St. Louis while Richard's family hailed from Wilkes County, Georgia, and moved to St. Louis. His birthplace is variously recorded as Georgia or Missouri.[2] Sometime in the 1880s, after Jessie's birth, the family moved from St. Louis to Peoria, Illinois. As a young girl, Turner had training in singing, painting, and sculpture, purportedly spending some time in Paris, where she attended sculpting classes at the Paris studio of Antoine Bourdelle (1861–1929), well-known sculptor and teacher.[3] Her high school education was at the Berkeley School in Peoria.

Turner's introduction to the world of women's intimate fashions began in the late 1890s in Peoria, where as a teenager she sought employment in Fischer Brothers, a local lingerie store, by suggesting to the owner that she could improve the quality and range of their merchandise. Soon afterward she obtained work in a larger arena as buyer for the lingerie department at Scruggs, Vandervoort, and Barney, St. Louis's premier department store known as the "Fashion Authority of the Midwest." At a time when fashion dictated heavy corseting, she became aware of her clients' intimate wear needs beyond what the store had to offer (Crawford 1941: 231) and sought out items (possibly more comfortable alternatives) to meet their requests with frequent trips to New York.

Recognizing that there was no possibility of advancement, Turner left the firm after three and a half years. After a hiatus in which nothing is known about her activities, in 1908 she was hired as the European buyer for the New York firm McCutcheon & Co., "The Linen Store," purveyors of high-quality household linens, lingerie, corsets, and related attire at 34th Street and Fifth Avenue. Her three-year stint there involved travels to Europe, broadening her horizons and knowledge of the lingerie and textile fields. In 1911, when she was 30 years old, Turner's talents caught the attention of Paul Bonwit, co-founder of the exclusive specialty store Bonwit Teller & Co., where she would be employed for the next ten years designing fashions that would make her famous. Having just moved his store from downtown to prestigious new quarters at Fifth Avenue at 38th Street, Bonwit hired her as European and Oriental buyer for the new department devoted to lingerie and intimate wear. During her extensive travels to Europe and Asia as Bonwit's representative, she visited museums and had access to private costume and textile collections. Her talents and experience with women's intimate wear soon led to more than buying; sometime between 1913 and 1915 Bonwit deployed her to the Philippines to establish and supervise a factory producing fine handmade cotton lingerie for Bonwit's (Advertisement 1916b). Around 1916, she also set up her own workrooms designing for private clients at 11 West 56th Street and established special workrooms at Bonwit's for "design and making Custom order teagowns & negligees" (Turner Notebook 1: 5). It is likely that she had her hand in the "Studio Negligees, an entirely new type of Robe d'Interieur evolved in the Bonwit Teller & Co. workrooms ... introducing rich and mystic themes of the Orient" (Advertisement 1916a).

Between 1918 and 1920 there were several displays of her negligees and tea gowns in Bonwit's windows representing such diverse cultural inspirations as East Indian clothing, Italian Renaissance velvets, and batik-dyed Javanese textiles. She had also by this time, probably when she opened her independent 56th Street workshops, incorporated her own business under the name of Winifred Warren, using the first name of her paternal grandmother, Winifred Pullin Turner.[4]

Her career was given an additional boost by Paul Bonwit's friend, fashion impresario Morris De Camp Crawford. Using his influence as fashion editor of the industry's trade paper, *Women's Wear*, and research fellow in the Department of Anthropology at the American Museum of Natural History (AMNH), he joined forces with influential New York museum personnel in a nationalistic campaign to create a distinctly American design style. The impetus was the onset of the First World War, precipitating the loss of materials and design inspiration from Europe (especially France) that the American fashion industry traditionally relied upon. The campaign's leaders contended that the wealth of objects in American museums from non-European indigenous (which they often referred to as "primitive") cultures would inspire American designers. Recognizing Turner's talents in textiles and fashion, Crawford chose her to be the featured designer for the campaign. Between 1918 and 1920, he promoted her work for Bonwit's in his column "Design Department" and recruited her for committees, design competitions, and textile exhibitions related to the campaign. In his December 1917 *Vogue* article promoting the campaign, Crawford included a photo of Turner's first design illustrating its central thesis. A luxurious free-flowing at-home gown of soft rose duvetyn and blue chiffon trimmed with fur, it was derived from a traditional dancing coat of animal hide, fur and bead work worn by the Koryak peoples of Siberia from the collection of the AMNH. The skillful transposition of the original artifact's ceremonial function and protective materials to a modern at-home gown of soft filmy fabric accented with luxurious fur trim expertly illustrated Crawford's mission to create a unique American design through mining the rich global resources of museum collections.

Through Crawford Turner also met the man who would become her most influential mentor, Stewart Culin, curator of ethnology at the Brooklyn Museum. From her first trip to the museum in 1918 until Culin's death in 1929, she studied the diverse ethnographic holdings collected by Culin, with exclusive access to him as her teacher. She later acknowledged his particularly strong influence on her design career, noting that she "owe[d] more to Stewart Culin than any other man I ever knew. He taught me the basic silhouettes of the Orient, and the nature and scope of ornament and color" (Crawford 1941: 274).

When Crawford and his museum colleagues organized a major exhibition at AMNH in late 1919 to illustrate the success of their campaign, they included Turner—the only woman—to serve on the planning committee comprised of New York museum personnel and wholesale fashion designers. The landmark exhibition, entitled "The Exhibition of Industrial Art in Textiles and Costumes," was on view for two weeks. It featured museum objects displayed side by side with the contemporary works they inspired produced by textile and embroidery manufacturers and artisans as well as fashion designers. Turner was given priority to show her work, which included luxurious at-home gowns inspired by Coptic, Turkish, and Bokharan sources, alone in one of seven special exhibition spaces.[5]

In the fall of 1919 she moved from West 56th Street and set up workrooms and showrooms in two adjacent row houses at 4 and 6 East 12th Street in the heart of Greenwich Village, New York's bohemian district that was mecca to the artistic and literary crowd that made up part of Turner's clientele. By this time Turner was ready to leave Paul Bonwit's employ, but reluctant to let her go, he negotiated with her to work half time for him for another year and devote the remainder to independent designing. Finally having completed her obligation to Paul Bonwit during 1920, in January 1922, at age 40, she went solo. A brief newspaper notice dated January 24 headlined "NEGLIGEES" proclaimed that "Announcements are in the mail … Jessie Franklin Turner will show her *intime* gowns direct to her patrons at her apartments" at 290 Park Avenue (unidentified clipping).

Turner's experiences as buyer and designer, her travels abroad, and close relationships with New York's top museum and fashion industry personnel as well as Bonwit's socially elite clients set her in a unique position when she went out on her own. The discernment she developed when buying textiles in other cultures honed her own design aesthetic. The special draw of her fashions emanated from exotic, often mystical, combinations of colors and the textures of her textiles, which were custom-woven, hand-decorated, and dyed with colors devised from formulae she developed in her own workrooms. She purportedly imported weavers and set up looms in Connecticut in 1928 (Bailey 1940). She also imported fine French textiles custom ordered to her color and weave specifications. Rich velvets, gossamer chiffons, butter soft wools, novelty weave crepes, glittering brocades, and original ethnic textiles and embroideries were the tools with which she worked her magic. In December of 1921, right before opening her first shop, *Vogue* published an editorial featuring five of her *robes d'interieur* that represent the remarkable diversity of sources that characterized her clothes. A mirror-embroidered Turkish textile made up the front bodice of one, the main body of another was styled from an embroidered Indian silk sari, a third was fashioned from indigo resist-dyed Japanese textile, and a fourth incorporated a gold brocade East Indian temple cloth as the back panel.

Her custom weaves sometimes copied the patterns of original museum artifacts and other times interpreted them. Silks brocaded with small half-drop repeat patterns typical of Persian textiles were favorites. Her collection of world textiles usually served as interesting trims and distinctive touches, but she also acquired pieces large enough to make dramatic one-off garments that, along with designs inspired by a specific work of art, she termed "document gowns." Three particularly stunning examples were fashioned in 1935 and 1936 from brilliant brocaded textiles repurposed from Russian priests' robes. One, a velvet tea gown with elaborate sleeves made from the brocade, was a direct copy of Antonio del

FIGURE 1.1 A page from Turner's scrapbook showing advertisements for two of her "Document Gowns"; left: purple velvet gown inspired by a portrait by the sixteenth-century Italian master Santi di Tito; right: model wearing a tea gown with antique Russian brocade sleeves. The photo replicates Antonio del Pollaiuolo's *Portrait of a Young Woman*. Beneath it is Turner's philosophy of clothes that aims at "distinction rather than fashion." Scrapbook 1, Jessie Franklin Turner Scrapbook Collection, The Irene Lewisohn Costume Reference Library, The Costume Institute, The Metropolitan Museum of Art, New York, NY. Photos by Alfredo Valente.

Pollaiuolo's *c.* 1465 *Portrait of a Young Woman* in the Staatliche Museum. Turner's ad depicting her model's upper torso in profile bears an uncanny resemblance to the Renaissance original.

Turner's influence on the fashion capital of the world could be inferred from an editorial pronouncement: "Word comes from Paris that everyone is bringing home native costumes from the Orient, having them slightly altered, and wearing them everywhere in the evening. Jessie Franklin Turner has been doing just this for years. In fact, her business is founded on it" ("Shopping Bazaar" 1935). A casual day dress Turner fashioned in 1938 is evidence of her commitment to bringing esoteric world cultures into the lives of her patrons. Made of linen custom-woven to simulate birch bark cloth produced by the Amur peoples of northeastern China, its blue and white patterning was adopted from textiles of the Gilyaks (also known as Nivkh) of Russia's Sakhalin Island (Spur 1938).

Turner's unconventional freedom with color led to frequent press raves: "Jessie Franklin Turner, the color genius, ... knows the greens and blues that are happy together, the yellows, the reds, the pinks" (Town and Country 1937). For the mystical effects of tea gowns in particular, she blended layers of chiffon in slightly different pastel hues of the same color or in off-beat combinations such as magenta and orchid, mauve and aquamarine, or peach and chartreuse. She dyed her ultralight wools in the same pastel colors and combined them in threes in her day dresses.

Just as adroitly, she combined vivid colors, bold on bold, especially in garments meant to evoke the fantasy of what was then referred to as "the Orient"—Chinese yellow and black, brilliant blue with bright red, deep rust with bright geranium pink. Bold jolts of color such as flame red, chartreuse, and magenta in belts and trims also offset the softness of her pastel gowns. A dress described in the New York Times in 1934 sums up her strategies: "Peach over Chinese yellow chiffon dress with Laurencin blue satin trims and peach satin scarf belt" ("Elegance" 1934). To emphasize the custom aspect of her dyes and give them personality, Turner named her colors. Cantaloupe pink, biscuit brown, epinard (spinach) green, golden thrush, Derain green, Peruvian ochre, and Malmaison pink appealed to the worldliness and cultural sophistication—not to mention the appetites—of her clients.

Turner's artistry with color and her appreciation of world textiles were used to great effect in her unique tea gowns. The form of robe d'interieur known as the tea gown originated in Victorian England as a type of relaxed dressing worn in the late afternoon hours to provide relief from the restrictive boning and corseting of fashionable dress. As an alternative, private form of dress, it was designed with more creative latitude than formal attire and street wear, often invoking the romanticism of past times and exotic places. By the time Turner began designing them, and their close cousins negligees,[6] fashion had become less restrictive, but the tea gown remained an important part of the well-dressed and socially active woman's wardrobe.

Still acceptable only in the daytime company of intimates or alone, lounging in a tea gown gave a woman time to relax, drape herself on a chaise, and let her imagination drift, perhaps to a far-off place where a hint of seduction was in the air. As Harper's Bazaar explained it: "If you have been rushing about hectically all day, nothing turns you into a woman again like a tea-gown" ("The Gown" 1933).

The tea gown was usually distinguished from other forms of intimate wear by an elegant trailing train; voluminous draping sleeves completed the languorous look. Pre-1920s examples tended to be loose fitting and one-piece, but by 1928—after a dip in popularity owing to the masculinized styles and hectic pace of the "roaring twenties"—the tea gown made a comeback. Announcing its reinvention in 1928,

FIGURE 1.2 Pictured in *Vogue* in April 1933, socialite Mrs. Julien Chaqueneau, wife of a theater producer, wears a tea gown ensemble: a slip cut like an evening dress with the addition of a train and a gossamer jacket with trailing sleeves, both requisite tea gown elements and indicative of the transition from tea to evening gown that Turner promoted. Photo by Edward Steichen/Conde Nast via Getty Images.

a *Harper's Bazaar* editorial featured three Turner tea gowns in a new two-piece format comprising an elaborate trailing coat-like outer layer and a simple body-hugging underdress. These were said to have attained a level of formality suitable for wearing not only at the tea hour but also as hostess gowns. An explanation of how these gowns were more "formal" than their forebears was suggested in the description noting the chiffon under layer had "a front godet which dispels any hint of the lingerie note" ("The Teagown" 1928).

From then on the tea gown's sphere expanded from private afternoon wear to attire for at-home entertaining—for bridge games, teas on the terrace, informal dinners—or at country house parties. Advancing shifts in social conventions and the general feminization of fashion beginning in the early 1930s, Turner's innovative ideas pushed the tea gown's boundaries out of the home into the public arena. By designing some of her tea gowns with under dresses that she referred to as slips, but which increasingly worked as stand-alone evening garments, she introduced the idea of separates in the form of interchangeable overbodices (Reeder 2010: 118–119) as well as wraps that could be worn as part of the ensemble or removed for evening glamour. "Most of [Turner's] tea gowns are completely suitable for evening dresses once the sweeping outer coat is removed after cocktails" (Long 1936: 56). A coat could also accomplish the reverse, as in the case of a 1933 ensemble with a black velvet low-cut evening dress and short silver lamé coat that could transform the dress into a hostess gown when worn, or serve as a light wrap to be removed for evening affairs ("Tailored" 1933: 58). By 1938 the tea gown's suitability for practically any occasion reached its apotheosis when Mrs. William Hendrick Eustice, owner of a ranch in Wyoming, columnist for the *Washington Evening Post* and a collector of Turner tea gowns, was photographed wearing one suspended midway up a ladder as she checked decorations at the Elbow Room, a celebrity nightclub in New York (LaRoche 1938).

The well-heeled clientele Turner attracted were from the upper echelons of America's social, artistic, and theatrical realms. As she put it, they were not necessarily the richest or involved in "the most spectacular phases of society," but "are the women who really make society in America" (Crawford 1941: 231). They appreciated clothing as art and sought to set themselves apart by wearing clothing that was apart from fashion trends, and as Turner put it, "independent of fashion." The socially elite hailed from the high-profile families who developed and sustained America's industrial, mercantile, and financial sectors with names such as Goodyear, Morton (salt), Whitney, Strawbridge (department store), Gould and Warburg. Well-known theater designer Aline Bernstein and Princess Martha de Bourbon, wife of the Archduke Franz Joseph, were also among her patrons.

Turner was already prominent in these rarified social circles by 1924, when she designed the clothes for the wedding of Cornelia Stuyvesant Vanderbilt and Sir John Amherst Cecil held at Biltmore, the family's estate in the Blue Ridge Mountains of North Carolina. The eight-ankle-length chemise-style dresses for the bride's attendants were signature Turner, a simple silhouette with skirts fashioned from Japanese silk figured with a large pattern of green and white begonias. At the time it was not customary to identify the designer of wedding clothes in the press, but because Turner included the rotogravure editorial spread in the *New York Times* about the wedding and everything in the scrapbooks pertains to her work, it can be surmised that she was the designer. Furthermore, the attendant's dresses made from Japanese silk are strongly indicative of her work. It follows that Cornelia's dress, a slim line in white satin with long sleeves and low back, was also designed by Turner, but not certainly. Ironically, the only designer mentioned is the French couturier Jeanne Lanvin, who designed the maid-of-honor's dress that was a significantly different style from the others. The day before the wedding, the bride was photographed at the train station greeting guests in a Turner day dress made of a silk textile embroidered with mynah birds copied from an Indian blouse. The first version of the dress, a tea gown, was shown in Bonwit's windows in September of 1919 and was reported on with great fanfare.[7]

Given their theatricality and distinctiveness, it is not surprising that Turner's designs attracted prominent actresses appearing on the New York stage during the 1920s and 1930s. They wore her fashions, mostly the elaborate at-home attire, on- and off-stage and posing in fashion editorials. The list is a who's who of marquee names: Ina Claire, Fay Bainter, Cornelia Otis Skinner, Barbara Stanwyck, June Knight, and Dorothy Gish were among the headliners. The publicity generated by these prominent displays of her elegant *intime* finery spread her fame beyond national borders, as an unidentified theater program from 1933 attests: "Nothing more readily induces an alluring languor than a trailing tea gown.... The fashioning of such gowns is a highly specialized field, and, although it's traditional that they do these things better abroad, it's a field led beyond question by an American—Jessie Franklin Turner of New York." The comedic actress Grace George was a devotee for nearly twenty years. For her star turn in "The Happy Husband" (1923) she wore a panné velvet negligee with a batik design, whereas a sporty belted spectator dress defined her character in a 1941 production of "Spring Again."

Turner's success was based not only on her artistry with dress but also on her astute business sense. At the heart of her client-centered business were the principles of exclusivity and personal client relations, producing a sense of intimacy, comfort, and luxury paralleling her clothes. This consistency of message between product and practice—the equivalent of a modern-day branding strategy—created the cachet and distinction that wearing JFT clothing signified for her clients. Turner never wavered from her focus on her customers' needs. Yet, ironically, she did not socialize with or for that matter greet them at the shop, preferring to concentrate on designing and allowing her salespersons to help with their selections. Intentional or not, her reclusiveness added to the cachet of exclusivity that she fostered.

Over the twenty years she worked alone as Jessie Franklin Turner, she had three different salons. The first, opened in 1922, was at 290 Park Avenue, at the corner of 49th Street, with workrooms and private living quarters in a house around the corner at 143 East 49th. Eight years later, in October of 1930, because of the disruption caused by construction of the new Waldorf-Astoria Hotel nearby, she announced that "For the convenience and comfort of our customers, we are going to make a new home." She leased a house at 23 East 67th Street between Fifth and Madison, where she showcased only her custom gowns, leaving ready-to-wear day, sports, and evening gowns at the 290 Park salon. This address too became problematic when in the fall of 1933 Elizabeth Hawes, by then a rival couturière, but still with ties to the wholesale business, moved in next door. Turner objected to the commercial atmosphere that surrounded Hawes' establishment as well as the lower social status (in Turner's opinion) of Hawes' workers.[8] Over time the more northern location also proved inconvenient to her clients, whose activities were centered in the fifties. Determining that Park Avenue was indeed a more suitable address, in November of 1935 Turner moved back, to 410 Park, where she stayed for the remaining seven years of her career. Workrooms were at 515 Madison Avenue at 53rd Street in the prestigious new Dumont Building.

The stunning interiors of Turner's salons reflected the daring use of color, aura of intimacy, and the alchemy of exotic, historic, and modern that epitomized her fashions. At 290 Park, gleaming silver-leaf walls and ceilings were complemented by an upholstered sofa of silver velvet accented with black and green piping, a dressmaking detail of Persian origin that she favored in her designs. Woodwork painted in vivid chartreuse with draperies to match, polished jade green floors, and a Buddha image above a black sofa emphasized the exotic. An art deco diamond-patterned glass panel in the ceiling and an ebony cabinet inlaid with a silver zigzag added contemporary notes. A boudoir-style vanity table underscored the intimate atmosphere.

In contrast, the décor theme of the East 67th Street house was Renaissance Italy, offering a subliminal connection between the sumptuous textiles portrayed in portraiture of the Italian masters and the artistry behind Turner's own creations. Antique Italian furniture was set off against pale walls illuminated by lamps made in Italy and designed by Turner. A distinctive wooden door with coffered paneling greeted patrons and served as a background for advertising photographs. A small garden at the back gave a cool ambience to the showroom and emphasized the home environment. By the end of 1933, *Fortune* magazine reported that several thousand women had visited the Renaissance rooms ("The Dressmakers" 1933: 38).

Turner decorated 410 Park with upholstered divans in Tunisian green and vibrant Chinese yellow curtains against stark white walls. But in 1939 she updated the interior with vibrant chartreuse and tomato red, prompting Lois Long to proclaim that "the woman knows how to use color. No one except La Turner could combine black, chartreuse and tomato red to create a restful shop interior" (Long 1939: 69).

Turner's business logo also melded modern Western and traditional Eastern forms. Modeled on the square seals used by twentieth-century Japanese artisans to identify their work, the design enclosed her monogram, drawn with letters overlapped, in a slightly rectangular border. The striking graphic was consistently present on all stationery and advertisements throughout her career.

FIGURE 1.3 The languorous elegance of Turner's tea gowns is captured in this advertisement published in *Harper's Bazaar* in March 1933. Turner's distinctive logo is at upper left. Photo by Alfredo Valente.

For the first ten years of her business Turner chose a personal approach to promote her designs. Eschewing the more commercial strategy of advertising, she sent out what she termed "announcements" informing clients of her latest designs or recent textile discoveries and stressing the distinctiveness and individuality of her creations. Prices, ranging from $45 for the simplest negligee to $275 for an elaborate gown, were usually included. Written in her distinctive left-slanted handwriting, or, later on, in typeface, the notes were printed on expensive heavy wove or translucent onion skin stationery and always included her handwritten signature and logo. Variously colored tissues evoking the rich hues of her designs lined the envelopes. As if addressing a friend, the tone of the message was always personal, with phrases such as, "Won't you come and see...?" (Turner Scrapbook 1, January 1, 1929) or, "Miss Turner collected on her trip many rare and exceptional fabrics from Morocco, Egypt, India and Spain. She would like very much to have you see the gowns made from them" (Turner Scrapbook 1, October 15, 1923). There was no particular regularity in the timing of the announcements; as many as six were sent in some years, fewer in others. Over two decades, no two were alike, assuring that the arrival of an announcement was always a source of surprise and novelty. On average Turner sent 2,000 or 3,000 at a time, but occasionally more, as in March of 1932 when 5,000 at a cost of $480 were dispatched.

After nearly ten years of doing business based on personal contact, Turner began advertising when the full effects of the 1929 stock market crash had brought the economy to a low ebb. She placed her first ads, a simple rectangular layout with her name in block letters and her distinctive logo, every month in *Vogue* between August 1931 and April 1932. The first pictorial ad, a drawing by the illustrator J. Pages, appeared in *Harper's Bazaar* and *Town and Country* in the spring of 1932. From then on she posted glamorous photographic ads (on average twice a year in *Vogue* and *Harper's*), along with the simpler formats in these and countless other local fashion magazines, theater programs, and influential theater magazines, including *Promenade*, *Spur*, and *Stage*. The brand identity Turner established reached its apex in the late 1930s when she designed a spectator dress with her initials, JFT, boldly displayed in an oval frame centered on the back, pajamas with her initials on the breast pocket, and a navy silk day dress embroidered all over in white with her logo and the date, 1939, beneath each one.

With signs of war once again appearing in 1938, the nationalistic campaign to support American design took on new urgency. Over the next four years, M.D.C. Crawford, collaborating with philanthropist Irene Lewisohn and theater designer Aline Bernstein, founders of the newly formed Museum of Costume Art, helped organize three exhibitions based on the same premise as the 1919 show in which contemporary designs were exhibited alongside the museum artifacts that inspired them. Turner not only actively participated in each show but also served as director of the Museum of Costume Art in 1940, following Crawford. Along

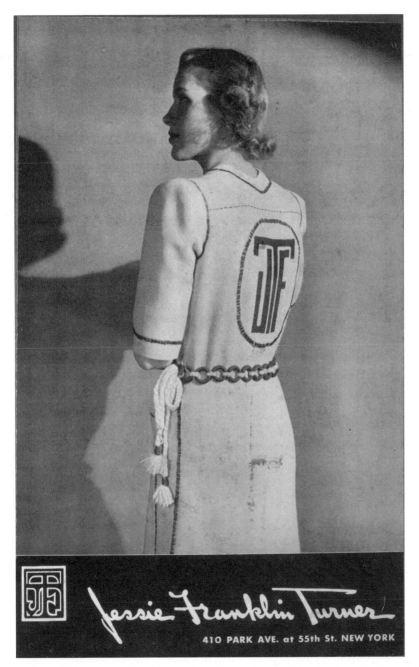

FIGURE 1.4 By the late 1930s the cachet of Turner's brand had developed to the point where she could boldly display her initials on pajamas and sporty day dresses. Scrapbook 2, Jessie Franklin Turner Scrapbook Collection, The Irene Lewisohn Costume Reference Library, The Costume Institute, The Metropolitan Museum of Art, New York, NY. Photo by Alfredo Valente.

with established designers, a crop of new up-and-coming American designers who would come into their own in the 1940s—Mark Mooring of Bergdorf Goodman, Fira Benenson of Bonwit Teller, Tom Brigance of Lord and Taylor, Norman Norell of Hattie Carnegie, and independents such as Jo Copeland, Helen Cookman, and Clarepotter—participated.

For the last of the three shows, an extravaganza entitled "Renaissance in Fashion" presented in the great hall at the Metropolitan Museum of Art in 1942, featured American designers working at the highest level of luxury wear. Most, such as Benenson and Mooring, were associated with department stores, but a few high-end wholesalers, and two pure couturières, Jessie Franklin Turner and Valentina, were invited to design garments inspired by the museum's Renaissance collections. Turner, in her element, showed four opulent gowns. One, like her famous "document gowns," was inspired by the costume depicted in a specific Renaissance portrait, the jerkin with detachable sleeves worn by the subject in Pinturicchio's 1490 *Portrait of a Youth*. It was a fitting finale, as she retired after the exhibition.

In her private life Turner was Mrs. Charles Hiram Ferguson. After a romantic whirlwind courtship initiated by a friend in 1919, she married Ferguson, an inventor, who became wealthy as the founder of Homelite Corporation, manufacturer of electrical devices used in aircraft engines during the world wars. The couple always maintained a residence in New York, but their private time was spent at their home, Walhalla, in the town of Valhalla, New York, where their marriage was by accounts a happy one. Jessie was said to have been an excellent hostess at Walhalla, where the couple made wine from grapes they grew on the property. They also owned a small home in a renovated carriage house at the edge of the Bois de Bologne in Paris. They died within six months of each other, he on March 1, 1956 and she, at age 74, on September 6.

As the first American woman to establish herself in New York and then to gain international acclaim as a leading designer, Turner set the stage for the next generation of women who would become prominent and successful with their own businesses and put their names on labels in the 1940s. Her astute understanding of how to develop and maintain a dedicated client base through the consistent messaging that is now known as branding was uncannily prescient. She also brought into sharp focus the decorative and creative benefits of introducing cuts and textiles borrowed from historic and traditional costumes into contemporary fashion, a technique that designers Carolyn Schnurer, Bonnie Cashin, and Tina Leser especially adopted in their work of the 1940s and 1950s.

But her greatest contribution was to the development of the relaxed attitude, ease, and convenience of the aesthetic that would come to define a uniquely American style in the next decades. From her innovative work in the field of loungewear that gradually blurred the lines between daytime at-home wear and public evening dress emerged the modern concept that clothing could be adapted for time and occasion through introducing interchangeable elements. This concept of versatility through separates dressing was the foundation of the American sportswear-based sensibility developed by the next wave of American women designers. It would become the country's most important contribution to twentieth-century fashion.

Archival Sources

Jessie Franklin Turner Scrapbook Collection. The Irene Lewisohn Costume Reference Library, The Costume Institute, The Metropolitan Museum of Art, New York, NY. The collection consists of two scrapbooks and three notebooks. Organized chronologically, the scrapbooks contain clippings from publications and ephemera documenting Turner's career. Scrapbook 1 covers the years 1918 to mid-1937. Scrapbook 2 continues from late 1937 to 1942. The three notebooks contain informal personal writings.
Stewart Culin Archival Collection, Brooklyn Museum.

Notes

1   In her 1938 fashion exposé *Fashion Is Spinach*, Elizabeth Hawes grudgingly acknowledged Jessie Franklin Turner's status as New York's first and only couturière when she set up her fledgling business in 1928.

2   At some undetermined point, Jessie or her family changed the name from Frankman to Franklin.

3   In her personal writings, which are at times unreliable, Turner makes casual reference to this, but it is not documented elsewhere.

4   No Warren surname appears in her genealogy. Bonwit's did not officially identify her work, but, from the time she incorporated, Morris De Camp Crawford referred to her alternately as either Winifred Warren of Bonwit Teller or Jessie Franklin Turner of Bonwit Teller. When she went out on her own in 1922, she dropped Winifred Warren and used her own name from then forward. However, she maintained Winifred Warren, Inc., as her corporate name for legal purposes throughout her career.

5   See Tartsinis (2013: 65–88) for an in-depth description of the campaign and exhibition.

6   The word "negligee" was sometimes used as a general reference to loungewear, but JFT always distinguished them as separate forms.

7   See Mears (1999) and Coleman (1998) for in-depth discussions of existing versions of the dress and textile.

8   At the housewarming in September, Hawes lined up dressmaker's dummies with signs proclaiming "Contractors are unfair to union labor" (Hawes 1938: 230).

Bibliography

Advertisement: Bonwit Teller (1916a), *New York Times*, October 15: 5.

Advertisement: Bonwit Teller (1916b), *New York Times*, December 31: RP4.

Bailey, G. (1940), "Gowns Ignore Tricks of Trade," *New York World Telegram*, December 9.

Coleman, E.A. (1998), "Jessie Franklin Turner: A Flight Path for Early Modern American Fashion," *Dress* 25: 58–64.

Crawford, M.D.C. (1917), "A New Source of Costume Inspiration," *Vogue*, December: 88, 168, 170, 172.

Crawford, M.D.C. (1941), *The Ways of Fashion*, New York: Putnam.

"The Dressmakers of the U.S." (1933), *Fortune*, December.

"Elegance at Home in Tea Gowns" (1934), *New York Times*, May 20: RP5.

"The Gown After the Javanese" (1933), *Harper's Bazaar*, November: 73.

Hawes, E. (1938), *Fashion Is Spinach*, 3rd printing, New York: Random House.

LaRoche (1938), "These Disarming Women Set Their Own Style," *Town and Country*.

Long, L. (1936), "And in New York," *The New Yorker*, August 22: 56.

Long, L. (1939), "On and off the Avenue," *The New Yorker*, May 27: 69.

Mears, P. (1999), "Jessie Franklin Turner: American and "Exotic" Textile Inspiration," in *Creating Textiles: Makers, Methods and Markets; Proceedings of the Sixth Biennial Symposium of the Textile Society of America, Inc.* Edited by Madelyn Shaw. Earleville, MD: Textile Society of America. 431–440.

Netherton Andusko, K. (2009), "Jessie Franklin Turner," Unpublished article written in connection with the Brooklyn Museum Costume Documentation Project. Brooklyn Museum Libraries and Archives.

Reeder, J.G. (2010), *High Style: Masterworks from the Brooklyn Museum Costume Collection at the Metropolitan Museum of Art*, New York: The Metropolitan Museum of Art.

"Shopping Bazaar" (1935), *Harper's Bazaar*, February: 27.

Spur 1938, April.

"Tailored Luxury" (1933), *Vogue*, November 15: 58–59.

Tartsinis, A.M. (2013), *An American Style: Global Sources for New York Textile and Fashion Design 1915–1928*, New York: The Bard Graduate Center.

"The Teagown Has Been Elevated to a Place of Formality" (1928), *Harper's Bazaar*, Summer.

Town and Country (1937), February.

2 VIRGINIA WOODS BELLAMY: THE POET AS KNITTER

ANN W. BRAATEN AND SUSAN M. STRAWN

American poet and knitter Virginia Woods Bellamy (1890–1976) established a career as a successful mid-century designer of innovative hand-knitted garments for women and children. Her rebellious nature, coupled with frugality, inspired her to invent the patented "no-waste" modular method of garment construction that she called number knitting. Despite the contemporary resurgence of hand knitting, Bellamy's work and career had been largely lost to history. The 2004 discovery of a rare copy of her book *Number Knitting* and twenty of her extant knitted garments spurred a collaborative exploration and documentation of her remarkable accomplishments.[1]

Bellamy was born on April 5, 1890, in Providence, Rhode Island, to Rev. Frank Churchill Woods and Virginia Lee (Hall) Woods. She graduated from what is now Moorestown Friends School in New Jersey. Her Quaker education espoused gender equality, education for women, and working for the betterment of society. As a young woman who considered herself first and foremost a poet and author, she established herself in New York City and married into New York literary circles. Her first marriage to author, gastronome, and New York literary figure Lawton Mackall ended in divorce in 1925, doubtless stressed by her confinement for tuberculosis and prolonged separation from her husband and infant son. In 1926, Bellamy married author, editor, and distinguished literary critic Francis (Frank) Rufus Bellamy, who served as editor of *The Outlook*, a well-respected weekly magazine of news and opinion (1927–1932), and executive editor of *The New Yorker* in 1933 ("Francis" 1972). Their son Rufus and daughter Jane were born in 1928 and 1931.

In 1932, Bellamy's son from her first marriage contracted polio and died suddenly. She struggled with personal depression from the loss of her son and with

FIGURE 2.1 Portrait of Virginia Woods Bellamy, *c.* 1948. Photo by Clara Cipprell. Courtesy of Jane Churchill Young.

the responsibility of caring for two small children during the nation's economic Depression. Her marriage to Frank Bellamy ended in divorce in 1945. She moved to Eliot, Maine, where she pursued knitting as a serious business from the late 1940s through the 1950s. She built her business on her technical innovation in hand knitting, coupled with her sophisticated flair for upscale women's clothing. Later in life, she and Frank Bellamy remarried (Young 2012). Virginia Woods Bellamy passed away in 1976, shortly before the publication of a book of her poetry (Bellamy 1976).[2]

Bellamy and knitting

Involvement with knitting as a practical, intellectual, and economic resource accompanied Bellamy throughout her lifetime. She first learned to knit during her teens but was too impatient to develop a love for the process. In her mid-twenties she learned to knit stockings for charities while being treated for tuberculosis (Bellamy 1952). At the time, it was common to confine tuberculosis patients to a sanatorium to effect a cure for the patient and isolate society from the disease (Rothman 1994). Sanatoriums regulated every aspect of patients' lives, and knitting may have offered Bellamy an escape from the sanatorium's stifling control and a way to cope with being away from her family. Handcrafts like knitting have proven useful in response to traumatic experiences, comforting for their rhythmic quality and connection with generational continuity (Adamson 2013).

During the 1930s, Bellamy continued to knit to relieve her suffering from depression after the death of her oldest son. She also turned to knitting to fulfill a need for practical, imaginative, inexpensive clothing for her two surviving younger children during the great economic Depression of the 1930s. She devised an original "way of dressing my two children from the skin out in knitted clothes—after my own easy designs—I was saving not only on the cost of clothes they wore, but on the laundry bills as well" (Bellamy 1952: 4). Her knitting method produced clothing light and porous enough to wash by hand and dry overnight. As her children grew, clothes that once fit over their diapers became their underclothing.

The children's clothing that Bellamy designed and knitted was consistent with a new philosophy of child development and new standards for children's clothing that had emerged during the early twentieth century. Nineteenth-century American children had worn clothing that mimicked adult fashions. Toddlers, both boys and girls, wore closely fitted dresses with petticoats. Complicated construction and fasteners created tight garments that restricted movement, raised concerns about hygiene, and discouraged self-reliance. Children could not dress themselves; an adult had to dress a small child in tight clothing fastened with hooks and eyes, snaps, bows, and elastic (Przybyszewski 2014).

Beginning in the 1920s, the emergent home economics and extension service movements espoused the importance of carefully selected clothing for children and conducted research on child development. Proponents of this philosophy claimed clothing influenced children's health, happiness, and development. Small children who could not put on their own clothes became passive, they believed, and basic styles with such simple fasteners as a few large buttons encouraged self-reliance. Concerned that tight clothing caused various disorders, including bacterial growth on skin, researchers recommended that children's clothing, including undergarments, allow freedom of movement for wholesome play and good hygiene. Clothing should also allow exposure to sun during summer months (Elder 1927; Przybyszewski 2014). These beliefs set the standards for twentieth-century children's clothing, and Bellamy's mid-century knitted clothing designs for children met the criteria. Her garments stretched in all directions, allowing freedom of movement. They laundered easily for good hygiene. Toddlers could dress themselves with ease. Her designs could be made at home using inexpensive materials, a bonus for Depression-era parents.

As a Depression-era mother herself, Bellamy wasted no time finding a way to sell instructions for her unique new knitted designs. A friend recommended her to *Woman's Home Companion*, where she had the "pleasure and profit of selling the idea to [editor] Martha Cobb Peabody" (Bellamy 1952: 4). In 1934, *Woman's Home Companion* featured a series of her designs dubbed *Puffbunny Wardrobes*, plus a thirty-six-page booklet sold separately (1934). Bellamy designed an economical wardrobe in a series of four practical layers: Skinbunnies (shorts and light shirts), Hopbunnies (short suits and dresses), Hugbunnies and Topbunnies (coats and hats), and Snowbunnies (snow suits). Bellamy used rib knits to provide stretch, resilience, and long wear life. The magazine required Bellamy to hire a professional photographer to capture her designs in an attractive manner (Young 2012). Her 4-year-old son Rufus and 2-year-old daughter Jane modeled their hand-knitted garments; an editor named Rufus and Jane "Master Four" and "Miss Two." Her daughter remembers the photo shoot as being very hot and that she and Rufus were a bit naughty by the end of the session (Young 2012). *Woman's Home Companion*, a widely circulated and popular periodical, introduced Bellamy's innovative design for children's hand knits to 2.8 million readers (Endres and Lueck 1996). Bellamy reported that she received "letters from women all over the country telling me of their enthusiasm for the idea" (Bellamy 1952: 4).

Eight years later, *Woman's Home Companion* published a wartime-era article by Bellamy that explained her first steps in the invention of number knitting. In later publications, she would attribute her earlier modular knitting project to a friend who asked her to design a child's coverlet using only knitted squares, a pattern she sold to *Woman's Home Companion* (Bellamy 1949; Casey 1945; "Knitting" 1952). However, writing in first person and a conversational voice for *Woman's Home Companion*, she gave credit to her daughter who had learned to knit small squares in school and wanted to make doll clothes. Bellamy wrote, "'All I know how to knit', mourned my daughter, 'is a little square. You can't make anything out of a square except a blanket'" (Bellamy 1942: 55). Bellamy found no knitting books for dolls, so devised a way to make doll clothing using only squares. Two squares made a boy doll's sun suit or cap and four squares a pullover. She worked out a geometric, modular method for stitching together many small squares in particular ways to construct wardrobes for her daughter's dolls:

Any creature, doll or what not, has a personal square. You can find it by measuring from shoulder to shoulder. Then you make a sample of any yarn you have, on any needles that are handy, and see how many stitches you knit to one inch. Then you multiply one by the other and you have the answer to how many stitches in my square. Presently you have a boxful, a bagful, a trunkful of squares. Then you put them together, with mother's help, the way we've suggested and you have a complete outfit. (Bellamy 1942: 55)

FIGURE 2.2 Bellamy's daughter Jane as "Miss Two" models a Snowbunny. She wears the rest of her Puffbunny outfit underneath: Topbunny coat, Hugbunny dress, and Skinbunny underwear. The unique design laces together the Snowbunny suit with matching mittens, socks, and hood that slip on and off as one whole piece. The wide collar turns up against wind and down for the sun. *Woman's Home Companion*, December 1934. Photo courtesy of Susan Strawn.

For 6 cents, a reader could order a "Knitting Square Table" from *Woman's Home Companion*, showing how many squares were needed for each garment, with directions for putting them together.

Bellamy's writing style is clear, personable, and distinctive—as her mature knitwear designs would become. Her written voice in articles reads like a personal letter to a friend, light-hearted and often humorous. The lightness of her written voice belies a seriousness of purpose for her knitting technique and the intentionality with which she would further develop her technical craft and establish a successful business.

After the Puffbunny Wardrobe publication, Bellamy had studied the history of knitting, although scant information existed at the time. She tested many knitting patterns and techniques to better master the craft of knitting. As she did so, she began to understand the potential of hand knitting and how it could be pushed into the realm of art. The purpose of machine knitting was not to "promote a craft, with its partnership of imagination and hand, but to produce saleable garments in profitable numbers" (Bellamy 1952: 5). Through her research, Bellamy concluded that hand knitting had lost much knowledge and originality to machine knitting and the commercialization of hand knits. She believed all hand knitters, given appropriate tools and techniques, could reclaim the opportunity to create garments of their own original designs.

Number knitting defined

Hand knitting, by definition, is the process of using two or more needles to create fabric by inter-looping strands of yarn across horizontal rows of stitches. Hand-knitted fabric grows vertically row-by-row. Knitting requires only two basic stitches, knit and purl. Positioning knit and purl stitches in specified ways creates textured surfaces on knitted fabric, and interlocking different color yarns creates color motif patterns. A typical knitted garment is knitted flat in several pieces in the final desired shapes that will be stitched together. Alternatively, a garment may be knitted in the round and openings cut into the fabric as needed (to accommodate space for sleeves, for example). Knitted fabric stretches in all directions and may be as porous or dense as the size of yarn and needles determines (Kadolph and Marcketti 2016).

Bellamy based number knitting on these standards for knitting and knitted fabric. However, true to her independent and creative nature she invented an innovative approach to modular knitted structure that defied conventions of knitting at the time. First, she used only knit stitches, a technique that produces garter stitch fabric. Two rows of knit stitches produce a characteristic horizontal ridge of bumps along both sides of garter stitch knitted fabric. (Garter stitch knitted fabric looks the same front and back, making it fully reversible.) Second, she applied geometric principles to modular garment construction. Each number-knitted garment is constructed of geometric units connected by picking up stitches along one straight side of another unit or combination of units. Units are completed and others added on each side until the finished size is reached: a modular method of constructing a garment with minimal seams. Repeated geometric units form the shape of the garment, and modular units produce a fabric with resilience that stretches in all directions. Third, Bellamy invented a new graphing system that can be used to plan and design a garment before knitting begins.

After her move to Maine in 1945, Bellamy found herself much in demand as an instructor of number knitting. Word of number knitting spread from such unlikely sources as her daughter's high school teacher and the director of the Kennebunk Brick Store Museum (Bellamy 1952). Encouraged by local interest and with support from *McCall Needlework Magazine* editor Elizabeth Blondel, Bellamy patented her unique knitting technique (1952: 10). She filed the patent application in 1945 and received a patent for "Number Knitting" on January 27, 1948 (Bellamy 1948). The introductory paragraph in the patent describes her invention:

The present invention relates to number knitting and comprises a method of hand knitting and articles produced thereby. According to this method an article is formed progressively in numbered units each of which, after the first, is picked up in the knitting from a previously knitted unit with a complete edge. Each of these units has a boundary of straight lines and is one of a plurality of fundamental shapes or combinations thereof. Yarns of different colors or characteristics may be used and very ornamental results attained. (Bellamy 1948)

Eight columns of descriptive text in the patent clarify objectives and detail methods used in her invention. The text emphasizes the "novel and advantageous" technique that allows for design in successive units, specifies graphs by which to plan knitted designs and produce finished articles with resilient shapes. The majority of the patent describes construction and application of six geometric units all knitted in garter stitch: (1) square, (2) right triangle, (3) parallelogram, (4) rectangle, (5) divided square, and (6) double parallelogram. A graph for a knitted blanket, one of her earliest designs, illustrates the method of planning the order in which successive units are knitted. The patent also elaborates on eight general rules for number knitting (Bellamy 1948).

After the patent was issued, Bellamy continued to experiment with techniques and designs for refined garments for women. She understood knitting as an artistic medium. Using a variety of yarns and needle sizes, she designed knitted garments with intriguing silhouettes and flattering drape. Her shawls and stoles, for example, were knitted of thin mohair yarn on large needles, achieving an airy, open fabric that allowed a glimpse of a gown beneath. Taken to an extreme, her hooded cloak resembled the winged outline of a butterfly, yet draped gracefully around the torso with hood over the head or falling in back. Modular construction of her fitted garments created unusual shapes for lapels, necklines, and edges. Her comfortable and versatile jackets, blouses, and capes adapted easily to different sizes and were light as leaves. A modular-knitted circle could become an evening hood, double cape wrap, or cape scarf. She experimented further with such unusual fibers as straw yarn for hats, bags, and belts and with copper, gold, and silver yarn for dramatic evening wear.

In 1948 she began writing her book about number knitting. In 1952 she presented her results in *Number Knitting: The New All-Way Stretch Method*, published by Crown Press, Inc. of New York City with an initial press run of 5,000 copies.[3] Interestingly, she expanded and redefined the geometric shapes to include (1) square, (2) rectangle, (3) triangle (left and right), (4) divided square, (5) divided triangle, (6) single wing (left and right), and (7) double wing. She also revised and elaborated on general rules for number knitting:

> Rule 1. The *basic square* is the smallest box on the graph page and must be numbered. This number equals stitches wide and ridges high.
>
> Rule II. *Cast on and off with extreme looseness.* The *cast on* row is counted as the first row. *Cast on* and *cast off* rows form the *flat edges.*
>
> Rule III. *Slip the first stitch and purl the last stitch* in every row, beginning with the last stitch of the second row. This forms a chain on edges of the work; these edges are the *rising edges.*
>
> Rule IV. To *decrease*, knit two stitches together; to *increase*, knit twice in one stitch—once in front once in back. Counting from either edge, every other row only, decrease on 2nd and 3rd stitches, increase on 2nd. Double decrease or increase when diagonal runs through center of unit. All decreases or increases are made regularly and in the same position, every other row, to achieve the diagonal line.
>
> Rule V. A *diagonal edge* may not be picked up and knitted from, or joined to, a straight edge; but must always be joined to another diagonal edge.
>
> Rule VI. To *join* edges of two units:... knit together the last stitch (first row) of each ridge with the corresponding ridge stitch of the adjoining unit; knit without further joining (not slipping the first stitch of return row).
>
> Rule VII. *Units of charts* are numbered. Pick up, knitting at the same time, these units in numbered order ... turning diagram so that unit being knitted is right side up.
>
> Rule VIII. *Tie contrasting yarn or key tag* on first unit, to indicate right side of work. (Bellamy 1952: 58)

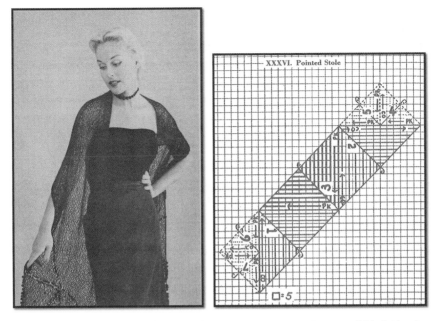

FIGURE 2.3 Bellamy's Pointed Stole design is composed of seven divided triangles. Numbers indicate the order they are knitted. PK indicates where stitches are picked up to begin knitting consecutive units. Photo by Douglas Armsten. Courtesy of Jane Churchill Young.

By the time she wrote *Number Knitting*, Bellamy had also devised new notations and knitting terms for graphs to further guide the number knitter. She termed cast-on edges of the work as *flat edges* and those edges vertical to the needles that rise as the work progresses as *rising edges*. A short line drawn on the graph represented the beginning of a unit, a longer line with a loop the end of that unit. An ellipse indicated a stitch in some patterns. An ellipse with a plus sign inside was a symbol to increase a stitch, an ellipse with a minus sign inside the symbol to decrease a stitch. A circle indicated a short strand of yarn of a different color tied into a free-floating loop and used as a stitch marker. Other symbols showed where to drop or break yarn (Bellamy 1952). Bellamy's system of graphs and notations is among the earliest attempts observed to date that present knitted pattern instructions using a format with charts and symbols.[4] Bellamy's charts provided a visual shorthand that broke with the traditional standard of lengthy written instructions for printed knitting patterns.

Number knitting inspiration

Bellamy recounted something of a perfect storm in her preferences and personality that inspired the invention of number knitting. First and foremost, she loved working with wool fiber. In the introduction to *Number Knitting*, Bellamy opined,

"Wool is a beautiful—and a live—medium" (p. 2). She compared its resilience with that of the human nervous system:

> Now this same "live" yarn under a microscope reveals the delicate and exquisite mechanism of a strand of yarn: it resembles the hinges of the spinal column. To knit too tightly can only result in strain—like the nervous tension in the spine—on the yarn! Pulled to its elasticity it can relax only in shrinkage, which is certainly the nervous breakdown of any fabric. (Bellamy 1952: 2)

Knitting experts at the time taught knitters that only tight, evenly knitted work would hold its shape. Bellamy disagreed and proved them wrong. She was by preference a knitter who worked her stitches loosely. Wool yarn knitted on large needles created fabric that also held its shape, thanks to the unique properties of wool fiber. Wool resists wrinkles and retains its shape through its natural resilience (Kadolph and Marcketti 2016). Wool yarn knitted loosely on large needles was perfect for the loose, open, stretchy knitted fabric at the heart of number knitting.

However, her rebellious and frugal personality drove much of the work of invention. A self-described frugal knitter, Bellamy considered efficient use of materials a top priority. Her resolve began in the 1930s when a self-designated knitting expert at a yarn shop sold her too much yarn to knit a cardigan for her two-year-old daughter. The expert estimated the amount of yarn based on the manufacturer's recommendation but then refused to reimburse her for leftover skeins. Incensed, Bellamy recalled, "Now I was a rebel against knitting. I took my leftovers home and looked at them resentfully. 'I'd like to knit my own way'" (Bellamy 1952: 3).

Yarn manufacturers not only spun and sold yarn but also published the majority of knitting pattern instruction booklets through the 1950s. Pattern instructions specified the varieties and amounts of yarn required to knit different styles. Most called for small needles and densely knitted work, which took more yarn for each piece. In addition, manufacturers encouraged styles that required more yarn: matching skirt and sweater sets during the 1930s and the craze of argyle stockings and knitting for the whole family during the postwar years (Strawn 2007). She did not hide her disdain for yarn manufacturers who dominated the knitting pattern market: "it is he [manufacturer] who manufactures the medium used by the craftsman, the knitter, and stamps the design with CHICKENFEATHER YARNS are the best yarns. Use CHICKENFEATHER YARNS when you are knitting CHICKENFEATHER DESIGNS" (Bellamy 1952: 5).

Bellamy believed yarn manufacturers had hijacked the knitting pattern industry and intimidated knitters into compliance with their specifications. Bellamy's number knitting, in contrast, relied on pattern graphs that closely estimated correct amounts of yarn. In addition, number-knitted garments required less yarn. Number knitting calls for modular units knit in a much looser stitch on larger needles than typical patterns of the mid-twentieth century.

Marketing number knitting

Doubtless needing to support herself after her move to Maine in 1945, Bellamy marketed number knitting for *income*, reminiscent of women throughout history and across cultures who have turned to making cloth for financial survival. Interestingly, she promoted and sold number knitting as an artisan handcraft rather than art or couture fashion. Her timing was excellent. For one thing, the hand-knitting market included millions of postwar American men, women, and children who had learned to knit for the war effort during the Second World War. Yarn manufacturers who sought civilian markets after the war predicted, correctly, that many wartime knitters would become avid postwar knitters (Strawn 2007).

Bellamy attributed to her established publishing connections the ease with which she was able to introduce number knitting to the world of handcraft. She wrote articles and sold instructions for her designs in periodicals that maintained offices in her former home, New York City. In 1946 alone, *McCall Needlework* published three features on number knitting and offered instruction pamphlets for "designs by Virginia Bellamy."[5] The articles show the development of simple knitted squares into more complex geometric shapes that were joined in similar ways to the doll and children's clothes patterns. The marketing appealed to women's fashion sense as well as to the practicality of the method and ease in making. The summer 1946 issue of *McCall Needlework* reported, "Thousands of our readers have already shown their interest in the new Number Knitting which was introduced in the previous issue of this magazine" (37).

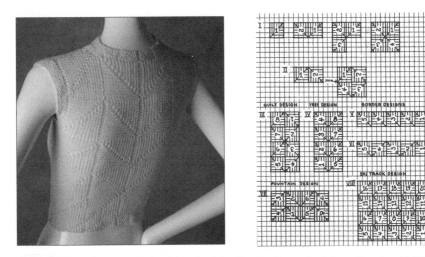

FIGURE 2.4 An extant knitted garment and instructions chart from *Number Knitting* demonstrate Bellamy's complex and sophisticated application of modular knitting. Photo by Mark Anthony. Illustration courtesy of Jane Churchill Young.

After her patent was issued, she turned attention to the larger world of handcraft. Her article for *Craft Horizons* elaborated on her process of discovery, modular knitting techniques, and the advantages of number knitting for the craftsperson wishing to create original hand-knitted designs (Bellamy 1949). Noted textile journalist Louise Llewellyn Jarecka praised the technical aspects of Bellamy's work as engineering and architecture in a feature article for *Handweaver and Craftsman* (1950). Knitters keen to learn more about the number knitting wrote her with questions, so many that she found herself "deluged with mail and in a quandary." The only way to keep up was to hire a secretary and develop a correspondence course to teach the principles of number knitting to a larger market. Spurring her market with correspondence course advertisements in *Craft Horizons* and *Handweaver and Craftsman*, she reported "subscribers living as far away as Alaska, Australia, England and South Africa" (Bellamy 1952: 11). She also worked on writing her book, no doubt relieved after its publication eased demands from correspondence course subscribers. *Number Knitting* presents Bellamy's original designs, each with graphs and photographs of finished products, but concludes with instructions for planning and designing original patterns. Bellamy traveled the country teaching number knitting and promoting sales of the book ("Knitting" 1952).

Bellamy and the mid-century Studio Craft Movement

Bellamy's approach to the craft of knitting is consistent with the mid-century studio craft movement, which emphasized the invention of new ways of working, new techniques and novel uses of traditional materials as the path to innovation (Adamson 2013; Koplos and Metcalf 2010). Mid-century handcraft was increasingly aligned philosophically with fine art, as witnessed in the launch of such periodicals as *Craft Horizons* and *Handweaver and Craftsman*, artistic periodicals dedicated emphatically to reviving and honoring a broad range of American handcrafts. (*Craft Horizons* included a feature article for needle workers in each issue.)

In *Number Knitting*, Bellamy acknowledged that yarn manufacturers needed to stimulate their market and then reflected, "This is fine as far as it goes. The trouble is it goes in a circle, for unless an artisan moves a craft into the realm of art, it will chase its own tail and wind up on the wheel of a machine" (5). With her new way of knitting, she intended to free knitters from slavish adherence to knitting patterns driven by yarn manufacturers. She encouraged knitters to follow her example and experiment with their own design variations. She wanted knitters to explore the capability of their tools and medium: knitting needles of every size and yarn of various kinds. Bellamy wrote to her readers, "no matter how you knit, something of yourself goes into it" (249).

Number knitting units: Influenced by art and fashion

Bellamy's use of geometric units in her designs reflected the vernacular of artists in the twentieth century. This approach was led by artists Pablo Picasso and Georges Braque, who abandoned the use of a perspective with a single viewpoint and instead used simple geometric shapes and interlocking planes to create a more abstracted form (Rewald 2004). Cubists liberated art from copying nature. They dissected and fractured objects into smaller geometric facets, then reassembled them into new forms. Most closely associated with painting, cubism also proved a major influence on architecture, sculpture, interior design, and fashion design (Rewald 2004). Cubism provided a new way of seeing abstracted forms filtered into the creative process.

Fashion designer Madeleine Vionnet divided the plane of her bias-cut gowns into units. Bellamy, too, manipulated units to take advantage of the fabric's drape that comes as gravity exerts its force on the fabric. Both Vionnet and Bellamy left garments unlined to allow the fabric to react to the body and to gravity in its own way (A.G. Nauta 2013). A separate slip or dress allowed each part to move independently as they shaped to and moved with the body. Their garments made women feel comfortable, flattered, and timeless.

Conclusion

Rebellious frugality, coupled with need for income, contributed to Bellamy's development and career as a designer. Uncomfortable with the conformity and submissive behavior expected of women during the 1950s, she explored independent attitudes toward clothing design and encouraged knitters to consider her patterns only as starting points in their own design work. Bellamy believed women were problem-solvers with the intellect necessary to understand the medium of knitting and to create their own designs rather than follow the dictates of the yarn industry. Her career takes on particular significance and interest because she worked as a freethinking designer in a time of mass fashion conformity. She protected her designs with a patent and name attribution on her publications during a time when most knitting designers worked in anonymity. Despite the initial press run of 5,000 books, few copies of *Number Knitting* remain on library shelves, and only an occasional (and costly) resale copy becomes available in bookstores or on Internet sites. Perhaps *Number Knitting* was among the many volumes weeded from library shelves over the decades, while personal copies may have disappeared into estate sales. Bellamy's case illustrates the fragility of design history and the illusive nature of innovative design processes.

Notes

1   The only publications on her life and work appeared in *Knitting Traditions* (2012) and *Piecework* (2017).

2   Bellamy also published poetry and short stories, several in *Fiction Parade* and *The Saturday Review of Literature*. In the early 1930s, Virginia had met E.B. White, editor of *The New Yorker* magazine. She described her frustration that none of the poems that she had submitted to the magazine had ever been published. White confided that his secretary/receptionist was responsible for reading the submitted poems and forwarding the ones she liked to him. He instructed Virginia to submit her poems directly to him, and he would personally select and publish the ones that he liked. Between 1932 and 1945, *The New Yorker* published twelve of her poems (http:// archives.newyorker.com /#).

3   The only reference to number of copies printed was found in the December 1, 1952 *Portsmouth Herald*. Library shelves in the United States, Canada, and the United Kingdom hold only fifty-one copies of *Number Knitting*, according to the library catalog database World Cat.

4   Charts had been used to show color patterns in knitting and cross-stitch embroidery throughout the nineteenth century and earlier, but the system of charts and symbols used in contemporary knitting instructions is generally attributed to the work of designers Dorothy Reade and Marianne Kinzel.

5   "McCall *Number Knitting* Pamphlet No. 2 for five designs by Virginia Bellamy" cost 25 cents (Bellamy 1946: 37).

Bibliography

Adamson, G. (2013), *The Invention of Craft*, London: Bloomsbury.

A.G. Nauta Couture: All About Fashion (2013), *Madeleine Vionnet, Master in Manipulating Fabric*. Available online: https://agnautacouture.com/2013/05/12 /madeleine-vionnet-master-in-manipulating-fabric/.

Bellamy, V.W. (August, 1934), "The Puffbunny Wardrobe," *Woman's Home Companion*, 61(8): 77.

Bellamy, V.W. (September, 1934), "Puffbunny Wardrobes II: The Hopbunny Suit," *Woman's Home Companion*, 61(9): 98–99.

Bellamy, V.W. (October, 1934), "Puffbunny Wardrobes III: Hugbunnies and Topbunnies," *Woman's Home Companion*, 61(10): 106–107.

Bellamy, V.W. (December, 1934), "Snowbunnies," *Woman's Home Companion*, 61(12): 90–91.

Bellamy, V.W. (December, 1942), "Look Mother, I Can Knit!" *Woman's Home Companion*, 69 (12).

Bellamy, V.W. (1946), "Number Knitting," *McCall Needlework*, Summer: 37, 54, 81–82.

Bellamy, V.W. (1946–47), "Number Knitting," *McCall Needlework*, Winter: 29, 53.

Bellamy, V.W. (1948), *Number Knitting*. Patent no. 2,435,068.

Bellamy, V.W. (1949), "Geometric Number Knitting," *Craft Horizons*, 9(2): 22–24.

Bellamy, V.W. (April, 1950), "Advertisement for Correspondence Course in Number Knitting," *Handweaver and Craftsman*, 1(1): 41.

Bellamy, V.W. (Summer, 1950), "Advertisement for Correspondence Course: Geometric Number Knitting," *Craft Horizons*, 1(2): 1.

Bellamy, V.W. (Summer, 1950), "Advertisement for Correspondence Course in Number Knitting," *Handweaver and Craftsman*, 1(2): 55.

Bellamy, V.W. (Fall, 1950), "Advertisement for Correspondence Course in Number Knitting," *Handweaver and Craftsman*, 1(3): 44.

Bellamy, V.W. (1952), *Number Knitting: The New All-Way Stretch Method*, New York: Crown Publishers.

Bellamy, V.W. (1976), *And the Morning and the Evening*, Freeport, ME: Bond Wheelwright.

Braaten, A.W. (2012), "Virginia Woods Bellamy: Poet, Designer, Knitter," *Knitting Traditions* (Fall): 22–25.

Casey, F.R. (June, 1945), "Knitting News," *Woman's Home Companion*, 72(6): 72.

Druchunas, D. (2010), *Successful Lace Knitting: Celebrating the Work of Dorothy Reade*, Bothell, WA: Martingale.

Elder, M.B. (1927), *Clothes for Little Folks*, Ames, IA: Iowa State College Extension Service.

Endres, K. and Lueck, T. (1996), *Women's Periodicals in the United States: Consumer Magazines*, Westport: Greenwood Publishing Group.

"Francis Bellamy, Author, Was 85" (1972), *New York Times*, February 4: 34.

Jarecka, L.L. (1950), "Number Knitting—A New Way with an Old Art," *Handweaver & Craftsman*, 2(1): 22–24, 64.

Kadolph, S. and Marcketti, S. (2016), *Textiles*, 12th edition, London: Pearson Education.

Kinzel, M. (1972), *First Book of Modern Lace Knitting*, New York: Dover. (First published in 1953.)

"Knitting Method Saves Time, Energy" (1952), *Portsmouth Herald*, December 1: 2.

Koplos, J. and Metcalf, B. (2010), *Makers: A History of American Studio Craft*, Hendersonville, NC: Center for Craft, Creativity and Design.

Przybyszewski, L. (2014), *The Lost Art of Dress*, New York: Basic Books.

Rewald, S. (2004), "Cubism," in *Heilbrunn Timeline of Art History*, New York: The Metropolitan Museum of Art. Available online: http://www.metmuseum.org/toah/hd/cube/hd_cube.htm.

Rothman, S. (1994), *Living in the Shadow of Death: Tuberculosis and the Social Experience of Illness in American History*, New York: Basic Books.

Strawn, S. (2007), *Knitting America: A Glorious Heritage from Warm Socks to High Art*. Minneapolis, MN: Voyageur Press.

Strawn, S. (2012), "Number Knitting: The New All-Ways Stretch Method," *Knitting Traditions*: 26–29.

Strawn, S. and Braaten, A. (2017), "Virginia Woods Bellamy and the Puffbunny Wardrobe," *Piece Work Magazine*: 25–30.

Young, J.A.C. (2012), Conversations with Ann W. Braaten, March 18 and May 1.

3 TINA LESER: GLOBAL VISION

APRIL CALAHAN

Fantasies of escape and the lure of exotic lands are woven into the work of American fashion designer Tina Leser (pronounced Lee-ser). Perhaps the happy result of a somewhat unorthodox childhood, Leser sought design inspiration from foreign shores and embraced small, artisanal textile producers from around the globe. At a time when the American fashion industry was still struggling to find its own identity, Leser's conceptualization of fashion was vaster than the polarizing discourse of New York versus Paris. Often associated with the development of "The American Look" alongside her contemporaries Claire McCardell and Bonnie Cashin, Leser's unique contribution to American fashion was her global perspective and her commitment to and belief in the generative power of the fashion industries.

The early years

Given the circumstances of her family life, Leser's creative talents were perhaps preordained. She was born Christine Buffington in Philadelphia in 1910 (Belyea 2004), yet her own biography (Biography 1 n.d.) as well as press produced by her contemporaries give her birth name as Christine Wetherill Shillard-Smith. The era's social stigma regarding adoption is likely the cause of this inaccuracy—as a small child, Leser was adopted by her mother's cousin (Howley 2009). Both Leser's birth mother, Mary Edith Cox, and her adoptive mother, Georgine Wetherill Shillard-Smith, belonged to the Wetherill family of Philadelphia, whose prominent

FIGURE 3.1 Tina Leser in the early years of her career, c. 1940. Source: Tina Leser Collection, Box Photos-1940s, Special Collections, Gladys Marcus Library, Fashion Institute of Technology, New York. Image courtesy of Fashion Institute of Technology|SUNY, FIT Library Special Collections and College Archive.

social status in the city dates back to the founding of the Philadelphia Free Quaker Society in 1781. Both Mary Edith and Georgine enjoyed privileged childhoods (Belyea 2004).

Shortly after Tina's birth, Mary Edith separated from her husband, Charles Buffington. His chronic alcoholism fractured the young family and, living in California, Mary Edith struggled to provide for her and her young daughter by working as a freelance artist. Leser's adoption was arranged when Georgine, and her husband Charles Shillard-Smith, spent several months wintering in California (Howley 2009). They were childless and had the means to provide young Tina with not only the best education but also a life of luxury. Buffington later perished in a trolley accident and Mary Edith happily remarried a few years later and became known in artistic circles as Mary Edith Cox Maison (Belyea 2004).

While Leser became Georgine's official charge—and later, heir—evidence suggests that the relationship between Mary Edith and Georgine was warm and relaxed. Leser enjoyed a bi-coastal upbringing, attending the finest private schools on both coasts, displaying a talent for art and music from a young age. This is not surprising given the fact that many of her family members were professional artists or musicians. Leser's aunt Eugenie was known to be such an impassioned, frenzied artist that she had difficulty maintaining her own household (Belyea 2004). Both Leser's birth mother and adoptive mother were skilled painters as well. The Coachella Valley was frequently the subject of Mary Edith's work, and her quick, impressionistic style won her the reputation for working "like a man" (Belyea 2004). Georgine's talents were honed under the tutelage of American artists James McNeill Whistler and Robert Henri, and her work was exhibited professionally in New York at the, now famous, 1913 Armory Show (Hoffman 1954: 10).[1] Georgine's investment in art extended beyond the scope of her own work, and her personal art collection included works by some of the great modern masters—Monet, Cezanne, Van Gogh, and Picasso (Ann 1940).

The Wetherill family was deeply committed to the arts, both personally and financially. The family's prosperity allowed them to direct significant resources toward funding public arts programs (Belyea 2004), and Leser's early immersion in philanthropic efforts went on to shape her views on fashion's role in the global economy. In 1915, Leser's aunt, Christine Wetherill Stevenson, established the Philadelphia Art Alliance, and converted the family's Rittenhouse Square mansion into its headquarters (Belyea 2004). Now one of the oldest arts centers in the United States, the Alliance has been the sponsor institution for many noteworthy presentations throughout the years, including Andrew Wyeth's first solo exhibition in 1936 as well as early experiments between John Cage and Merce Cunningham in 1950 (Philadelphia Art Alliance 2009).

In the early 1950s, Georgine undertook her own philanthropic endeavors, founding the Belleair Art Center in Clearwater, Florida. The Art Center provided not only a permanent home for Georgine's extensive art collection but also community arts programming including classes, residencies, and workshops. Leser was instrumental in aiding her mother (who was then in her mid-seventies) in establishing the Center (Belyea 2004). The institution would go on to play a significant role in Leser's adult life; she once noted that the Center "holds the center of my heart" (Albert 1965). Many of the benevolent projects implemented by Leser over the course of her life owe their inspiration to the example set by Georgine and her extended family (Albert 1965).

While Leser was brought up as a member of Main Line society—a world of breeding, elegance, and traditional good manners—there was also a strong bohemian streak among the women of the Wetherill family. Her freethinking birth mother, Mary Edith, was a devoted member of Mary Baker Eddy's Church of Christ, Scientist, while Georgine's convictions ran more toward the metaphysical. She was a theosophist, a believer in a philosophy that draws on the mystical tenets of, among other beliefs, Hinduism, Zoroastrianism, and the Kabala. Georgine's original vision for the Art Center was of a self-sustaining artist's commune governed by the tenets of theosophy. While practical concerns prevented Georgine's little utopia from materializing, one can see how she relied on theosophy in her altruistic endeavors. She was a committed believer, and her theosophical studies led her around the globe, frequently with young Tina in tow.

It was this informal education Leser received circumnavigating the globe as a child that made the greatest impact on the aesthetic she would later develop as a fashion designer. Leser's widower, Jim Howley, related an amusing anecdote of Georgine and Tina's relationship. Georgine and young Tina were in Maine at the family's house in Winter Harbor. Approximately aged 10, Tina was taking her daily bath when Georgine barged in and proclaimed, "Get out of the bathtub! We're going to India!" The pair *immediately* departed for Madras, where they remained for the winter. Georgine studied at the theosophical center located there, while young Tina, enthralled with the colorful pageantry of the Maharajas—who were still in power at this time—developed a deep, abiding love of textiles and a keen sense of color (Albert 1965). Leser later remarked about this time period, "after seeing an elephant in India with a ruby necklace, I thought anything is possible" (Miscellaneous notes n.d.).

In 1929, Leser made her formal debut into Philadelphia high society. Two years later, she married Curtin Leser, a marine biologist. The newlyweds relocated to Honolulu in the early 1930s, where Curtin worked for the Academy of Science, and Tina took up spearfishing and diving with the Hawaiian locals (Carson 1945). She quickly realized her East Coast wardrobe did not fit her new lifestyle and recognized a ripe market in Honolulu for chic sportswear and gossamer evening gowns befitting warm weather (Carson 1945).

In 1935, Leser opened a specialty shop that catered to the unique needs of island life. She sold high-end ready-to-wear lines such as Nettie Rosenstein and Germaine Monteil as well as her own custom designs, which she created with the help of a French dressmaker (Bailey 1940). A shipping strike in the early years of the business tested Leser's creativity. She was unable to receive the wholesale garments she ordered from New York, nor was she able to acquire the materials she ordinarily used in her own designs. She improvised and turned to the materials at hand. Sailcloth, ropes and grommets, and other materials readily available on the island were used in her early play clothes (Carson 1945). She used native textiles such as *palaka*, a shirting worn by Hawaiian fieldworkers, and began creating her own hand-painted and printed textiles, which frequently featured tropical motifs of bright island botanicals or underwater seascapes.

Leser's boutique, Tina Leser Gowns, was located directly across the street from the Royal Hawaiian hotel, which attracted a wealthy, jet-setting crowd (Howley 2009). Her client base at the Honolulu shop included socialites such as Mrs. George Vanderbilt and celebrities such as The Dolly Sisters and Joan Crawford. While Leser's professional life was beginning to blossom, her personal life was less auspicious. Her marriage to Curtin was unraveling, and sometime between 1936 and 1938 they divorced. With the marriage dissolved, it was everyone's expectation that Leser would return to the mainland and resume her life as a Main Line socialite—particularly Georgine, whose correspondence pleaded for her daughter to come home (Howley 2009). But an independent spirit was strong among the Wetherill women, and Leser was no exception. She decided to remain in Hawaii and try to make a go of her small business, and having already made a name for herself, she kept Leser as her professional name for the remainder of her career, even after she remarried in 1948 (Howley 2009).

As Leser's designs returned stateside in the suitcases of some of the world's most photographed women, opportunity came knocking. Department stores, including Bonwit Teller and Saks Fifth Avenue, clamored for her designs which sold out in a matter of days (Biography 2 n.d.). Leser's Hawaii workrooms strained under the flurry of incoming orders. Her staff, at this time, consisted of six Japanese seamstresses, and this new explosion in business required new production capabilities (Howley 2009). In the ensuing months, Leser scrambled to resolve her production problems. Manufacturing garments in Hawaii and shipping them halfway around the world was cost-prohibitive; she needed manufacturing capabilities stateside if the business was to expand. Troubles seemed to lurk around every corner. Technical difficulties surrounding the hand-painted and printed textiles had to be resolved before they could be launched into a wider market.

In the early 1940s, she expanded her business to the Mainland—to much critical acclaim. But her troubles were not entirely over. She had union problems, and her business manager died unexpectedly. Knowing little about business in general, Leser's operations slid into the red; she said, "The more we sold, the more we lost" (Stiles 1950). Leser was splitting her time between her New York atelier and the Honolulu boutique until 1942, when she was required to close the shop and leave the island just after the bombing of Pearl Harbor (Howley 2009).

What was on one hand a bane for Leser's business turned out to be her salvation. With the war came drafts and enlistments, and one inductee was the American fashion designer Tom Brigance. His departure into the army left New York–based manufacturer Edwin H. Foreman without a designer. Friends and buyers told Foreman about Leser's work and recommended he meet with her (Howley

2009). The resulting partnership lasted ten years and encompassed some of the most fruitful years of Leser's career. In 1945, Leser won both the Neiman Marcus Award and the prestigious Coty, Inc. American Fashion Critics' Award (Pope 1945). Her work was covered extensively by the American fashion press during the 1940s, 1950s, and 1960s, frequently pictured in *Vogue* and *Harper's Bazaar*, and newspapers of the period were rife with department store ads for her designs. The June 1945 issue of *Collier's* magazine affirms Leser's pervasive influence on American visual culture, noting that "Now you see Leser-clad beauties everywhere, from magazine front cover to nail polish ad on the back" (Carson 1945). Indeed, Leser's work was featured in countless advertising campaigns during the 1940s and 1950s, ranging from Coty cosmetics to Coca-Cola and Ford.

Global inspiration

Throughout her career, Leser flavored her designs with elements picked up in the course of her extensive travels, perhaps a pant leg inspired by the *dhoti* of India or a shoulder treatment borrowed from garments depicted on an ancient Greek vase. The exoticism of Leser's designs was acknowledged by the fashion press, and Leser asserted that while many considered them bold, "anyone can wear my clothes. It might be said that they are daring only in that they are different from the usual run... What gives a person the idea that a certain dress is extreme is usually not the dress itself but *how and where it is worn*" (Roberts n.d.). Above all, Leser—who once described her work as "half Asiatic and half just pretty and feminine"—wanted her clothes to be fun ("Tina Leser" 1986). She adapted her global inspirations into the sort of fresh, easy-to-wear garments that came to exemplify the American approach to sportswear.

From her earliest days in Hawaii, swimwear comprised a major segment of Leser's creative output, and an innovative two-piece suit dubbed "the most daring attire to appear on beaches to date" was a runaway success for Leser in 1944–1945 ("Scanty Swim Suits" 1944). Her eye-catching design featured an asymmetrical strap on the bandeau top—an idea borrowed from the traditional costume of Bali—and was offered with matching bottoms in the way of high-waisted shorts or a short sarong with built-in shorts. The design was a sensation, featured in magazine after magazine in both editorial and advertising spreads. It was produced in a myriad of textiles ranging from two-tone jersey knits to whimsical conversational prints and even an authentic Scotch tartan. The popularity of this suit opened doors for Leser, who was soon approached by the swimwear brand Gabar, and her swimwear designs were available exclusively through a highly profitable partnership with Gabar for more than twenty years (Biography 2 n.d.).

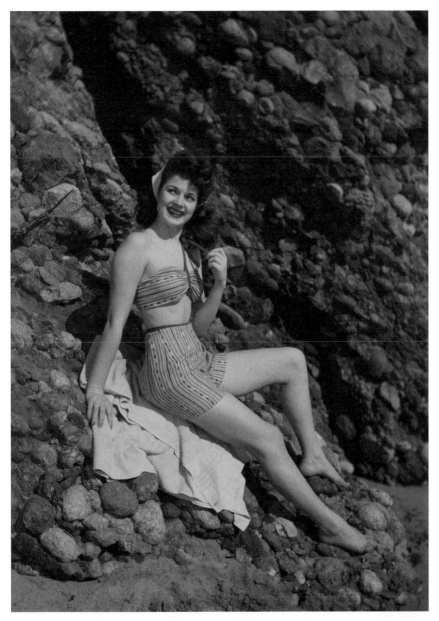

FIGURE 3.2 Miss America 1942, Jo-Carroll Dennison, modeling Leser's two-piece bathing suit inspired by traditional Balinese costume. This particular version of the suit was realized in striped Guatemalan cotton. Source: Tina Leser Collection, Box Photos-1940s Transparencies, Special Collections, Gladys Marcus Library, Fashion Institute of Technology, New York. Image courtesy of Fashion Institute of Technology|SUNY, FIT Library Special Collections and College Archive.

A beautiful example of Leser's ability to deftly integrate ethnic inspirations into the lexicon of American sportswear took the form of a 1945 white jersey "dinner dress" that blended these seemingly disparate approaches to great success. The silhouette of the skirt is unmistakably non-western, inspired by traditional Indian *dhoti*. What appears to be complex drapery is actually quite simple; "the skirt consists of one piece of material two and a half yards long which is passed through the legs from front to back, then drawn up around the waist and tied at the front" ("Southern" 1946: 86). This ingenious wrapping technique allowed the wearer to adjust the fit to her own body, solving the problem of sizing ever present in

FIGURE 3.3 Leser's white jersey dinner dress appeared in the January 14, 1946 issue of *LIFE* magazine. Photo courtesy: Estate of Phillippe Halsman/Magnum Photos.

the ready-to-wear trade. While Leser's "strapped-and-wrapped" silhouettes were specifically cited when she won the Coty Inc. American Fashion Critics' Award for 1945, she was not the only designer employing the concept (Press Release 1945). Other American designers of the era, such as Claire McCardell, also used knots, halters, and spaghetti string ties to allow the wearer to customize size and fit—so much so that these devices became a defining feature of "The American Look." Combined with a simple short-sleeved bodice with wide-scooped neck, the *dhoti* dinner dress only hints at an exotic origin, while its humble fabric and

FIGURE 3.4 Leser's original sketch for a dinner dress inspired by Indian *dhoti*, 1945. Source: Tina Leser Collection, Box Resort 1945, Special Collections, Gladys Marcus Library, Fashion Institute of Technology, New York. Image courtesy of Fashion Institute of Technology|SUNY, FIT Library Special Collections and College Archive.

ease keep it comfortably rooted in the ethos of American sportswear. Unlike some designers, whose ethnic inspirations called to mind indigenous costume rather than high fashion, Leser filtered her inspirations, delineating dress from fashion by adhering to a policy that privileged either the cut or the cloth; her ethnic-inspired garments were exotic in *either* their choice of textile or their silhouette, rarely both!

From her youth, indigenous textiles were near and dear to Leser's heart. Her early success using native Hawaiian textiles paved the way for her patronage of small exotic textile producers from around the globe; she used exquisite silks from Thailand, sturdy Guatemalan cottons, and airy Indian gauzes. Whenever possible, she preferred to commission these textiles directly from local artisans, as in the case of a black hand-woven cotton Leser commissioned from the Nadachada tribe in Assam, India, which was additionally hand-embroidered with motifs of modes of travel common within India. She used this textile for a skirt, which retailed in 1960 at the price point of $70 (Advertisement 1960). Leser saw these partnerships as mutually beneficial situations; she not only received a unique, high-quality product, but she was also able to provide income to (frequently disadvantaged) artisans working outside the system of commercial manufacture. However, production limitations or the logistics of import/export were sometimes too daunting to make these types of collaborations possible. In these cases, Leser bought liberally from the original artisans and had the textiles copied or adapted and then mass-produced—according to her own specifications—in the United States.

Shortly after Leser married her second husband, Jim Howley—a Pan Am pilot—in December of 1948, the couple embarked on a four-month around-the-world honeymoon tour. She returned from the trip with nineteen suitcases packed with costumes, fabrics, books, artwork, jewels, and accessories collected during their stops in Hawaii, Japan, India, China, Turkey, Italy, France, England, and the Persian Gulf (Robin 1949). Her 1949 collections reflected all of these influences. The Indian sari became a fixture in her collections, as did both Thai and Japanese silks. Leser was one of the first American designers to adopt the luxurious Thai silks produced by spy-turned-textile entrepreneur Jim Thompson; the two Americans being of like mind in their desire to introduce them to the U.S. wholesale market as a way to reinvigorate the faltering Thai silk trade.

Likewise, during the Japan segment of her honeymoon trip, Leser had a revelation about the state of the textile arts in postwar Japan and seized an opportunity when the presence of a famed American fashion designer caused a stir in the press. Leser explained:

> There I could hardly leave my hotel room for the stream of people who came to see me to find out what we were wearing in America. They wanted modern new styles, suited to their way of life, yet they felt they could not break with the

traditional kimonos devised by their ancestors. It was then I suggested a national design contest. The Mainichi Press, the largest Japanese press, publicized the contest all over Japan. Thousands of sketches came in and these were carefully narrowed down to 200 and sent to New York for Judging. (Dean 1949)

Only a few years after the end of the Second World War, Japan was in the throes of its rebirth as a modern nation. Leser's hopes for the competition were that contestants could "devise their own modern styles, using their beautiful fabrics and their own traditional background of styles to start from" ("There's an Oriental Air" 1949). At least half of the materials for the proposed designs were required to be of Japanese origin, which brought much-needed publicity to Japan's centuries-old textile traditions.

In September of 1949, twenty winning sketches were announced. The winning designs were made up into garments that were modeled in the first national fashion show ever held in Japan ("New Style" 1949). Monetary prizes were attached to each award, and they were sponsored by American fashion industry insiders, including Leser, Edwin H. Foreman, and the noted publicist Eleanor Lambert. Michiko Konishi of Ashiya, Hyogoken, and Toshiko Koide of Toyonakashi, Osaka, were awarded the top two prizes of $400 for their modern interpretation of the sartorial traditions of Japan ("New Style" 1949). With the success of the contest, it was established as an annual event, and the prizes eventually expanded to include full scholarships to study design in the United States. An intriguing byproduct of this contest, the Japanese press would later cite Leser's instrumental role in laying the foundation for the Japanese modeling industry (Biography 2 n.d.).

During the 1950s, Leser placed an increasing emphasis on the versatility of her clothing with the playsuit often serving as the foundation and basic building block. It was an idea that she had been working with for years, and now she advocated it wholeheartedly. (Perhaps this was the result of changes to her business model—in 1953 Leser was again designing under her own label, Tina Leser Originals, after Foreman had retired and closed his manufacturing facilities the previous year.) In sketch after sketch from the 1953 Resort collection she illustrated her thoughts on the viability of the playsuit. It adapted easily from beachwear to daywear and even eveningwear with the addition of coordinating skirts. Chic efficiency was Leser's goal for all of her Resort collections, and she frequently offered advice in the press about planning travel wardrobes. When asked about packing for Hawaiian vacations, Leser offered this advice: "You will need a lot of sun dresses with an apron-skirt, and a playsuit with a skirt. Sun dresses with jackets are perfect for luncheon" (Babette 1947). To this effect she created easy-to-pack, modular capsule collections specifically for the lady traveler.

For city wear during the 1950s, Leser expanded her base of inspiration to include the history of both art and fashion. She studied resources offered by the costume collections at both the Brooklyn Museum and The Costume Institute at The

Metropolitan Museum of Art, and her Fall 1950 collection was an amalgamation of her studies (Bender 1961). She said,

> The glamour that I've borrowed from Spain includes such colors as rich El Greco brown, soft greens and blues taken from Velasquez's paintings, and several Spanish olive tones. I've adopted the lovely Infanta neckline, which bares the shoulders in a new straight across line, for little evening blouses and sweaters, I've made cloaks instead of coats. (Leser 1950)

Like many designers before her, Leser also found French fashions of the eighteenth and early nineteenth centuries irresistible. The pleats of Watteau and fichus inspired by the Jacobin period of the French Revolution appeared in her summer collections of 1955 and 1956. A 1955 window display at Bonwit Teller prominently featured Leser's light-as-air dress with a sweetheart neckline, cap sleeves, and a bouffant shin-length petticoated skirt. Rendered in white cotton with a pink and red arrow-through-the-heart motif, the dress featured a long pleat trailing from the center back—recalling the draped and pleated backs of the eighteenth-century *robes volantes* frequently depicted in the paintings of Jean-Antoine Watteau. As was common in her work, Leser used the same textile and similar, much-shortened silhouette for a coordinating skirted playsuit. Leser used textiles and silhouettes democratically, utilizing them throughout entire collections with little prejudice as to what time of day they would be worn. "Denim … cut respectably as chiffon," noted one advertisement for her designs (Advertisement 1949).

A new chapter of Leser's career began in 1966—Tina Leser International. During a two-year break following the adoption of her own daughter, Georgine, in 1964, a daring plan had been put into motion, one she called "IDEA," shorthand for "International Design Educational Association." She spoke of her dream of making fashion international: "Today the world is very close. We no longer work in or for just one country. … All have something to give each other and the designer must see how they fit in" (Albert 1965). Leser had been working with textile artisans from abroad for decades, but IDEA took things one step further—outsourcing the production of her garments to international manufacturers. She said in 1964, "I still think that is the thing to come. … I hope it (the idea) will work with China, Japan, Portugal and other places. I HOPE it will work that way. That is why I'm working so hard at it. But these are dreams. I can only report what exists" (Osgood 1965).

In 1965, Leser implemented IDEA, choosing India as her first manufacturing destination. Years earlier, via mutual charity work, Leser had developed friendships with several prominent Indian women (Howley 2009). Premilla Wagle, daughter of the former Indian Ambassador to the United States, and Dina Wadia, daughter of a Pakistani statesman, joined Leser as business partners in the Neville Wadia Factory in Bombay. Leser owned a half interest and the remainder was split equally between Wagle and Wadia (Wagner 1965). Ever philanthropically minded, Leser's newest venture was as much about benevolence as it was about business. She recognized fashion's potency in the global economy and saw a mutually beneficial relationship in the Indian partnership. She explained, "Their workmanship is better, and they need more work to allow them better standards of living. I hope this will help promote the angle of international thinking and economic co-operation" (Albert 1965).

Evidence suggests Leser was among the very first "big-name" American designers to internationally outsource garment production. Treading unfamiliar territory was not without problems; at this time there were no precedents for manufacturing abroad, but Leser retained her sense of humor, laughing later about the challenges: "At first we couldn't get the men tailors too interested in working on dresses. Then I gave them some French dress dummies and showed them how to match dress seams. Now it's become a big game. Why, in one week they got so carried away they made over 100 dresses" ("Made-in-India" 1966). The India-made designs debuted in January of 1966 and included slim brocade suits and silk day dresses with vibrant botanical motifs (Wagner 1965). The brocade used for a stunning set of at-home pajamas was inspired by an Italian ecclesiastic textile but realized in a riotous 1960s color palette of green, gold, and purple (Meredith n.d.).

In 1967, the hues of Leser's Indian textiles were electric, "bright enough to turn night into day," declared *Vogue*. With these fabrics, she produced voluminous jeweled caftans in cotton and silk that honored her vision of "quality and simplicity" ("American" 1967: 204). An editorial photo essay in *Vogue* the same year featured one of Leser's voluminous golden silk caftans—modeled by Marisa Berenson on the island of Sardinia—made from two layers of silk, a solid slip and a gauzy overdress. The cuffs, neck, and hemlines were adorned with faux jewels of the same hue ("Vogue Patterns" 1967: 146).

By 1968 it was becoming evident that Leser's hopes for IDEA were perhaps a bit too premature. The system for manufacturing abroad was not quite viable yet. She was having problems with production delays, and buyers were becoming impatient for their promised stock (Howley 2009). She dejectedly scrapped IDEA and returned to more traditional models of manufacture in the United States. While the IDEA endeavor failed, Leser's dreams for the internationalization of the fashion industry proved prescient. Soon after, increasing numbers of American designers began to cast their sights farther and farther afield in search of cheaper manufacturing alternatives.

Following the disappointment of Tina Leser International, the company was scaled back and reorganized as Tina Leser Couture sometime during the mid- to late 1970s. Leser produced custom garments for long-time customers as well as ready-to-wear for select high-end boutiques such as Philadelphia's Nan Duskin. While her business model may have changed slightly, she continued to relish art and costume from around the globe. Her Fall 1975 collection was prototypically postmodern, combining the look of Toulouse-Lautrec's paintings of the Belle Epoque with "the glowing colors and elegant fabrics worn in the Chinese Empire at the time of the Boxer Rebellion" (Press Release 1975). As the decade progressed, production tapered off as Leser—now approaching seventy—also began to slow. She was spending more and more time at her Sands Point, Long Island, home and in 1982, after nearly fifty years in the fashion business, Leser made the decision to shut her doors permanently. Shortly after her retirement, Leser's health took a turn for the worse, and the designer passed away in January of 1986, but not before passing along the baton to the next generation of American fashion designers, having given Liz Claiborne her first job in fashion as a sketch artist (Howley 2009).

"Always, everywhere, for me, it is the fabrics that excite and inspire. ... Long ago I worked to bring the beautiful brocades, the kimono silks, the sari and hand-woven silks into the wholesale operations of American designers. Now they are very much a part of many firms' collections," remarked Leser in 1967 (Dennis 1967). Indeed, Leser's early immersion in her family's philanthropic endeavors shaped her views on the American fashion industry's generative power. She saw fashion as not only a business but also a means of improving the lives and working conditions of textile artisans worldwide. Her views on fashion's role in the global economy were in the vanguard; she understood that the world was changing and soon both the aesthetics and business of fashion would become international.

Leser's wanderlust and love of the leisure lifestyle were reflected in the clothing she produced. Her designs speak to the complexity of the period between the 1940s and the 1960s, a period when modernism began to embrace multicultural points of view, heralding the rise of the postmodern aesthetic, which gleefully blends temporal and cultural references at will. From this eclectic cultural melting pot, Leser drew her inspiration for chic clothing, which met the modern woman's needs for a versatile wardrobe, while simultaneously indulging her longing for fun, fantasy, and escape.

Archival Sources

Eleanor Lambert Collection. Special Collections. Gladys Marcus Library, Fashion Institute of Technology, New York.

Tina Leser Collection. Special Collections. Gladys Marcus Library, Fashion Institute of Technology, New York.

Tina Leser Vertical Files. Irene Lewisohn Costume Reference Library, The Costume Institute, The Metropolitan Museum of Art, New York.

Note

1   The article contains an error in the date assigned to the Armory show; it says 1912, but the show was first mounted in 1913.

Bibliography

Advertisement: Bonwit Teller (1960) [labeled "Inquirer"] April 26, Tina Leser Collection, Box A5.

Advertisement: Gidding's (1949), *Cincinnati Enquirer*, March 17.

Albert, I. (1965), "Tina Leser at Work," *Clearwater Sun*, May 2.

"American to the Life: Sundown Brights" (1967), *Vogue*, May: 204.

Ann, B. (1940), "Hawaiian Designer Brings New York New Dress Ideas," *Milwaukee Journal*, September 29.

Babette (1947), "Wardrobes for Vacation," *San Francisco Examiner*, June 4.

Bailey, G. (1940), "Hula Girls Inspire Fashion Collection," *New York World Telegram*, October 29.

Belyea, M. (2004) "Mary Edith Cox Maison." Paper, annual meeting of The Fortnightly Club, Easton, PA, October 10.

Bender, M. (1961), "Fashion Historian Eyes the Future for Stylists," *New York Times*, November 21.

Biography 1 (n.d.), Tina Leser Collection, Box A1.

Biography 2 (n.d.), Tina Leser Vertical Files.

Carson, R. (1945), "Girl," *Collier's*, June.

Dean, J. (1949), "Eastern Garb Takes on New Western Air," *Detroit Times*, September 12.

Dennis, H. (1967), "Designer Tina Leser Renews Island Ties," *Honolulu Adviser*, December 5.

Dodge, A. (2009), Comment on: L Is for Leser, *Lulu's Vintage Blog*. Comment posted on November 30. Available from: http://lulusvintage.typepad.com/blog/2007/04/l_is_for _leser.html

Hoffman, M. (1954), "Designer Helps Mother Start Art Center," *Christian Science Monitor*, January 25: 10.

Howley, J. (2009), Telephone Interview with April Calahan, May 2.

Leser, T. (1950), "Designer Uses Spanish, Moroccan Motifs," *Houston Post*, August 17.

"Made-in-India Fashion Charm Radio-TV Women" (1966), *Washington Post*, May 20.

Meredith, A. (n.d.), "Elegance with East," Tina Leser Collection, Box A7.

Miscellaneous notes (n.d.), Tina Leser Vertical Files.

"New Style for Japanese Modernizes Kimono" (1949), *Louisville Courier-Journal*, September 10.

Osgood, N. (1965), "Look for More of Leser Designs," *St. Petersburg Times*, March 25.

Philadelphia Art Alliance (2009). Available online: http://www.philartalliance.org/space .htm

Pope, V. (1945), "Fashion Awards Bestowed Upon 3," *New York Times*, February 15.

Press Release (1945), Coty-AFCA 1945 Winners Eleanor Lambert Collection, Box 33.

Press Release (1975), Tina Leser Collection, Box 25.

Roberts, C. (n.d.), "Creator of Daring Design," Tina Leser Collection, Box Press Clippings.

Robin, T. (1949), "Global Fashions," *Holiday*, November: 114.

"Scanty Swim Suits" (1944), *Click*, July, Tina Leser Collection, Box Press Clippings.

"Southern Resort Fashions" (1946), *LIFE*, January: 86.

Steinle, D. (2009), "Largo's Gulf Coast Museum of Art Falls to Lack of Visibility," *Economy*, February 1.

Stiles, S. (1950), "Famous Designer a Study in Contradictions," *St. Louis Post Dispatch*, February 19.

"There's an Oriental Air in New Fashions" (1949), *Salt Lake City Desert News*, September 24.

"Tina Leser, a Designer, Dies; Headed a Sportswear Concern" (1986), *New York Times*, January 27.

"Vogue Patterns: Homme fires—Feathering the Nest with Velveteen" (1967), *Vogue*, November 15: 146.

Wagner, R. (1965), "A Dream in Technicolor," *Washington Post*, December 12.

4 SANDRA GARRATT AND MODULAR CLOTHING

DANIEL JAMES COLE

In June 1988, *Texas Business* asserted that 37-year-old Sandra Garratt "may just be the hottest fashion designer in America" (Herold 1988b).

That same month, *People* spun the designer's story as a rags-to-riches narrative:

> Just two years ago Sandra Garratt was cleaning kitchen floors and scrubbing toilet bowls for $5 an hour. This year she's cleaning up in a bigger way—with a projected $1 million in royalties as the designer of Multiples, a line of mix-and-match clothing that is rattling the racks in about 600 stores across the country. Garratt's threads will pull in an estimated $110 million in sales this year for Jerell Inc., the Dallas-based firm that bankrolled the designs, and company president Jerry Frankel sees bigger days ahead. "It's not just style, it's concept." (Shapiro and Demaret 1988)

While the press emphasized Garratt's perceived meteoric rise, the success of Multiples actually represented years of hard work and setbacks.

Garratt was born Sandra Howower during a blizzard in South Milwaukee, Wisconsin, in the wee hours of December 16, 1951, to a Scottish father and an English mother. Her father accepted a position at Lockheed and moved the family to Southern California. Garratt took an interest in sewing and made some of her own clothes as a teenager, often inspired by Mary Quant. However, she was also attracted to dance and attended the Royal Winnipeg Ballet School on scholarship and subsequently performed in Europe. With dual citizenship in the United States and the United Kingdom, she headed for London. Having just arrived the morning of December 31, 1971, while waiting for a friend at a café, Garratt had a chance encounter with a financial backer for the trendy boutique Quorum.

The dapper gentleman (in need of a shop girl) encouraged her to come to work there; the offer gave the young Garratt the opportunity to work with Ossie Clark and Celia Birtwell, then at the pinnacle of their relevance to the London fashion scene. While calcium deposits in her foot ended her ballerina dreams, her love for clothes flourished at Quorum.

Garratt returned to California in 1974 enrolling in an accelerated program at the Fashion Institute of Design and Merchandising. Initially her school projects reflected a theatrical aesthetic, and she had thoughts of a career in costume design. But her mentor, FIDM department chair William Pearson, encouraged her to "design a line contrary to her baroque interest in couture dressing" (Hockswender 1988). Garratt developed a modular wardrobe as her graduating project based on rectangular shapes, utilizing yardage with a minimum of waste, with both woven and knit fabrics primarily of silk and cotton; she thought of the individual pieces of the collection as "units." Garratt recalled, "it was so far from anything I wanted to do. This was problem-solving, as opposed to fantasy" (Hockswender 1988), and the project prefigured the ideas that would later define Garratt as one of the great innovators of late-twentieth-century fashion. Some industry professionals who attended the graduating fashion show derided Garratt's work, but, despite their negative opinions, she won the top honor, the FIDM Bob Mackie Award for outstanding achievement; Mackie himself was encouraging to the young designer (Garratt 2016a). Her first real industry job out of school came at the high-end design shop Dinallo of Beverly Hills—known for its celebrity clientele—where she strengthened her skills and her enthusiasm for the industry.

Venturing to New York in 1976, she freelanced in a variety of jobs for notable industry figures including textile design for Mary McFadden and illustration for Giorgio di Sant'Angelo. An interview for a design assistant position at Zoran proved fortuitous: Zoran was creating "a line based on one simple square shape" (Ennis 1982), and Garratt, with the FIDM project in her portfolio, clearly "understood his simple concept" (Garratt 2016a). Another crucial job—doing display design for Halston—also came along, and Garratt remembered:

Halston ... gave me a new direction. Halston offered a basic way of dressing that seemed suited to Americans. His clothes were realistic in the sense that they worked for you instead of your having to adopt the characteristics of the clothes. (Walker and Dixon n.d.)

Garratt would later acknowledge many other important influences:

Both Jean Muir and Zandra Rhodes have influenced me throughout my career but my favorite designer of all times is Paul Poiret. ... Other inspirations ... come from Rudi Gernreich, who was also trained as a dancer, and Giorgio di Sant'Angelo. (Walker and Dixon n.d.)

The aesthetic of the Bauhaus was inspirational as well, and futuristic thoughts (encouraged by Garratt's love of science fiction) were also clearly present (Garratt 2016b).

While in New York, she married Michael Garratt in 1977 (whom she met at Halston, and who also worked for Andy Warhol) and she took his surname. Their son Wesley was born in February 1978. The couple began a clothing line, CMS Spectrum, that included printed scarves and sarongs, and "peasanty" separates and loungewear, including pieces with modular components. At an open call at Henri Bendel, Geraldine Stutz (Bendel's president) favorably received the collection and the line was merchandised in the store. But the loss of financing precipitated the end of the venture.

The couple relocated to Dallas at the suggestion of Michael's brother who lived there. Garratt took a job working as display manager for Marie Leavell, a high-end dress shop popular with Dallas's fashionable elite; her innovative and avant-garde window displays generated buzz, but the windows shocked the "proper clientele" and she was let go after "creating a provocative display based on the Seven Deadly Sins" (Ennis 1982).

At a crossroads, Garratt bought some poly-cotton jersey on sale at Cloth World, a fabric store that was across the street from Marie Leavell, and the purchase proved fortuitous: with her extremely limited funds, she bought enough fabric to create a group of "units" along the lines of her FIDM project, founding Sandra Garratt Design. Garratt's 1979 debut in Dallas placed her in a vibrant local fashion scene. Soon her designs could be found at some of Dallas's edgier boutiques and were promptly featured in the local press: the *Dallas Morning News* featured some of her innovative designs. Garratt's mix-and-match collection of units was dubbed "Group V" (as she had originally envisioned five different lines); Group V included "briefs, bandeau, cloche hat, leggings, one-seam bias cut pants, chemise, wrap jacket, square-cut dress and detachable sleeves" ("Sandra Garratt Jumps" 1979). Garratt proclaimed in the article: "It's a way of dressing. You can be totally monochromatic, or you can have a real field day with colors and stripes. I think because they're so funny, people can't help but like them" ("Sandra Garratt Jumps" 1979). Garratt also offered edgy outerwear by special order, including a "modacrylic shag coat ... and a clear vinyl raincoat" ("Sandra Garratt Jumps" 1979). While a few readers wrote to the newspaper disapproving of the clothes—even calling them "gutter" fashion (Anderson 1979)—in a matter of weeks Group V was "hotter than a Dallas summer" (Shapiro and Demaret 1988). The local boutiques promptly sold out the clothes, and Garratt scrambled to keep up with sudden demand from other cities. Journalist Keith Anderson observed: "It depends on your point of view. Sandra Garratt is either always ahead of her time or she's merely out in left field" (Anderson 1979).

Simultaneously, her special occasion dresses, "ornate ... like Viennese pastry" (Dallas Morning News 1979), were offered by stores as diverse as the established retail giant Neiman Marcus and funky Dallas boutique Eclectricity. These dresses reflected Garratt's taste for elaborate costuming and the aesthetic of Quorum. Garratt didn't really see a contradiction between different lines: "When I stopped being in the manner of everyone else—which is easy to get into—ballerina dresses and knit types were what I thought of" ("Sandra Garratt Jumps" 1979). Michael, however, encouraged her to concentrate on modular ideas, as he considered those to be her true calling, and discouraged her work in the romantic vein cautioning her not to become a "second rate Zandra Rhodes" (Garratt 2016b).

In 1980 the young couple separated but remained friends. By 1981, Garratt was operating under the name "Units," and over the coming years the label would grow to nationwide distribution. *Dallas Morning News* showed continued interest in the fashion designer and frequently profiled her in its style section. By 1982, Garratt had outgrown the cottage industry approach of local seamstresses and moved to factory production (but would stress made-in-USA production for her clothes her entire career). Units were now available not only in the home base of Dallas but also in New York, Chicago, and Los Angeles. Stanley Marcus of Neiman Marcus— the elder statesman of Dallas fashion—gave his stamp of approval to the endeavor by serving on Units' advisory board.

> Among Dallas's most progressively dressed working women, a Sandra Garratt [garment] became a symbol of high fashion consciousness. The underground popularity … proved that Garratt's seemingly esoteric theories were practical. Her line consisted of only four or five tops, a couple of cardiganlike, buttonless wraps to go over them, a jump suit, and shorts, skirts and pants in a couple of styles each. All had the same boxy construction, were in cotton-polyester t-shirting or sweat-shirting, and came in black, white, red, and a few other colors that Garratt chose each season. The discount house prices and the unwad-it-and-wear it practicality of the line were bonuses. (Ennis 1982)

While innovative "convertible" garments had been pioneered in the 1930s and 1940s by American women—Valentina on the couture level, and Claire McCardell among others in sportswear—Garratt's modular designs pushed the concept beyond her predecessors' with pieces that could transform even further into different garments, such as tubes of fabric that could morph from a dress to a skirt to a cowl and so on. Each piece of the line had transformative potential— "Erector Set functionalism" declared *Texas Monthly* (Ennis 1982). Units expressed "individuality through apparent uniformity" (Walker and Dixon n.d.) as the wearer could be creative in styling and accessorizing. Units were described as "a simple design, a stretchy canvas, perfect for a decade when hair was the undeniable centerpiece" (Carlson 2016). Garratt's jersey pieces were compared to Norma Kamali's designs, but Garratt pointed out that "Norma was a '40s baby who was at an impressionable age in the '50s. I was a '50s baby who was at an impressionable age in the '60s" ("In Quotes" 1982). Garratt's glib remark was actually quite apt: Kamali often favored curvaceous defined waists and peplums, while Garratt favored tubular silhouettes.

Units were popular as workout clothes, their flexibility reflecting Garratt's years as a dancer (Walker and Dixon n.d.). Units were also used for maternity wear prefiguring the 1990s maternity "systems." Noted choreographer Jerry Bywaters Cochran utilized Units as costumes for dance pieces, and the Los Angeles Philharmonic purchased over 100 jumpsuits and dresses for its female musicians. A Units children's line was created inspired by Wesley, who served as fit model for his mother as the line developed.

A Wisconsin native of British parentage and California upbringing, Garratt would seem an unlikely candidate to be recognized as the cultural property of Dallas, Texas, but soon the young designer was a fixture in the town's creative life and society press. Garratt's 1983 holiday party for Units was a notable event for the Dallas social set and made the pages of the *Dallas Morning News* in a story punningly titled "Expression of Unity":

The trendy mix of fashion plates, artsy rebels and local glitterati swelled to almost 500 strong before the morn. Notable ensembles: a generous smattering of Units.... the best use of basic black and white we've seen in a long while. (1983)

Expanding quickly, but running a deficit and not able to keep up with demand, Garratt took on local partners for financial backing, inking the deal in January 1986. The newly formed corporation called itself Stinu Corp. ("Units" spelled backward); while Garratt was promised 100 percent creative control, she had only 45 percent interest in the corporation, the new partners a combined 55 percent. The arrangement did not prove to be harmonious, and Garratt was not consulted on all the decisions she thought she should have been, while the partners were horror-struck that what they thought were "ladies" garments had been marketed as unisex. Mere weeks after Stinu Corp. was formed, an April 1986 meeting with the partners and the employees deteriorated into shouting and thrown clothes, with Garratt and her crew walking out. Garratt maintained that she was forced out, while Stinu Corp.'s Don Rhoden claimed that Garratt "resigned in a huff" (Mangelsdorf 1988). Whatever the truth, the Dallas flagship store carried on without her leaving "Texas money-men dressed in jeans and cowboy boots to scramble around ... helping customers with red leotards, black jumpsuits and white slit skirts" (Herold 1987). During the settlement litigation, Stinu Corp. began negotiations to sell Units to the J.C. Penney Corporation. Pending the sale, Garratt was prohibited from working in fashion in any way in Dallas for six months. Desperate for an income to support herself and Wesley, Garratt went to work for a housekeeping service. Looking back thirty years later, Garratt commented that the work was in its way "therapeutic" after the tribulations of the previous months (Garratt 2016a). But a judge found

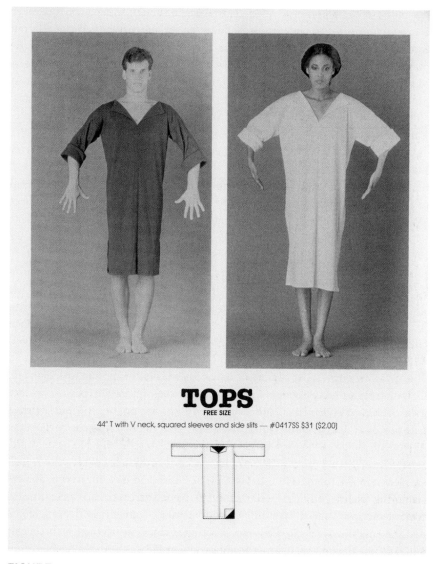

TOPS

FREE SIZE

44" T with V neck, squared sleeves and side slits — #0417SS $31 ($2.00)

FIGURE 4.1 By the mid-1980s, Sandra Garratt's Units were in full swing, and the modular line was marketed with unisex potential. Photo by Michael Moore.

prohibiting Garratt from working was in violation of Texas state law and as the sale to J.C. Penney was completed and she awaited her monetary settlement from Stinu Corp., she was free to compete against her former business.

Thus Garratt's new modular line, Multiples, was born in 1987. Initially announced as "Baseline," that name was unavailable by copyright so "Multiples" it became. Like Units, Multiples offered one-size cotton-polyester jersey knit mix-and-match pieces that could be worn multiple ways, but the new line reduced the number of options: whereas Units had almost fifty pieces, Multiples was conceptually leaner with twenty-two. To produce and market Multiples, Garratt entered into an agreement with Dallas dress manufacturer Jerell Inc., whose previous products had been conservative styles popular in mid-western markets. Meanwhile, J.C. Penney was increasing the number of Units stores in malls across the country, and Garratt later remarked, "for a while I was actually competing with my former company, … like a Star Trek episode … which is the real Spock?" (Carlson 2016)

Multiples quickly built both momentum and revenue. Instead of stand-alone stores, Multiples boutiques were placed in department stores, eventually in hundreds of stores across the United States. Some Multiples boutiques were located on the first floor, unusually prominent merchandising for a women's clothing line. By mid-1988 Multiples captivated the press, including the *People* profile. Amy Kline, a buyer for Marshall Field and Company, declared "it's one of the hottest things in ready-to-wear right now" (Mangelsdorf 1988), and *Women's Wear Daily* declared Multiples a "retail phenomenon," adding that the line was putting Dallas back on the fashion map with Jerell "riding tall in the saddle" (McFarland 1988). Widespread print and television ads proclaimed "modern modulars for modern living" and, with a fresh hip appeal, Multiples vastly surpassed the sales of rival Units. By October, Jerell was shipping an estimated 47,000 pieces a day, and Multiples was one of the most successful U.S. sportswear labels, with an estimated 150 million in sales surpassing well-established lines such as Anne Klein. Coordinating accessories were added, including specially licensed hosiery. Other industry leaders chimed in: "Multiples and I are like kissing cousins" said designer Donna Karan, "I did … a tube skirt with a roll-down cuff waistband in black jersey. They've made … a brilliant business, out of a few wonderful pieces that work" (Hockswender 1988). The *Wall Street Journal* called Multiples "a spectacular hit" and "one of the biggest fashion trends in years" going on to assert that "stores are clamoring for [the] designs" (Mitchell 1989). Apparel areas in department stores typically averaged annual sales of $250.00 per square foot for a clothing line or department; with a Multiples boutique that figure could be as staggeringly high as $1100.00 per square foot, essentially unheard of in 1988.

Multiples was called "a line of casual-but-dressy, funky-but-chic separates" (Herold 1988a) and merchandised in a correspondingly trendy way, "sold folded up in slim plastic bags which would hang from a metal rod affixed in a pegboard" (Carlson 2016). The innovative merchandising was recognized with a citation from *VMSD* (*Visual Merchandising and Store Design*) magazine (Carlson 2016). The merchandising included demonstrations from Multiples-clad sales staff, specially trained for showing how to style and restyle the pieces.

"Versatility is our magic, our abracadabra," says Alice Berthelsen, who trained the 30 trainers who have in turn trained 1200 store employees. Ms. Berthelsen

FIGURE 4.2 Multiples were at the height of their popularity when this advertisement ran in *Vogue* in April 1989. Photo by Les Hall.

and her disciples sing the praises of the soft, durable Multiples from Dallas to Boston to Minnetonka. (Herold 1988b)

Writing in 2010, a fashion blogger remembered the modern grid-like display of Multiples and watching in awe the demonstrations of effortless styling:

This was fresh, Multiples was in line with electronic music, videos, and graphics of that time. It was clean, simple and smart right down to the presentation. Even better, was that it was sold in flat packaging like an efficient commodity that belied its versatility, this was clothing of the future. (Gaby 2010)

Fashion shows wowed crowds as models transformed the pieces in front of the audience's eyes and took ensembles from day into evening. "The splashiest opening yet was at the New York Macy's in November. Ms. Garratt and eight models did live fashion shows in the 34th Street windows that drew crowds and made the evening TV news" (Herold 1988a).

Because "[c]ustomers tend[ed] to look slightly bewildered at first" (Hockswender 1988), the press often included guidelines on how to wear the pieces in different combinations and configurations; *Women's Wear Daily* pointed out that the wearer potentially "mixes, matches, layers, rolls, tucks, ties or turns the pieces upside down to get the desired look" (Hoffman 1987). The practical virtues were praised, noting that a piece of Multiples "takes up little room in the washer, the dryer or suitcase" and that "six colors are sold year-round: black, white, red, gray, navy and olive. Pastels, stripes and polka dots are mixed in seasonally, and one size fits all" (Herold 1988a). While Multiples's one-size didn't really fit *everybody* ("one size fits most" was the motto), it *did* fit a very wide range and the cut took into account size averages of American women, with the tube skirt, for example, able to accommodate hips up to 60 inches. The "Multiples Memo" on the back of each package educated the purchaser on the potentials of the piece and also provided a checklist for pieces the customer already owned and those she wanted to buy, and pamphlets provided guides on how to choose and pack one's multiples for a vacation. "The line's success stems from its quick-and-easy fashion answers for today's busy women" (Herold 1988b). In Garratt's own words,

Simple clothes, for most people most of the time. For me it was work, play and after 5 p.m. … all the pieces had to work at any time. Depending on what pieces and colors were used, that made it all about creative personal choices for that person at that time. [They were] flexible applications for busy on-the-go women with active modern lives. (Carlson 2016)

With Multiples, modular dressing reached its zenith—in concept, in execution, in media coverage, and in public consciousness. And many boutiques across the nation attested that its appeal was widespread. The *New York Times* confirmed "in a time of escalating clothing costs and fashion ennui, 'modular dressing' is catching on across the nation" (Hockswender 1988), and the same week the *Los Angeles Times* asserted that "even stodgy old Boston, which doesn't take kindly to fashion trends, is abuzz over modular dressing" (Young 1988). Garratt herself noted its potential appeal to different parts of the country: "the conservative

FIGURE 4.3 Multiples for Kids allowed children to experiment with their own creativity.

girl in the Midwest will wear it differently than trendy clubgoers in New York" (Hockswender 1988).

As with Units, a children's line—"modern modulars for modern kids"—was introduced in February 1988, leading the *New York Times* to quip that the children's line enabled "mothers and daughters to share, trade and argue over pieces of their wardrobes" (Hockswender 1988). Garratt later recalled:

> PBS/*Sesame Street* came as close to a commercial endorsement … that they could [given] their non-commercial policies. We were invited to be in the big twenty-five-year anniversary of *Sesame Street* held in Central Park, [and we] dressed the kids who sang and danced and performed that weekend. The significant part was that they felt that the clothes were actually learning tools for kids.… . putting things together in creative ways (like Legos), plus very young kids could dress themselves without help which is good for building their confidence, … [as well as being] non gender specific. (Garratt 2013)

Even though the women's Multiples were conceptually unisex garments (as Units had been), a men's line was created, and a women's plus-size line was developed. Multiples boutiques opened in Japan and Australia, and in Europe boutiques operated under a licensing agreement. Following the London opening at Debenhams, Garratt was invited to be part of a fashion show benefitting Prince Philip's World Wildlife Fund (Garratt 2016b). Shortly afterward, Garratt was honored at the Baha'i International Community Representative Offices to the United Nations for Multiples' ethical labor policies. Multiples were celebrated by the inclusion of Garratt's work in several museum exhibitions, including at the Musée des Arts décoratifs, Paris, and The Natural History Museum, Los Angeles.

While acknowledging Garratt as the pioneer of modular clothing, the press also noted the emergence of copycat lines that appeared on the scene, including

"26 Designs," "Bubbles Plus," "Linkup," "Switches," and "Symmetry"; the Spiegel catalogue got in on the trend with "Equasions" (Hockswender 1988; Groves 1988). Also in 1988, Multiples's manufacturer Jerell introduced "Singles." While somewhat different in cut and feel from Multiples—"unsized unconstructed dresses" (Hockswender 1988) that the wearer could accessorize and adapt—Singles was nonetheless conceptually similar to Multiples, and in some ways competitive, often merchandised in very close proximity to Multiples in stores.

Despite the success of Multiples, and the lofty stamp of approval from major museums, Garratt was not making the royalties she expected off of the reported sales figures, and she pursued legal action to sever from Jerell. Garratt alleged that Jerell was "violating the licensing agreement" (Anderson 1995) withholding over 4 million dollars in royalties, and that Singles was derived from her ideas. Frankel contested the charges. Garratt was soon financially drained by legal fees, and in October of 1989 she was forced to file for bankruptcy protections. The bankruptcy case was rolled into the lawsuit, and ultimately a settlement was reached where Jerell paid off a fraction of the royalties allegedly owed, and was awarded exclusive rights to the line. Jerell was also allowed to continue using Garratt's name through January 1991, asserting the extent of labeled inventory and packaging that had not yet been shipped.

While designing Multiples, Garratt also maintained her own Dallas shop, selling a line of fine sportswear with her name on the label, and she began developing other lines before the litigations. Projected activewear and bodywear lines suitable for dancers had Capezio on board to sell in their New York City flagship store (Ward 1989). When the litigation with Jerell forced Garratt into bankruptcy, she took on private investors to back a new venture operating as Perfection of Design, Inc., announced in *Women's Wear Daily* in November of 1989. Noted for innovative uses of fabric, in addition to cotton and lycra interlock, the line included "matte and shiny rubber; puckered nylon and nylon Supplex in black, neon and tie-dye colors, and a metallic snakeskin print in polyester and Lycra" (Haber 1989). Also on the drawing board under the same corporation was a new "clothing system" labeled "Whole," made of cotton interlock and conceptually very similar to Units and Multiples. Nordstrom, Macy's, Saks, and Bloomingdales were among the retailers lined up to sell the POD lines with preferential floor space, but the investors withdrew merely weeks after *Women's Wear Daily* announced the new venture, after garment construction was underway and shipping had begun (Garratt 2016b).

"Garratt concedes her talents lie in the cutting room, not the boardroom," reported the *Wall Street Journal*. "'I wouldn't call myself naïve' … Garratt says ruefully. 'I was foolish, which I think is worse. When you're naive, you just don't know better, and I do. It's like some kind of perverse artistic streak. You feel like if you succeed, you've sold out'" (Mitchell 1989). *The Los Angeles Times*, writing in 1990 about the Multiples litigations, noted, "for Garratt … this isn't the first time. . . . she says she has repeatedly been outmaneuvered by the manufacturers who once backed her" (Reischel 1990). Such outmaneuvering placed her in the unfortunate company of other notable designers who fell victim to the hostile takeover mentality of the 1980s, including Halston, Norma Kamali, and Ronaldus Shamask (Reischel 1990).

With Units, Multiples, and Perfection of Design all behind her, in 1992, operating as Sandra Garratt Design, she launched New Tee, a line of T-shirts and other simple separates that utilized 100 percent organic fibers and non-toxic silk screen inks that began as a Dallas T-shirt boutique; a signature logo tee was an especially popular item. New Tee was at the leading edge of the sustainable clothing movement and, in an early use of the term, the clothes were described as "green":

> The green theme carries throughout the shop's design. Fixtures are made of scrap metal from cars, and the store's paint is not toxic. Recycled paper is used for bags and hangtags, and customers who buy four or more items get a free cotton tote to carry the goods. (Haber 1992)

The original boutique lasted about a year, receiving another *VMSD* citation for the sustainable and eclectic store design (Garratt 2016c). Garratt reorganized into two sportswear lines that included not only T-shirts but also dresses and separates maintaining the organic principles, sold under the labels Sandra Garratt Design, and New Tee/Sandra Garratt. The lines grew into distribution in stores nationwide. While maintaining some of the edginess of Units and Multiples, New Tee embraced a softer spirit, including hand-knit sweaters fabricated from Fox Fibre naturally colored cotton, and bias-cut silk dresses. Romantic baby dolls, tiered skirts, and corset belts were prescient of the "boho" vogue of the 2000s. Garratt noted the clothes could work for "a woman for a day at the office, and evening out and even a cruise" (Haber 1994). Although the line was successful, a significant financial backer was caught up in legal trouble following the savings and loan crisis of the 1990s, and by 1998 Garratt lost the capital to continue production. New Tee was nonetheless a *succès d'estime* given that the sustainability principles espoused were just beginning to take hold in the garment industry, and an environmentally conscious line on this scale, this early, was particularly important.

Meanwhile, J.C. Penney closed its chain of Units stores in 1994, which had been performing unsuccessfully for a few years. Jerell continued to sell Multiples into the 1990s, but in direct marketing only. In 2000, Garratt joined the Spiegel Catalog as head designer for new lines, but after a year Garratt and the rest of the design staff were laid off while the company declared bankruptcy and the business was sold. Garratt returned to her *alma mater* FIDM to teach from 2008 until 2012.

Garratt also began creating a modular clothing system on a small scale, Mod Box, which continued her Units and Multiples ideas. In 2009 she launched

FIGURE 4.4 These looks from 1994 New Tee/Sandra Garratt embraced a softer feel that prefigured the "boho" style of the following decade. Photo by Tim Boole.

DUGwear ("dual utility garments"), which was at its core an urban wear line with performance fabrics, with a distinctly West Coast vibe and color palette. But what made some of the garments in the collection genuinely distinctive was that they were offered with solar collection panels to charge the wearer's phones and other devices, a venture initially partnered with electronics expert Doug Holmes. Casual outerwear and pants with large pockets were the most typical garments for the solar panels. The endeavor not only continued Garratt's "green" thinking but also reinforced her role as fashion's true futurist, and the line was hailed by earthtechling.com in 2011 as "by far the closest thing we've seen to stylish in this emerging category of portable power" (DeFreitas 2011).

At this writing, Garratt operates as SGDBOX, which produces several "box" options, all embracing sustainable principles. These include the already established Modbox, Luxbox with high-end organic materials, Bodybox for activewear and loungewear, Euwbox ("eco-chic urbanwear" essentially a continuation of DUGwear), a modular children's line Kidbox, and—in typically Garratt spirit—Chefsbox, aprons from organically grown fibers, Dogbox for modern canines, and Chocbox, hot chocolate mixes. Garratt is "amazed and gratified daily that so many of my long time customers track me down and patiently wait for their orders to arrive" (Carlson 2016).

In 1982 Garratt remarked, "I always thought that the best thing you could ever do was to out-design Levi's or Fruit of the Loom" (Ennis 1982). In retrospect in 2016 she assessed her career vision: "modern clothes for modern people sums up my personal design point-of-view" (Sandragarratt.com 2016).

Acknowledgments

Special thanks to Randy Bryan Bingham and Ruel Macaraeg.

Bibliography

Anderson, K. (1979), "Close to the Edge," *Dallas Morning News*, October 31: 79.
Anderson, S. (1995), "Susan Powter's Wallet Gets a Nasty Workout," *Bloomberg*, January 23. Available online: http://www.bloomberg.com/news/articles/1995-01-22/susan -powters-wallet-gets-a-nasty-workout
Carlson, J. (2016), "Meet The Creator of the Greatest 1980s Modular Clothing," *Gothamist*. Available online: http://gothamist.com/ 2016/04/25/sandra_garratt_modular _multiples_1980s_fashion.php#photo-1
DeFreitas, S. (2011), "Solar Pants Charge Your Cell W/Style," *Earthtechling*, January 1. Available online: http://earthtechling.com/2011/01/solar-pants-charge-your-cell -wstyle/
Ennis, M. (1982), "The Empress' New Clothes," *Texas Monthly*, September: 152.
"Expression of Unity" (1983), *Dallas Morning News*, December 21: 10E.
Gaby (2010) "It's a Modular World: Interview with Sandra Garratt," *Stars We Are*, January 18. Available online: https://starsweare.wordpress.com/2010/01/18/its-a-modular -world-interview-with-sandra-garratt–2/

Garratt, S. (2013), Email to D.J. Cole, March 30.

Garratt, S. (2016a), Email to D.J. Cole, July 31.

Garratt, S. (2016b), Interviews with D.J. Cole, June 30, July 18, August 8.

Garratt, S. (2016c), *Sandra Garratt's Website*. Available online: www.Sandragarratt.com

Groves, M. (1988), "Modular Puts Shape Back in Fashion Profit: Southland and U.S. Wrapped Up in New Look, but Imitators May Unravel Trend," *Los Angeles Times*, February 1. Available online: http://articles.latimes.com/1988-02-01/business/fi-26785_1_modular-line

Haber, H. (1989), "Garratt Gets 2nd Shot at Launching Her Line with New Backers," *Women's Wear Daily*, November 6: 2.

Haber, H. (1992), "New Tee Shop Aims to Reap Budding 'Green' Awareness," *Women's Wear Daily*, July 2: 7.

Haber, H. (1994), "Sandra Garratt Ready to Go Nationwide," *Women's Wear Daily*, October 19: 9.

Herold, L. (1987), "Picking Up the Pieces," *Dallas Morning News*, February 1: 8.

Herold, L. (1988a), "A Designer Is Reborn," *Dallas Morning News*, January 6: 1E.

Herold, L. (1988b), "No Hang-Ups," *Texas Business*, June: 25.

Hockswender, W. (1988), "Modular Clothes: Count the Ways," *New York Times*, October 18, 1988. Available online: http://www.nytimes.com/1988/10/18/style/modular-clothes-count-the-ways.html

Hoffman, T.Z. (1987), "Multiples Catches on as Flexible Dressing Out of the Southwest," *Women's Wear Daily*, August 19: 9.

"In Quotes" (1982), *Dallas Morning News*, April 11: 157.

Mangelsdorf, M. (1988), "Dressed for Success," *Inc.*, August. Available online: http://www.inc.com/magazine/19880801/5902.html

McFarland, K. (1988), "Jerell Riding Tall in the Saddle," *Women's Wear Daily*, April 27: 1.

Mitchell, C.F. (1989), "Riches from Rags," *The Wall Street Journal*, March 20: 1.

Reischel, D. (1990), "Units Creator Wrapped Up in Legal Woes," *Los Angeles Times*, May 4. Available online: http://articles.latimes.com/1990-05-04/news/vw-403_1_legal-woes

Rogers, S. (1982), "One of a Kind," *Dallas Morning News*, July 28: 74. Available online: sandragarratt.com http://0348617.netsolhost.com/sgdboxhome.html

"Sandra Garratt Jumps into the Dallas Designer Game" (1979), *Dallas Morning News*, April 4: 49.

Shapiro, H. and Demaret, K. (1988), "Style: Success Comes in Many Forms for Mix and Match Designer Sandra Garratt," *People*, June 20. Available online: http://www.people.com/people/archive/article/0,,20099252,00.html

Walker, M. and Dixon, J.G. (no date), "Sandra Garratt," *Fashion Designer Encyclopedia*. Available online: http://www.fashionencyclopedia.com/Fr-Gu/Garratt-Sandra.html

Ward, P. (1989), "Garratt to Launch Line of Activewear," *Women's Wear Daily*, April 25: 6.

Young, K.N. (1988), "Modular Looks Go Their Separate Ways," *Los Angeles Times*, October 14. Available online: http://articles.latimes.com/1988-10-14/news/li-4139_1_separate-ways

PART TWO

DEVELOPING AN INDUSTRY

5 MARION McCOY AND PAULINE FRACCHIA: MID-TWENTIETH-CENTURY ORIGINATORS

JEAN L. PARSONS AND SARA B. MARCKETTI

The U.S. ready-to-wear industry has long clothed women fashionably at all price points. By the mid-twentieth century, thousands of designers created clothing ranging from high-priced originals to low-priced copies. These designers remain largely unknown today as the company or department store label seldom included their names. Through the industry trade press, patent records, and advertisements, it is possible to discover the lives and contributions of these individuals, expanding our knowledge of the women's U.S. ready-to-wear apparel industry. As a group, no single profile of the designers exactly fits; they had various educational backgrounds and followed a variety of career paths, working in all the major garment centers in the United States, including New York, Chicago, St. Louis, and Kansas City. But, like their counterparts who designed at higher price points or for a custom market, many were just as concerned about protecting their original design ideas through intellectual property protection.

The dual focus of this chapter is two American wholesale designers whose distinct paths exemplified the varied experiences of designers of the time. Pauline Fracchia (1889–1989) was head designer at Rosenthal & Kalman (later R&K Originals) from its founding in 1932 to at least 1962. Despite its name, R&K Originals specialized in style adaptations or saleable variations of prevailing French fashions. Fracchia's frequent trips to Paris for style inspiration were recorded in the pages of *Women's Wear Daily*. Marion McCoy (1912–1960) began her career in the junior market in Cleveland and later moved to the thriving St. Louis junior market. She was head designer for the Carlye Dress Corporation from its founding in 1938 until she left to start her own business, Marion McCoy Originals, in Los Angeles in

1945. Rather than Paris, McCoy traveled to South America and Mexico for design inspiration. Although neither Fracchia nor McCoy's names appeared on the labels of the companies they worked for, both filed design patents with the U.S. Patent and Trademark Office for a significant number of dress designs under their own names. The careers of these two women span critical periods in the development of the U.S. ready-to-wear industry during the mid-twentieth century, as well as major industry centers in New York, St. Louis, and California. Their stories also reveal the blurry lines of design inspiration, originals, and adaptations and further our understanding of American democratic fashion.

Design patents and American designers

Pauline Fracchia's early years at R&K and the years that McCoy designed for Carlye Dress Corporation coincided with the tumultuous rise and fall of the Fashion Originators Guild of America (FOGA), a group of women's dress manufacturers producing goods in the higher price brackets, which remained in existence from 1932 to 1941. In order to protect and popularize original style, the FOGA built its foundation on retailer–manufacturer collaboration. With its system of labels, self-reporting, and "red-carding" or preventing retailers and manufacturers that created, purchased, or sold pirated designs, the FOGA became the most successful industry-run program of self-regulation against piracy (Marcketti and Parsons 2016). By 1936, however, the FOGA was fighting for its existence in the courts, largely because of its extension into lower-priced lines. As the organization was challenged through the legal system, they encouraged their members to seek design protection through design patents ("Design Patent" 1941). This type of patent provides short-term protection to inventions and designs that meet the requirements of novelty when viewed through the eyes of a hypothetical designer skilled in the art (Silverman 1993). The novelty resides in the visual aspect of the object, and not in the structure or function of the item, as is necessary with utility patents. Thus, for a dress design patent, only the appearance of the product is protected.

The years during which FOGA transitioned from self-regulation to dependence on design patents witnessed a dramatic increase in the number of design patents for dresses, from 48 in 1932 to a high of 1,276 in 1941 (Parsons and Marcketti 2014). It is to be noted that in 1941 the Supreme Court found the FOGA in restraint of trade and ordered them to cease and desist. Both Fracchia and McCoy patented numerous dresses during this period; the patent documentation provides evidence of a significant body of work that helps to place their personal creative styles into context and highlights the designs each considered to be original.

Marion McCoy

Marion McCoy was a ready-to-wear fashion designer whose career path began at the age of 18 in Kansas City and ended with ownership of her own company in Los Angeles. Born on July 13, 1912 in Missouri, she had a relatively short career, dying at the age of only 47 on May 5, 1960. Although little can be known about her early life, by 1930 at the age of 18, she was living with her grandparents and her brother Frederick in a relatively modest home in Kansas City, Missouri. The census lists her occupation as designer in the dressmaking trade at this point. At the time there were many ready-to-wear apparel companies in the Kansas City area producing women's apparel, including the Nelly Don Dress Company. Given that McCoy was already earning a living as a designer at 18, it is unlikely that she had formal training. Sometime in the mid-1930s she went to work as a designer for Cartwright Junior dresses in Cleveland, Ohio. Cartwright was a prominent junior ready-to-wear company whose label included the designer/owner's name, Martha Gates. Most likely McCoy worked with a team of other designers for the company, although she may have had some autonomy. Like many designers, her career and education began through learning her craft on the job. By 1938, the still young McCoy, aged just 26, was ready to move to the next phase of her career.

The Carlye years

Marion McCoy began as head designer for Carlye Dress Corporation in St. Louis upon its founding in 1938 ("Carlye Dress Co." 1938). When McCoy joined Carlye, she was one of a group of young designers generating new attention to junior dresses in the burgeoning St. Louis market. As far as can be determined, McCoy's appointment at Carlye meant her first opportunity to express her own design ideas and establish her creative style. Many of the St. Louis designers took a different educational route than McCoy. By the early 1940s, the St. Louis industry was recruiting designers from the Washington University Fine Arts program as soon as they graduated. The assumption was that the students had an immediate and clear connection to the needs and wants of the junior market, one that was young, but included girls and women from the teen years through college age and even into their early career years. Although McCoy had a different educational background than many of the other junior wear designers, she brought both a youthful and experienced outlook.

McCoy had a team of designers at Carlye, although how many at any given time is unknown. The mostly very young designers in the St. Louis market demonstrated one side of the ready-to-wear industry in the 1930s and 1940s—that there was considerable movement from one firm to another. For example, one of the designers that McCoy likely worked with at Cartwright Juniors was Louise Mulligan. Mulligan also worked for Townley Frocks and Flora Dress Company, briefly tried her hand at her own business, and in 1945 became the head designer for Carlye when McCoy left. Another designer, Virginia Spears, originally worked in Chicago, designed briefly on McCoy's team at Carlye, but soon left to become the head designer for Minx Modes in St. Louis (Surrarrer 2016).

McCoy joined Carlye at a pivotal time in the apparel industry in terms of creativity and protection of designs. Indeed, the idea that they were creating unique designs is demonstrated on the label "Carlye Originations," although use of the terms "original" and "originations" was common during the mid-twentieth century and tossed about relatively freely. Carlye Dress Corporation sought design protection initially as a member of the FOGA. The company also participated in a unique style protection service that existed in St. Louis, the Style Piracy Bureau ("St. Louis Garment Industries" 1937). However, when the FOGA lost its case in the Supreme Court, Carlye took out a full-page advertisement in *Women's Wear Daily* announcing that they planned to "protect Carlye designs with U.S. Patents" ("Carlye Dress Corporation" 1941). With the company commitment to design protection, Marion McCoy patented ninety-seven designs during her time there, all filed between March 1941 and August 1944. These provide a unique opportunity to evaluate the development of her design style. In addition, for about half of her six years at Carlye, McCoy was designing under the Second World War regulations of Limitation Order L-85. For those years it is possible to see how she adapted her designs to meet requirements for reduced materials.

Marion McCoy designed within the silhouettes of the period and the junior target market of Carlye. However, she also developed her own distinctive design details as head designer and an approach to design inspiration research that she retained throughout her career. Several design details tend to repeat in her patents, including trim radiating out from, and around, the neckline, either as pin tucks or as added ornament, one of which was described in an ad as "nailhead studs" (Advertisement 1941). One of McCoy's most distinctive design details was appliqué or embroidery accents. Just over one-third of her patented designs were created with appliqué decoration, including flowers, bows, umbrellas, and birds. Although appliqué was a detail found on other designs of the period, McCoy's frequent use of certain motifs added individuality to her designs. Reports in *Women's Wear Daily* and the *Retailers Market News* (a St. Louis trade publication) provide the source for some of her design trim and appliqué ideas. Rather than going to Paris for ideas or to adapt French designs (something not possible anyway from 1941 to 1944), McCoy traveled south for inspirations. She visited South America at least twice before the Second World War, in 1939 and 1940. *Women's Wear Daily* editors described her interest in new colors, new silhouettes, and interesting details of line and ornamentation ("Marion McCoy En Route" 1940). In the summer of 1943 she visited Mexico, looking for additional inspirations for color and decoration.

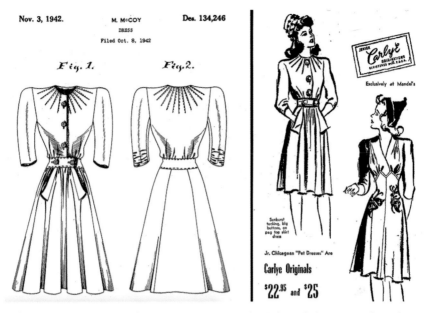

FIGURE 5.1 Marion McCoy dress patent on the left and the same dress in an advertisement. Note the radiating neckline stitching on the patented dress and the floral appliqué on the far right dress, described as "parakeet green." In addition, this dress was designed under the WW II L-85 regulations. McCoy, M. 1942, Design for a Dress, U.S. Patent 134246 and Advertisement: Mandel Brothers 1942, *Chicago Daily Tribune*, November 21: 9. Image out of copyright/authors' collection.

According to a *Retailers Market News* reporter, she returned with color inspirations, embroidery motifs, rickrack trims, and new yarn embroidery design ideas.

McCoy's interest in South America and Mexico for design inspiration was not entirely unique as other designers of the period also looked south for ideas, particularly as South American tourism was promoted as part of Franklin Roosevelt's "good-neighbor policy." McCoy was an early adopter of this fashion theme however. In addition, the St. Louis junior market as a whole often proclaimed their freedom from French design influences. Indeed, according to the fashion coordinator for department store Stix, Baer and Fuller, "St. Louis designers have never copied Paris, and they have created design so original that it is marked American" ("Department Store Stylist" 1944). This is undoubtedly an overstatement, given that the Style Piracy Bureau had written specific regulations for designers who were importing models from Europe for adaptation or reproduction. However, McCoy appears to have preferred non-French sources of inspiration.

Some of her appliqué and embroidery patterns appear clearly drawn from her travels, including birds such cockatiels, and tropical flowers. Rows of ruffles and of rick-rack trim can be seen on several dresses, and she created skirts with tiered ruffles. Another inspiration drawn from Mexico was use of certain types of fabrics, including what was described as a "butcher" type linen ("Juniors Not as Concerned" 1943). One of her best-selling designs in 1943, sold at Woodward and Lothrop in Washington, DC, was a two-piece dress with a large plume and rhinestone embroidery along one side ("Juniors" Choice Runs to "Grown-Up" 1943). McCoy traveled to Washington, DC, to promote her designs, answer questions, and discuss trends. While there she also introduced a "bride's suit" design in response to demand from youthful war-time brides. In addition to this design, her most obvious adaption to the wartime L-85 regulations was to create skirts with the fullness only in the front (see Figure 5.1).

The two-piece dress was another consistent theme in McCoy's designs throughout her career. These were dresses either with a separate jacket or with skirt attached to the jacket or an underbodice. It was sold as a single unit with one price. Patented as dresses and not dress ensembles, in one advertisement, a Carlye design was described as a "two-piece dress" (Advertisement 1943). In another it was also described as two-piece, but with the added description, "skirt hung on a bodice to keep that hemline straight" (Advertisement 1942).

Marion McCoy Originals of California

Marion McCoy resigned from Carlye Dress Corporation in May 1945. According to the announcement in *Women's Wear Daily*, she went to California for a rest and "had not made plans" ("Marion McCoy Resigns" 1945). However, by August, McCoy reported that she was forming her own firm in Los Angeles, including a factory and showrooms. It was to be known as Marion McCoy Originals, selling junior street and dinner dresses that wholesaled at $10.75 and up (at Carlye the prices were generally in the $8.75-10.75 range) ("Marion McCoy Forms Own Firm" 1945). In addition, her stated plan was to sell to only one store in a city, thus maintaining a level of selectiveness for her line. Again, this was not unique in this period—other designers also tried to create a sense of exclusivity for the customer by selling a specific design to only one store in a city or town. By October 1945, the first reports of her designs appeared in *Women's Wear Daily*, which suggests that the company was ready to begin production quite quickly. At some point McCoy married Morrison Miller, who became the president of the company.

California designers began to exert an influence in the 1930s; however, there were still not many junior dress manufacturers by the 1940s when McCoy started her business. As part of her move to California, McCoy chose to operate her own factory. She had at least 100 employees in 1951, as described in a letter to *Life* magazine when the entire company donated a day of work as part of a charity event ("Letters to the Editors" 1951). She quickly became part of a group of relatively young manufacturing designers in southern California. Some of these designers formed a professional organization called the Fashion Guild of Southern California to promote the California market. Described as "leading apparel designers," the initial group of nine included swimwear designer Rose Marie Reid. Among their plans was coordination of dates for openings, presentation of traveling style shows, and assistance with the needs of visiting buyers. There were other California associations, including the California Apparel Creators and the Affiliated Fashionists of California, but the group claimed they were not in conflict with these other organizations (Kaplan 2011). Whether or not that is true is unclear, as the organization does not appear to have lasted very long.

With her new business, McCoy retained elements of the design style developed during her years with Carlye, but she also evolved new signature approaches, as well as a California persona. Advertisements often stated that McCoy dresses were California creations, or the company was advertised as Marion McCoy Originals of California. She increased the price point of her designs, producing both medium and better dresses, with retail prices ranging from $22.75 to as high as $49.75. That she moved her line into a higher price and quality level is demonstrated by a department store advertisement where she is listed as part of a group of designers included in their Debutante Shop, along with recognized designers Ann Fogarty and Emily Wilkens ("Julius Garfinkel & Co." 1951). While debutante certainly suggests a junior market, another ad from the same time period states that one of her dresses was for either "college or career life" ("Marion McCoy Originals" 1948: 10). In addition to her appliqué and embroidery work, her designs included decorative elements intended to look like jewelry applied to the wrist, waist, or neckline, many of them removable. Many dresses also included rhinestone buttons down the front or on sleeve cuffs or collars, as well as rhinestone appliqués.

Marion McCoy died after what was described as a short illness at the age of 47 on May 5, 1960. She created a very successful business that continued after her early death. Her husband had died in 1953, but at some point her brother Frederick became a co-principal/owner in the firm. The company she started remained in business under the direction of her brother, who continued to produce dresses with the Marion McCoy label into the early 1970s.

Pauline Fracchia

Unlike Marion McCoy, Pauline Fracchia was employed by one company throughout her entire fashion design career. Fracchia was also inspired, like many New York designers during the early to mid-twentieth-century period, by Paris for style ideas. This dependence on France was evidenced by the hundreds of names of retailers, designers, and manufacturers, including Fracchia, reported in *Women's*

Wear Daily when they returned from inspiration and buying trips abroad on the *Queen Elizabeth*, the *Queen Mary*, and SS *America* (and later into the 1950s on airways such as Pan American) ("Arrivals from Paris" 1949).

Fracchia (née Ferretti) was born in Tizzano, Italy in 1889 and arrived in the United States in 1904. She married Italian-born husband John and bore her son Alfred at age 19 and her daughter Vivian at age 22. In 1932, at the age of 43, Fracchia joined the nascent apparel company Rosenthal & Kalman Dress Corp. (later Co., Inc. in 1936; then R&K Originals in 1946), staying with the firm as its head designer until the age of 73 (Sheinman 1962). Fracchia died in Queens, New York, at the age of 99 in 1989. Daughter Vivian would follow in her mother's footsteps becoming an apparel designer herself.

The company Fracchia worked for was the creation of Henry Kalman, former manufacturer for Adorable Frocks, Inc., and David Rosenthal of David Rosenthal, Inc., and Rosanna Junior Frocks ("Rosenthal, Kalman New Organization" 1932). The manufactured price of their misses and junior women's goods was in the moderate to popular range. They were an extremely successful organization, creating $12,000,000 in annual volume production by 1948. By the early 1950s,

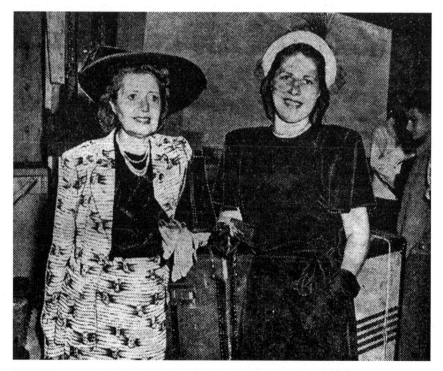

FIGURE 5.2 Pauline Fracchia and daughter Vivian returning aboard the *Queen Mary* from their overseas trip for Rosenthal and Kalman. "Couture Visits Not to Revive Second Lines," 1947, *Women's Wear Daily*, August 26: 8.

the organization, sometimes referred to as R&K Dress Corp., consisted of many subsidiaries and required at least eight floors of a twenty-three-story penthouse and basement building at the northeast corner of the Avenue of the Americas and 39th Street ("Dresses" 1953). By 1960, R&K Originals produced over $20 million dollars in annual volume with tagline reading "for the girl who knows clothes." The company was acquired in 1963 by Jonathan Logan, Inc., the then largest manufacturer of women's junior wear clothing. In 1984, United Merchants & Manufacturers acquired Logan, which had diversified into sportswear and swimwear, with divisions including Rose Marie Reid, Modern Juniors, and R&K Originals.

In their early years, Rosenthal & Kalman were one of the few manufacturing members in the moderate $6.75–8.75 price range to join the FOGA in 1935 ("Guild to Vote" 1935). Within two years, the FOGA would fine and sue Rosenthal & Kalman for failure to comply with their strict regulations against design piracy, alleging that the dress company sold merchandise to retailers who sold copied goods. During the time of this Guild dispute, Rosenthal & Kalman filed numerous design patents through their lead designer, Pauline Fracchia. From 1937 to 1941, Fracchia received over 250 design patents for her dresses. Every one to three months, she filed from four to twenty distinct dress patents. Based on the filing dates of the patents, these dresses clearly represented groupings within a season. For example on December 8, 1937, Fracchia filed seven design patents for dresses; three months later, on March 30, 1938, Fracchia filed six design patents, and then a bit over one month later, on May 7, Fracchia filed six design patents. While distinct, the patents show similar design elements such as dominance of one-piece dresses with embellishments of gathers, pleats, and trims centered at the sleeves, neckline, center front, and inclusion of decorative belts.

Although the patents were filed individually by Fracchia, Rosenthal & Kalman routinely sued fellow dress manufacturers that they believed infringed on these designs. As reported on June 23, 1939 in *Women's Wear Daily*, the company sought injunctive relief and financial settlement against Littman's Thirty-Fourth St. Corp., for infringing on patent number 115,108. This design patent was issued to Fracchia less than three weeks earlier on June 6, seeming evidence that American apparel designers trolled the patent record for sources of inspiration. In several of the cases filed by Rosenthal & Kalman, the presiding judge found the filed patent valid, agreeing that their designs were infringed; in others, the defendant agreed to a consent decree or settlement to resolve the dispute without admission of guilt. Interestingly, in one case filed by Rosenthal & Kalman against Golden Ray Dress Company, a representative of the defendant claimed that the dress patent in dispute had been purchased by an outside designer. Golden Ray Dress Company asked for a dismissal of the case, stating they would stop manufacturing all dresses in discussion ("Dresses: Seeks Dismissal" 1937). Despite the proclivity for filing patents and the suing of those who possibly infringed, there is no record within

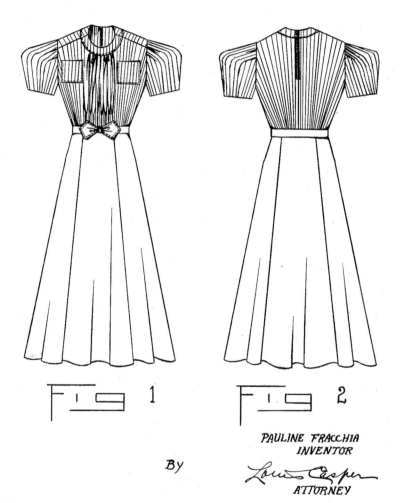

PAULINE FRACCHIA
INVENTOR

By

ATTORNEY

FIGURE 5.3 Design patent typical of Fracchia and the late 1930s, showing skirt fullness, short full sleeves, and greater embellishments on the top than bottom of the dress. Image out of copyright/authors' collection.

the U.S. Patent Office of a design patent for Pauline Fracchia past 1941, the date that the FOGA was found in violation of the anti-monopoly Sherman, Clayton, and Federal Trade Commission Acts.

From the 1940s through the 1950s, the discussion of Rosenthal & Kalman and Pauline Fracchia shifts in the trade press. Rather than the coverage of their design protection processes, the emphasis was on the trips abroad in which they, and other firms, searched for new styles, fabrics, and accessory ideas to bring back for use or adaptation in the United States ("U.S. Contingent" 1952). In larger retail units, employees from diverse lines within the store, such as the better coat buyer, women's, men's, and children's department heads, and men's haberdashery, all coordinated their travels to Europe. In the case of Rosenthal & Kalman, though a large and complex firm, it was typically only Pauline Fracchia, who was occasionally accompanied by her daughter, whose trips were recorded in the trade press.

While Americans asserted some design independence during the Second World War, following the war the press stated that Paris would once again serve as the greatest source of inspiration. Reports throughout this time indicated trends such as skirt length, fabric type, and other design details. Fracchia was often cited alongside industry professionals such as Claire Carnegie of Hattie Carnegie and Mildred Custin, then divisional vice-president of John Wanamaker, Philadelphia, as expressing their likes and dislikes from the foreign offerings ("European Arrivals Cite Barrel" 1957).

In 1947, the pivotal year in fashion history of Dior's New Look, Fracchia was quoted as emphatic about the "fabulously full skirts and tiny boned waistlines." However, she exclaimed, "we can't leave padding out of the shoulders of the popular price range and the tiny waistline would not work with the full range of figure types" ("Down to Earth Approach" 1947: 23.) This quote indicates the sensitivity designers such as Fracchia had toward their target market. It also highlights the delicate line between direct copying and American adaptations. Her designs from the late 1940s and early 1950s demonstrate clear elements of a French influence described as "daringly nipped in at the waist to emphasize full, swirling skirts" ("Marshall Field" 1948).

Throughout the 1950s, after viewing the Parisian couture collections, Fracchia was reported to make judgments and assertions regarding elements to keep and adapt to the American market. For example, Fracchia praised the corselet midriffs shown by Fath in 1954 as "for the young" but questioned whether boning should be repeated in the junior wear market ("Praise Easy Lines" 1954: 3) In 1959, *Women's Wear Daily* stated Europe pleased the U.S. market by showing wearable styles and no drastic changes. This was discussed as easier for the Americans to immediately utilize and adapt than the more radical changes, such as attempts to greatly shorten the hemline ("Apparel Men" 1959). If a dramatic line was introduced, designers and manufacturers discussed how to modify it for greater consumer acceptance. Following the introduction of Dior's 1920s inspired H-line in the Autumn/

Winter collection of 1954, one manufacturer spoke of recommending a belt "at the natural waistline in first American interpretations, to enable the consumer to get accustomed painlessly to the new line." Fracchia concurred, insisting that for widespread consumption, the long-waisted silhouette needed a belt for all but the most fashion-minded (Taub and Bianco 1954). Indeed, belts were a frequent addition to her dresses, showing up in a variety of styles and widths, including a wide corselet style belt described as a "wide waist cinch."

Toward the end of Fracchia's career, there was clearly less importance placed on the Parisian design houses. Many buyers returning from the European showings indicated a general disappointment in the Paris collections for their lack of individualism. They stated that Paris designers were trying to make clothes for the American market and were losing the "creative genius that typified previous collections" ("Junior Sources" 1958: 37).

It is unclear how long Fracchia continued to design, but certainly she found great success at Rosenthal & Kalman. Early in her career, the 1940 census lists her salary as $5,000 or 3.6 times greater than the average annual salary (Petro 2012). By 1960, a *Life* story describes her, at the age of 71, as senior designer of R&K Originals and includes a photograph of her working on a dress. The author goes on to explain that she was still creating four lines annually, with about 300 styles per season ("Seventh Rules" 1960).

Conclusion

There are many differences between Marion McCoy and Pauline Fracchia: McCoy's reliance on Mexico and South America for design inspiration and her several career changes; Fracchia's reliance on Paris and lifelong career at one organization. They represent different regional markets and the uniqueness of each geographic area. There are also similarities.

Both women entered the junior wear market during the Great Depression, a time that impacted the desire and need for more moderate to lower-priced clothing, although after the Second World War McCoy moved into a higher price point. This period also coincided with the effort of American manufacturers and retailers to regulate against design piracy. It is clear from the design patent record that both McCoy and Fracchia believed their designs were original and valuable enough to seek intellectual property protection. However, both women sought design protection for a short period of their careers, Fracchia seemingly when Rosenthal & Kalman was at odds with the FOGA, and McCoy in the window following the FOGA's demise until late 1944. While Fracchia and McCoy do not represent all American fashion designers, facets of their careers—working in various markets, and the recognition that their designs had to have widespread

HAYMAN'S

newest news for
fall is the curvaceous
skirt, simple and flattering.
Left, wool-and-rabbit's-hair dress
by Marion McCoy, 39.98;
right, rayon taffeta by R. & K., 22.98.

FIGURE 5.4 Although different price points, both designers were carried by the same retailers. Hayman's, 1957, *The Washington Post and Times Herald*, September 12: D5. Image out of copyright/authors' collection.

appeal—were shared across the industry. An uncovering of the stories of both women reveals much about the American apparel industry, particularly the diversity of experiences by the relatively unknown yet successful designers for the wholesale manufacturing firms of the mid-twentieth century.

Bibliography

Advertisement: Mandel Bothers (1941), *Chicago Daily Tribune*, November 4: 3.
Advertisement: Mandel Bothers (1943), *Chicago Daily Tribune*, December 18: 9.
Advertisement: Woodward and Lothrop (1942), *The Washington Post*, January 21: 5.
"Apparel Men Are Warned of Europe Threat" (1959), *Women's Wear Daily*, August 12: 1.
"Arrivals from Paris Openings Stress Panels" (1949), *Women's Wear Daily*, February 17: 1, 3.
"Arrivals Praise New Paris Silhouettes" (1953), *Women's Wear Daily*, August 12: 3.
"Carlye Dress Co., of St. Louis, Chartered" (1938), *Women's Wear Daily*, July 13: 20.
"Carlye Dress Corporation" (1941), *Women's Wear Daily*, April 22: 17.
"Department Store Stylist Takes Advance Peek at St. Louis Summer Fashions" (1944), *Retailers Market News*, January 15: 11.
"Design Patent Keystone of New FOGA Plan" (1941), *Women's Wear Daily*, June 3: 13.
"Down to Earth Approach" (1947), *Women's Wear Daily*, September 2: 23.
"Dresses: R&K Dress Corp. Buys Building on Ave. of Americas" (1953), *Women's Wear Daily*, May 5: 30.
"Dresses: Seeks Dismissal of Injunction Action" (1937), *Women's Wear Daily*, October 27: 26.
"European Arrivals Cite Barrel" (1957), *Women's Wear Daily*, August 14: 1.
"Guild to Vote on 29 Applications" (1935), *Women's Wear Daily*, October 18: 9.
"Juniors' Choice Runs to 'Grown-Up' Styles, Designer Comments" (1943), *Women's Wear Daily*, September 8: 11.
"Juniors Not as Concerned About Width of Skirt as 'Oomph' to a Frock" (1943), *Retailers Market News*, September 25: 6.
"Junior Sources Cite Paris as Inspiration for Trends" (1958), *Women's Wear Daily*, August 19: 37.
"Julius Garfinkel & Co." (1951), *The Washington Post*, February 27: F5.
Kaplan, W. (2011), *California Design, 1930–1965: "Living in a Modern Way,"* Cambridge: MIT Press: 265.
"Letters to the Editors" (1951), *LIFE*, December 24: 2.
Marcketti, S.B. and Parsons, J. (2016), *Knock It Off: A History of Design Piracy in the US Women's Ready-To-Wear Apparel Industry*, Lubbock, TX: Texas Tech University Press.
"Marion McCoy En Route to South America" (1940), *Women's Wear Daily*, March 19: 21.
"Marion McCoy Forms Own Firm on Coast" (1945), *Women's Wear Daily*, August 29: 12.
"Marion McCoy Originals" (1948), *The Californian*, August: N10.
"Marion McCoy Resigns as Carlye Designer" (1945), *Women's Wear Daily*, June 8: 17.
"Marshall Field and Company" (1948), *Chicago Daily Tribune*, January 20: 7.
Parsons, J. and Marcketti, S. (2014), *Finding the Unsung Design Heroes of the 1930s*. Costume Society of America Annual Meeting, proceedings of a conference, Baltimore MD.

Petro, D. (2012) "Brother, Can You Spare a Dime? The 1940 Census: Employment and Income." *Prologue*, 44, no. 1. Available online: https://www.archives.gov/publications/prologue/2012/spring/1940.html

"Praise Easy Lines, Ribbon Hats" (1954), *Women's Wear Daily*, February 24: 3.

"Rosenthal, Kalman New Organization" (1932), *The New York Times*, July 18: 18.

"Seventh rules nation's style" (1960), *LIFE*, October 3: 66–73.

Sheinman, M. (1962), "Seen and Heard in the Market," *Women's Wear Daily*, July 17: 21.

Silverman, A.B. (1993), "What Are Design Patents and When Are They Useful?" *Journal of the Minerals, Metals & Materials Society*, 45(3): 63.

"St. Louis Garment Industries Operate Own Piracy Bureau" (1937), *Retailers Market News*, October 23: 1.

Surrarrer, C.A. (2016), "Behind the Labels: Libby Payne, Fashion Designer for 'Mrs. Main Street America,'" MA thesis, Kent State University, Kent, OH.

Taub, B. and Bianco, M. (1954), "Straight, Eased Line: Daytime Chateau Influence," *Women's Wear Daily*, August 11: 1, 5.

"U.S. Contingent on Way to Paris Openings" (1952), *Women's Wear Daily*, January 15: 13.

6 FIRA BENENSON: THE PEOPLE'S COUNTESS

MICHAEL MAMP

Fira Benenson, whose career spanned more than four decades, was a prolific designer of women's fashion based in New York City. Benenson was first a purveyor of designer garments, then an in-house buyer and designer for Bonwit Teller, and finally the creator of a successful ready-to-wear line sold at retailers such as Bergdorf Goodman, and Lord and Taylor. Clothing designed by Fira Benenson is characterized by impeccable craftsmanship and refined, edited elegance. Benenson, who was "perennially attired in black," possessed a sophisticated sense of style focused on quality fabrications, which were often monochromatically manipulated via shirring, pleating, or tucks (Solomon and Litvinoff 1984: 155). These creations, which were simple but classically elegant in form, fabrication, technique, and color usage, were not only fashionable but also wearable and therefore appealed to a diverse clientele including mature and larger-sized women. Benenson's creations graced the pages of the fashion magazines of the period, including *Vogue* and *Harper's Bazaar*. Celebrities, including Grace Kelly, who included a dress by Fira Benenson in her wedding trousseau, favored the designer's work ("Grace Kelly" 1956: 4F).

Despite her many accomplishments in the fashion industry, Fira Benenson's achievements, until now, have been mostly undocumented. Yet from the 1920s through the 1960s, Benenson skillfully adapted her design process and business plan to account for the impact of world events such as the stock market crash of 1929, the Great Depression, and the Second World War. Benenson intuitively determined how to reinvent her business every decade or so in order to remain competitive. She was a successful buyer of luxury goods and designed haute couture in New York City when only a handful of designers such as Charles Kleibacker attempted to do so domestically (Bissonette 2012). Benenson was a

FIGURE 6.1 The Countess Illinski: Fira Benenson c. 1948. Image courtesy of Fashion Institute of Technology|SUNY, Gladys Marcus Library Special Collections.

true couturière, but she also recognized a need to shift her business post–Second World War to focus on ready-to-wear. She was a skilled designer, a strict business owner (her sister would describe her personality at work as that of a despot), and a colorful member of the New York social register (Solomon and Litvinoff 1984). Whatever the outcome, whether it was purchased goods for resale, couture gowns, ready-to-wear, or sew-at-home patterns, the Benenson aesthetic of understated wearable elegance remained consistent.

Imperial Russian roots

Fira Benenson was born in 1899 to Gregori and Sophie Benenson in Baku, on the Caspian Sea (Solomon and Litvinoff 1984). Fira was the third of four children; with two sisters, Flora and Manya, and a brother Jacob. Gregori Benenson settled in Baku where he "interested himself in the development of oil lands ... and in a few years made a fortune" ("Grigori Benenson" 1939: L25). Baku in the early twentieth century suffered from political and social unrest. The Benenson family was Jewish, at a time when many Jewish families in the area were asked to convert to Christianity as a means to avoid possible persecution. However, Gregori Benenson, while not a particularly religious man, remained steadfast and refused to abandon his cultural heritage and sought new business ventures elsewhere (Solomon and Litvinoff 1984).

The family moved to St. Petersburg, where they occupied a palatial apartment on the Moyka River. Grigori's business success provided his family with the means to live a sophisticated life in the twilight of Imperial Russia. After the abdication of Nicholas II in 1917 and Lenin's rise to power, the Benenson family, who lived within view of the Winter Palace, survived on a tightrope of anxiety. According to a biographical press release,

> for two years after the Bolshevik revolution she [Fira] remained there, with guards almost daily ransacking the house for money and jewels which had already been smuggled out of Russia. The Benenson family finally escaped dramatically, first to Scandinavia and then to England. (Lambert 1951: 1)

At first the family separated to confuse any pursuers. Grigori and Flora settled in London; later Fira and Manya joined them there.[1] Grigori worked feverishly to protect his financial interests. After a few years, the opportunity to seek a new life and fortune called; Fira and her father made their first trip to the United States in 1919 (Solomon and Litvinoff 1984) and two years later decided to make a new permanent home in New York City (Lambert 1951).

New York City

On their first trip to New York City in 1919, Grigori purchased a real estate parcel including 165 Broadway and the "leasehold of the southwest corner of Broadway and Cortlandt Street," for 7 million dollars ("165 Broadway" 1919: 24). When Grigori and Fira settled in New York City in the early 1920s, America was in an economic upswing. As the decade progressed the Benenson holdings grew to include significant properties in Brooklyn and Manhattan. Several of his new acquisitions included street-front retail development ("Heads" 1927). This allowed Fira to open an exclusive dress shop.

According to Fira's sister Flora, in America, "rich women indulged their love of clothes to the degree of rendering New York the glamorous reality behind the shadows of the cinema screen" (Solomon and Litvinoff 1984: 130–131). Therefore, Fira, along with her business partner Vera Heller, established Verben, a high-end women's boutique in the heart of New York City's luxury fashion district between 5th and 6th Avenues on 57th Street.[2] From the mid-1920s, Verben focused on classic but cutting-edge fashion for New York City's most fashionable and wealthy women. At Verben, Fira was a buyer and relationship builder with couture houses almost exclusively in Paris. Her selections for Verben demonstrated an appreciation for quality and timeless elegance that would steer her aesthetic for the rest of her career. According to *Women's Wear Daily*,

> A certain specially developed gift of selection by Miss Fira Benenson, directrice of Verben, Inc., equips her to sustain the character of unhackneyed imports which are associated with the firm's collections. The Verben clientele is definitely one that is conservative, but at the same time aware of the fundamental changes of smart fashions. Line supersedes all else, in every phase of the mode, whether daytime or evening, and in this connection Miss Benenson leans toward the particular techniques of Vionnet, Augustabernard, Dormoy, Chanel, Molyneux, Paquin, and in daytime styles, Schaparelli. ("Verben Favors" 1933: 6)

According to Eleanor Lambert, "her taste and ability soon became her fame" (Lambert, n.d.). Exclusive women's boutiques in New York City catered to a well-traveled clientele in between their annual pilgrimages abroad. Economic conditions that resulted from the crash of 1929 prompted shop owners such as Benenson to provide even more fashion-forward product for their consumers as some chose to shop domestically rather than make frequent, expensive European excursions. As explained during the period by a self-proclaimed expatriate on her return to the United States from Europe,

> the most exciting thing in New York is the shops ... here everything is conceived to save time ... the day before I sailed, I saw Lady Aby at lunch making a sensation with a regular bell-boy's cap sitting high on her semi-grown hair ... from Chanel ... I was telling a friend about these delightful absurdities one day as we were stepping into Verben's on Fifty-Seventh Street. My thunder froze on my lips. There were the tarantella stocking caps in white and black string and also Agnes's angora and jersey turban with tails that you bind about your head yourself! ("Your Thrilling" 1930: 60)

Verben's main competitors included shops such as Franklin Simon, Best, and Stern as well as high-end department stores. Benenson worked with her clients to achieve their desires, even in the case of wedding gowns. According to *Vogue*,

Verben is an Apostle of Modern Chic In Its Simple Terms

At left, Chanel's version of the ensemble for evening wear, developed in a fancy soft, sheer woolen all the smarter for its choice of string color.

After Augustabernard is a frock almost naïve in its simplicity, but made altogether sophisticated by the use of black broadcloth.

From the Imports of Verben, Ltd.

FIGURE 6.2 Verben advertisement with ensembles by Chanel and Augustabernard. Image out of copyright/author's collection.

"the most attractive wedding dress that we have seen in years ... was of white tulle, infinitely simple and infinitely chic, with tiers of knife-pleated ruffles and rows of cording ... the dress came from Verben" ("The Latest Excitement" 1932: 25). Fashions from Verben suited a variety of occasions from daytime to evening. For example, "Augustabernard's black broadcloth dress, fitted sleekly, with puffed rolls on the shoulders, nice for bridge, for Sunday afternoons, or for dining out in a restaurant" ("The New Conventions" 1933: 36). Verben carried a wide assortment of accessories and dresses for daytime through evening occasions:

> with the same quality that is associated with clothes worn by the private clientele of the Paris couturiers ... the quality of exclusiveness is understandable since one model after another confirms the statement made by Miss Benenson ... that handwork of a precious kind is the feature that the customer who patronizes a private dressmaker demands. ("Production" 1932: 3)

Fira's livelihood was greatly affected by her father's dwindling fortune. While Verben was well received, Benenson's father owned the building in which the store was located and she relied on him to help cover her living expenses. Benenson's sister remarked that Fira's "difficulty was to manage within her copious dollar allowance ... her stamina, sophistication and extravagance never failed to amaze me" (Solomon and Litvinoff 1984: 130). Fira also had social aspirations and married at age 36 on March 19, 1931 to Count Janusz Illinski, a Polish expatriate and aristocrat who had also served as a general in the Polish military ("Fira Benenson" 1931). After the marriage Fira became known in her personal life as the Countess Illinski, the nomenclature of aristocracy achieved. While her Count was handsome and aristocratic, he came with a title and not much else. Fortunately for the newlyweds, Grigori was incredibly generous, as evidenced by his philanthropic pledge of $24,000 per year to the Palestine Appeal in March of 1929 ("Aids Palestine" 1929). However, by 1932 his business took a turn for the worse resulting in auctions of properties, foreclosures, and lawsuits ("Finding" 1931). Following the crash of October 1929, real estate value plummeted. "The real estate downturn coincided with the stock market crash ... many businesses and hotels went bankrupt". The Benenson family lifestyle, which included residence suites at the Plaza hotel, was on the brink of ruin (Nicholas and scherbina 2013: 300).

Bonwit Teller

In 1934, Hortense Odlum became the president of Bonwit Teller, a large-scale women's specialty store located at 56th Street and 5th Avenue in New York City (Odlum 1939). Paul Bonwit started Bonwit Teller in 1895. Until the Great

Depression, it was an exclusive store only for women that offered luxurious, expensive fashion; truly a leader in New York's high-end fashion retailing (Crawford 1941). Bonwit's occupied several different locations before settling at the corner of 56th Street and 5th Avenue in 1930, a short distance from Verben on 57th Street. Although Paul Bonwit had successfully guided his namesake in the past, in this new seven-floor location he found it difficult to maintain adequate inventory levels while also weathering the storm of the Great Depression. Unfortunately, by 1931, business declined at Bonwit's to the point of loan default, and Floyd Odlum, Hortense's husband, acquired the store ("Mrs. Odlum; Bonwit Teller's Chief" 1934).

Odlum's company, Atlas Corporation, liquidated many investments just before the stock market crash of 1929, leaving plenty of capital to acquire holdings post-crash at a fraction of their prior value. In fact, in the early 1930s, Floyd Odlum amassed a fortune placing him among the top ten wealthiest Americans ("Atlas" 1941). Bonwit Teller was one such business acquired by Atlas Corporation in the detritus of the Great Depression. A woman's store was not in the usual purview of Odlum's organization; however, he recognized that prior to the crash the store had achieved respectable profits ("Lady from Atlas" 1934). On a whim, he asked his wife Hortense Odlum what to do with Bonwit Teller (Odlum 1939).

In contrast to Fira, Hortense came from a very modest upbringing in St. George, Utah, where her family was farmers and members of the Mormon church (Mamp 2015). Hortense Odlum stepped on every imaginable rung of the socioeconomic ladder, from scrimping on her husband's 75-dollar monthly salary to her position in the 1930s as the wife of one of America's wealthiest men (Mamp 2014). This put Hortense in a unique position to understand specifically what women, in a variety of economic positions, wanted out of their own store. She was not armed with education or even experience. Instead, she knew intuitively how to meet the diverse economic needs of women shopping for clothing. Hortense Odlum was not a customer of Bonwit's. Upon visiting the store for the first time in 1932 she quickly discovered that assortment was lacking. In her own words, "there isn't a dress ... that a well dressed woman would want to wear, I've never seen so many Christmas tree ornaments on clothes" (Odlum 1939: 72).

Hortense Odlum served first as a consultant and became the president of Bonwit Teller in 1934 ("Mrs. Odlum Heads Bonwit" 1934). Women continued to shop during the Great Depression; they just did so differently by looking for bargains, repurposing, and applying American thriftiness. Retailers and even government responded by providing a greater variety of clothing price points to meet the needs of a stressed economy (Marcketti 2010). Odlum created a variety of new departments at Bonwit's to cater to women of all economic backgrounds, from the extremely wealthy to those on a strict budget.

While she hadn't been a Bonwit's customer, Odlum did shop at Verben, an experience that led to another innovative department. Benenson had the clientele but no money, Odlum had the money but no clientele; hence the *Salon de Couture* was conceived. Despite its difficulties, Bonwit Teller had one good thing going for it: *location*. Just a block from Verben, next door to Tiffany's and across the street from Bergdorf Goodman—the epicenter of New York City's luxury fashion retail district (Neimark 2006).[3] According to the *Jewish News Wire*,

> There is news in the very air of Bonwit Teller. The first act in the drama was the arrival of Fira Benenson who, as Verben, has been dressing many of the most sophisticated women you see in New York. She is a bosom friend of the brightest stars in the Paris dress world. She stays in Paris after the other buyers go and shares from these friends of hers very special models, designed for the private clientele. The result is collections of dresses which you don't see elsewhere. A whole floor of Bonwit Teller is given over to her. The collection is divine. ("Shop Talk" 1934: 1)

In 1934, Benenson was paid a salary of 10,000 dollars per year as the director of the Salon de Couture, the equivalent of about 180,000 dollars in 2016 (Solomon and Litvinoff 1984; U.S. Inflation).

The *Salon de Couture* occupied an entire floor in the Bonwit Teller building, and it was a success from day one. The Verben clientele followed Benenson, and the Bonwit Teller publicity machine now under the direction of another Odlum new hire, Sara Pennoyer, attracted new customers ("New Bonwit" 1935). The salon was also a means to compete with other in-store couture and made-to-order salons such as the *Salon Moderne* at Saks Fifth Avenue headed by Sophie Gimbel ("Sophie" 1969). At first, the objective was to facilitate orders between New York customers and Paris. Bonwit Teller used the services of Gladys Tilden, who was positioned in Paris on behalf of the company to facilitate orders and to report fashion trends. Telegram correspondence between Benenson and Tilden documented orders from prestigious fashion houses such as Chanel and Mainbocher (Tilden 1934). By mid-1935 Tilden's services were no longer required as Benenson was already better connected to the European fashion scene via her work at Verben. However, as the threat of war loomed in Europe it became clear that the salon needed to do more than just order couture; they needed to produce it.

Odlum "insisted that we have the facilities to create exquisite gowns which would always be remembered by their wearers" (Odlum 1939: 116). Benenson's exposure to the finest couturiers of Europe, not to mention her own privileged upbringing, familiarized her with quality garments. However, she had never actually made one before. Benenson hired workers for her atelier, mostly Russian and Jewish refugees who were less fortunate than her but highly skilled (Lambert 1951). She learned more about garment engineering and construction along the way. Slowly, and quietly, Benenson went about perfecting her skills in garment design and supervised construction until the German occupation of Paris in 1940 effectively shut down the French couture industry. In the fall of 1940, Benenson showed her first small collection of dresses and ensembles in the *Salon de Couture*, and from that point forward did so twice a year until 1948 (Lambert 1951). Her approach to design involved detailed construction and fine handwork and was perfectly suited for wartime. Despite facing regulations imposed on the fashion industry to reserve materials for the war effort, Benenson insisted, "we mustn't

FIGURE 6.3 Fira Benenson (seated middle) at work in the Salon de Couture atelier, August 1, 1940. Image © [Alfred Eisenstaedt]/[The LIFE Picture Collection]/Getty Images.

allow clothes to be dull and stale ... let's make a springboard of our difficulties and let our imaginations put into clothes the liveliness and movement that we require" ("Fira Benenson's Silhouette" 1945: 3). As her collections progressed for Bonwit Teller she further refined her approach of using elegant, simple silhouettes and basic colors (especially black), and painstaking handwork such as "sawtooth edges, narrow shirred insets, cutouts lined with sheer cordiage for more surface interest, faggotting and puffed rows of shirring" ("Fira Benenson's Silhouette" 1945: 3).

The Benenson collection for the *Salon de Couture* gained notoriety, enhancing Benenson's status as a leading American fashion designer during the 1940s. Benenson also supported the war effort through her design of the uniforms for the American Women's Voluntary Services ("Counter Espionage" 1942: 33).[4] In 1943 she provided fashion predictions and reflections on wartime in a profile of ten of America's top fashion designers. According to Benenson,

> I believe the seriousness of the times has made women softer and more feminine. A woman today wants clothes that are useful, yet becoming to her womanly beauty. By creating a simple silhouette, I have tried to design clothes that may be worn from day to night. I do think that skirts must be manipulated in such a way as to allow ample freedom of movement, during times when women must not only look pretty but must walk and board buses and trains and climb subway stairs. ("Ten Designers" 1943: SM18)

Ready-to-wear

In 1948, after fourteen years, Benenson decided to leave Bonwit Teller. During her time at the store she successfully grew the *Salon de Couture* business first through relationships with Paris fashion houses and later through the development of her made-to-order items. From 1940 she and her team developed a reputation for amazing craftsmanship, clean elegant style, intricate detail, comfortable fit, and versatility. Benenson garments were worked with a very delicate hand. According to Virginia Pope, "Benenson has the faculty of making her trimmings a part of the dress rather than making them seem superimposed. It is rare that she makes use of another material for trimming" (Pope 1948a: 36). Instead, she manipulated the fabrication to create details such as cording, shirred panels, ruching, and pleats. It seems this focus on surface interest developed during the Second World War when due to rationing she worked primarily with plain wools and crepes (Pope 1944).

Through her years at Bonwit Teller, Benenson retained the building at 37 W. 57th Street where Verben was originally located, so in February 1948 she opened her new Fira Benenson showroom and ateliers in the same spot she had started in twenty years earlier (Pope 1948b). In the new space she not only maintained a made-to-order business but also worked on the development of her ready-to-wear line. A fashion show in her salon in February 1948 presented made-to-order models. However, in September of the same year she showed her first ready-to-wear collection in a fashion show at Lord & Taylor in New York City.

In September 1948, the new ready-to-wear collection was offered exclusively at Lord & Taylor. This first collection included over forty-six models with "wool dresses and suits, dressy wool crepes, creations for the cocktail hour and for dinner and evening" with price points starting at $110 (Pope 1948a). The work was extremely well received; Benenson effectively "translated into ready to wear the exquisite detail that made her custom fashions famous" (Pope 1948a). She followed up this success with another collection shown in January 1949 at the Pierre Hotel, as part of a charity benefit for the New York Heart Association. This spring collection featured "widely cut or plunging necklines" and skirts that were full but not cumbersome (Pope 1949: 26). Dorothy Shaver, President of Lord & Taylor, promoted American designers; Benenson was one of many, such as Nettie Rosenstein and Clare Potter, who benefited from Shaver's American Designer Program (Amerian 2011).

The stylish, finely made Benenson collection sold very well and was picked up by other retailers, including Marshall Field and I. Magnin ("Furred" 1948). The brand was available at retailers from 1948 throughout the 1960s. It also expanded to include a higher-priced bridge line of mostly evening clothes available at retailers such as Bergdorf Goodman, Hattie Carnegie, and Elizabeth Arden (Warren 1964). Consumers outside of New York City were also interested in Benenson designs. In February 1949 her wholesale collection was shown in Atlanta at the opening of a new Franklin Simon store. Dinner dresses were sold for around $235 ("Fira Benenson" 1949). Benenson offered many items in sizes ranging up to a twenty, and her expert skill at tailoring and surface detail proved flattering on a variety of women (Warren 1964). Only a few extent examples of Benenson's work from her early years of design at Bonwit Teller exist in collections. Benenson's garments were distinctly not trendy but rather well made and classically fashionable. Clothes by Benenson were worn over several years. Fortunately, a small collection of her design sketches dating from 1940 until about 1960 was saved.[5] The sketches reveal designs that were very wearable by women of varying ages and sizes. They are in line with fashion of the period but not overtly trendy (Emerson 1958). Perhaps, the lack of surviving garments is due to the fact that Benenson clothes were *worn*.

A testament to Fira Benenson's ability to design for a wide range of customers, starting in the 1950s her designs were also offered to the home sewer by the America's Designer Patterns Company of James and Jean Miller Spaeda.[6] These "were cut directly from a master pattern which was taken from the original garment," and the consumer received a Fira Benenson label to sew into their finished work (Bramlett n.d.).

FIGURE 6.4 Fira Benenson cocktail dress *c.* 1960 with three-quarter sleeves, and full skirt. "Fashion and Costume Sketch Collection. Fira Benenson sketch." Brooklyn Museum Libraries. Fashion and Costume Sketch Collection. Special Collections.

Conclusion

Fira Benenson continued working into her seventies. Her husband Count Janusz Illinski passed away in 1961; the couple had no children. Benenson's accomplishments were remarkable considering her lack of formal training. Benenson built a large and diversified fashion business that weathered the Great Depression and the Second World War. Her passion was her work, and her razor-sharp focus on an edited, elegant, hand-worked aesthetic never faltered. Fira Benenson passed away in 1977 at the age of 78 (Fowle 1977).

Fashion editor Carrie Donovan once said that Benenson created "the illusion of perfect sophisticated chic" (Fowle 1977: 32). Benenson's brand of sophisticated chic appealed to thousands of women over a period of more than forty years. She knew who her customers were, and she never disappointed them. The work of this accomplished woman was lucrative and widely praised, yet her story remained untold. Her brand of wearable sophistication never failed her or her customer.

Acknowledgments

Thanks to April Calahan at the Fashion Institute of Technology's Special Collections Archive, Sandy Wallace at the Brooklyn Museum Library, and Suzanne LeSar at the Iowa State University Textiles & Clothing Museum for their assistance. This research was funded by Central Michigan University.

Archival Sources

Eleanor Lambert Collection. Special Collections. Gladys Marcus Library, Fashion Institute of Technology, New York.

Fira Benenson fashion illustrations, Special Collections, Gladys Marcus Library, Fashion Institute of Technology, New York; Designer Files, Brooklyn Museum Library, New York.

Fira Benenson file at Irene Lewisohn Costume Reference Library, Metropolitan Museum of Art: New York.

Gladys Tilden papers, BANC MSS 88/229c, the Bancroft Library: University of California, Berkeley.

Spadea's American Designer Patterns. Book 2 (n.d.); *Spadea Patterns by World Famous Designers*. Book 14 & 17 (1957, 1960), Iowa State University Textiles & Clothing Museum.

Notes

1   Flora remained in London and had one son, Peter Benenson, who founded Amnesty International. She worked at Marks & Spencer department store. Her other sister Manya translated Russian literature, most notably *Doctor Zhivago*. Their brother Jacob died in a concentration camp during the Second World War.

2   See the London Bureau of *Women's Wear Daily* (April 15, 1932): 10. Vera Heller was a knitwear designer who after working with Fira at Verben established a "handknitted garment" business in Paris. In 1932 Vera Heller and her sister Eva Lutyens opened their own fashion house in London. Lutyens was an accomplished designer who counted Wallis Simpson as one of her clients. Heller and Lutyens were the nieces of Chaim Weizmann, President of the Zionist Organization in America, and in 1949, the first President of Israel.

3   Donald Trump demolished the building and built Trump Tower.

4   See http://fashionweekdaily.com/confessions-american-fashion-icon-stan-herman/. Stan Herman, an early employee of Benenson, went on to design uniforms for Pan Am and McDonald's.

5   See Fira Benenson fashion illustrations, Special Collections, Gladys Marcus Library, Fashion Institute of Technology, New York; Designer Files, Brooklyn Museum Library, New York.

6   See *Spadea's American Designer Patterns*. Book 2 (n.d.); *Spadea Patterns by World Famous Designers*. Book 14 & 17 (1957, 1960), Iowa State University Textiles & Clothing Museum.

Bibliography

"165 Broadway Sold to London Banker" (1919). *New York Times*, December 19: 24.

Abraham, R. (1987), *Alexander Kerensky the First Love of the Revolution*, New York: Columbia University Press.

"Aids Palestine Appeal" (1929), *New York Times*, March 4: 22.

Amerian, S.M. (2011), "Fashioning a Female Executive: Dorothy Shaver and the Business of American Style, 1893–1959," PhD diss., Los Angeles: University of California.

"Atlas into Hearst" (1941), *Time*, March 10: 86.

Bissonette, A. (2012), "Savoring the Process: Designer, Educator, and Curator Charles Kleibacker, 1921–2010," *Dress*, 38(1): 1–23.

Bramlett, L. (no date). Spaeda Patterns. Available online: http://fuzzylizzie.com/spadea.html.

"Buys Havemeyer Building" (1928), *New York Times*, August 7: 38.

"Counter Espionage" (1942), *Vogue*, July 1: 33, 72.

Crawford, M. (1941), *The Ways of Fashion*, New York: G.P. Putnam's Sons.

Emerson, G. (1958). "Realistic Approach to Fashion Is Suggested for Middle-Aged Women," *New York Times*, November 10: 35.

"Finding in Benenson Suit" (1931), *New York Times*, September 18: 41.

"Fira Benenson Cites Response to Showings on Atlanta Trip" (1949), *Women's Wear Daily*, February 21: 31.

"Fira Benenson to Wed" (1931), *New York Times*, March 19: 27.

"Fira Benenson's Silhouette of Motion for Bonwit Teller" (1945), *Women's Wear Daily*, March 9: 3.

Fowle, F. (1977), "Fira Benenson, Fashion Designer," *New York Times*, October 24: 32.

"Furred Evening Suits" (1948), *Vogue*, September 15: 162–163.

"Grace Kelly Will Sail Today for Monaco with Many Clothes" (1956), *Chicago Daily Tribune*, April 4: 4F.

"Grigori Benenson, Noted Financier" (1939), *New York Times*, April 6: L25.

"Heads New York Dock co." (1927), *New York Times*, March 25: 30.

"Lady from Atlas" (1934), *Time*, October 22: 61.

Lambert, E. (1951), Fira Benenson. Retrieved from Fira Benenson file at Irene Lewisohn Costume Reference Library, Metropolitan Museum of Art: New York.

Lambert, E. (no date), Fira Benenson, Eleanor Lambert Collection. Special Collections. Gladys Marcus Library, Fashion Institute of Technology, New York.

"The Latest Excitement as Seen by Her" (1932), *Vogue*, August 15: 25, 64.

Mamp, M. (2014), "Female Presidents of Bonwit Teller: Hortense Odlum (1934–44) and Mildred Custin (1965–70)," PhD diss., Ames: Iowa State University.

Mamp, M. and Marcketti, S. (2015), "Creating a Woman's Place: The Bonwit Teller Presidency of Hortense Odlum, 1934 to 1940," *Fashion Style & Popular Culture*, 2(3): 301–319.

Marcketti, S.B. (2010), "The Sewing Room Projects of the Works Progress Administration," *Textile History*, 41(1): 28–49.

"Mrs. Odlum; Bonwit Teller's Chief Began 2 Years Ago" (1934a), *Newsweek*, October 20: 34.

"Mrs. Odlum Heads Bonwit Teller" (1934b), *New York Times*, October 9: 14.

Neimark, I. (2006), *Crossing Fifth Avenue to Bergdorf Goodman: An Insider's Account on the Rise of Luxury Retail*, New York: SPI Books.

"New Bonwit Teller ad Director" (1935), *New York Times*, January 24: 37.

"The New Conventions for Bridge" (1933), *Vogue*, January 1: 36.

Nicholas, T. and Scherbina, A. (2013), "Real Estate Prices During the Roaring Twenties and the Great Depression," *Real Estate Economics*, 41(2): 278–309.

Odlum, H. (1939), *A Woman's Place the Autobiography of Hortense Odlum*, New York: Scribner & Sons.

Pope, V. (1944), "New York Designers Have Created Style Distinctive of World War II," *New York Times*, September 10: 46.

Pope, V. (1948a), "Detail Is Marked in Style Showing," *New York Times*, September 16: 36.

Pope, V. (1948b), "Sweep of Skirts Enhances Designs," *New York Times*, February 22: 26.

Pope, V. (1949), "New Styles Bring a Touch of Spring: Fashions by Fira Benenson Are Augmented by Hats Shown by Mme. Vittu" Virginia Pope, *New York Times*, January 27:26.

"Production of Handwork Details of Paris Models Keynote of Verben Collection" (1932), *Women's Wear Daily*, March 24: 3.

"Shop Talk" (1934), *The Jewish News Wire*, August 23: 1.

Solomon, F. and Litvinoff, B. (1984), *Baku to Baker Street: The memoirs of Flora Solomon*, London: Collins.

"Sophie Is Retiring and So Is Her Custom Salon at Saks" (1969), *New York Times*, May 26: 50.

Suny, R.G. (1972), *The Baku Commune, 1917–1918; Class and Nationality in the Russian Revolution*, Princeton: Princeton University Press.

"Ten Designers Predict" (1943), *New York Times*, March 21: SM18.

U.S. Inflation Calculator. Available online: www.USinflationcalculator.com

"Verben Favors Imports with Bias Developed Silhouette" (1933), *Women's Wear Daily*, March 31: 6.

"Verben Is an Apostle of Modern Chic In its Simple Terms" (1932), *Women's Wear Daily*, October 25: 8.

Warren, V.L. (1964), "Few Shops Put Stress on Size 18," *New York Times*, July 11: 12.

"Your Thrilling New York Shops" (1930), *Vogue*, September 1: 60, 61, 84.

7 HELEN LEE AND SUZANNE GODART: CHIC FOR CHILDREN

JENNIFER FARLEY GORDON AND SARA B. MARCKETTI

Robert Love, children's wear executive and designer for the family-run firm Joseph Love, Inc., asserted that the children's wear industry developed in distinct phases: as he told *Women's Wear Daily*, the first was the formation of large children's wear firms during the late nineteenth and early twentieth centuries. Like the U.S. garment industry at large, these companies pioneered the field of affordable readymade clothing. According to Love, the second phase was the promotion of specialist children's wear designers during the 1950s and 1960s (A.M.S. and C.H. 1966). Designers like Helen Lee and Suzanne Godart ushered in this new era. Bolstered by consumer affluence, these designers strove to position children's fashions on a par with the clothing of adults, bringing a fashion perspective to a growing demographic. After the Second World War, a large number of Americans had more disposable income than ever before, and they used that money to purchase goods for their homes and families (May 1999). As historian Lizabeth Cohen wrote, "consumer spending ... helped secure an historic reign of prosperity," and accordingly, production of goods skyrocketed (2003: 121). Consumer cash was coupled with the rising population of infants and children. The latter, observed sociologist Daniel Thomas Cook, "from the outset ... was framed as a business opportunity" (2004: 123).

Designers of children's wear fought to legitimize their field, to bring distinct points of view to children's clothing design, and to be acknowledged as creative and business talents. Fashionable clothing for children became a recurring theme in the fashion and trade presses, marketed as a status symbol to the aspirant middle-class customer. According to a 1954 *New York Times* report, "Fashion magazines, newspaper fashion pages and other media now devote a fair amount of space [to children's wear], mainly as a result of the newness of color and design that is available"

("Children's Styles" 1954: F7). By the 1960s, the children's wear market was lucrative enough to attract industry players from the women's wear market. High-profile designers, such as Claire McCardell, Bill Blass, and Arnold Scaasi, all experimented with children's clothing lines, often collaborating with prominent children's wear production firms. The designer name became valuable during the 1950s and 1960s in generating children's wear sales as well as business prestige, just as it increasingly did within the women's wear market. This chapter will examine the evolution of specialist children's wear designers from anonymity to prominence during the mid-twentieth century, using designers Helen Lee and Suzanne Godart as its primary examples, and placing their rise in stature in the context of these industry events.

The American ready-to-wear designer and the rise from anonymity

Children's wear designers, like most of their counterparts in the U.S. women's ready-to-wear industry, were largely unrecognized through the 1940s. According to scholar Veronica Manlow, the rise in status of fashion designers during the early and mid-twentieth century required a shift in the perception of the value of the designers' work, as well as a break from the traditional anonymity under which many clothing creators labored (2007: 93). Fashion designer Elizabeth Hawes argued that beleaguered designers were not just hidden; they were under the thumb of more powerful members of the industry—the executives of their wholesale firms as well as the clients to whom they sold (1942: 7). In the case of children's wear, the large manufacturing firms established during the first phase of the trade's expansion were initially reluctant to yield power to the individual designer. Industry-wide twentieth-century American ready-to-wear designers faced difficulty in asserting their value (Anspach 1967). Many, as JoAnne Olian pointed out, were thought of as "mere technicians" (121). While their counterparts in France might be respected as artists, any underperforming American designer was "replaceable"; she was "valuable only as long as she designs garments that sell" (Anspach 1967: 202).

By the mid-twentieth century, however, a number of notable exceptions in the U.S. women's ready-to-wear industry had emerged from the shadow of the companies for which they worked. During this period, prominent figures like department store executive Dorothy Shaver at Lord & Taylor helped to push forward the status of New York's fashion talents, hoping to "create a cult of personality around American fashion designers similar to that surrounding French couturiers" (Webber-Hanchett 2003: 83). Strong industry advocates, effective promotion, and genuine talent helped designers like Muriel King, Vera Maxwell, and Claire McCardell become far more recognizable to the public (Webber-Hanchett 2003; Arnold 2009). By around 1940–1941, the latter had even negotiated for her name to appear on the label of her garments, although she shared the label space with manufacturer, Townley Frocks (Yohannan and Nolf 1998). Further impetus for American design came in the form of global conflict, as information from the long-dominant Parisian industry became unavailable over the course of the Second World War (Buckland 1996; Manlow 2007).

Nevertheless, designers like McCardell were still *exceptions*. It was only for "a very few original high fashion designers" that "the role of the manufacturer has been eliminated or at least left unmentioned," argued writer Edith Heal (1966: 100). For American designers of children's clothing, this problem was magnified and the process of recognition slower. Fashion historian Rebecca Jumper Matheson (2015) noted that Emily Wilkens, who designed for the teen market, was both pioneering and highly unique in having command over her line, and her own name on its label during the 1940s.

Specialist children's wear designers

In 1956, *Good Housekeeping* wrote that "*name* designers with the same high talent as designers of adult fashions [were] working exclusively on children's clothes," listing Lee and Godart among the top tier ("Report" 1956: 42). Suzanne Godart herself noted, "The children's fashion designer is a key figure in the growing children's wear industry" (1966: 68). These designers were specialists, meaning their primary or exclusive field of design was that of children's clothing. Although some eventually had their own labels, most worked under the auspices of large first-generation children's wear firms such as L. Wohl and Company or Joseph Love, Inc., or by the 1960s, at newly launched brands like Alyssa.

Despite such praise, the quest for name recognition for specialist designers, as well as overall respect for an industry often considered secondary, permeated the discussion of mid-twentieth-century children's wear. For the individual children's clothing designer, the achievement of one's own name on the label was a significant step, much as it had been for their counterparts in women's ready-to-wear. The use of the designer's name, even under the auspices of another brand, promoted several of these specialists out of relative anonymity. Children's wear specialists Helen Lee and Suzanne Godart were among "the first" to be promoted, with their names on labels, by mass market children's wear firms or retailers. Both women were significant in their lasting impact on the children's wear industry and representative of the rise of the specialist children's wear designer.

Helen Lee

The single most repeated name in specialist children's wear design during this period was that of Helen Lee.[1] *Good Housekeeping* called her "the dean of the field," indicating her authority and influence ("Report" 1956: 42). Publicist Eleanor

Lambert claimed that Lee "conquered one of the garment industry's largest and most 'unconquerable' branches, the sprawling children's dress field" (Lambert *c.* 1960s: 1). In discussing the rise of fashion in children's wear, the *Saturday Evening Post* singled Lee out for recognition among a larger discussion of the new children's lines by women's ready-to-wear designers. None of the other designers mentioned were exclusive to the children's wear field (Black 1962).

FIGURE 7.1 Helen Lee at Work, Fall 1962. Image courtesy of Saks Fifth Avenue Publicity Collection, 1954–1974, The New School Archives and Special Collections, The New School, New York, NY.

Part of Lee's significance lay in what trade paper *The Infants' and Children's Review* called her "double vantage point" on the creative and business ends of the children's wear industry. The designer rose through the ranks of the children's wear business, and by the 1960s she was an "internationally acclaimed designer, and associate in a multimillion dollar company" ("About Helen Lee" 1963: 24). At the height of her career, Lee achieved what one writer called "triple-barreled success ... commercial, critical, and popular" (Williams 1956: 91).

Helen Lee left her birthplace in Knoxville, Tennessee, for New York City around 1926, at age 18. She studied her craft at the Art Students League and the Traphagen School of Design (Lee 1983: 5). Lee recalled that children's wear held great potential for an aspiring designer during this period, and the advice she received from a manufacturer, Louis Borgenicht, motivated her decision to enter the burgeoning field. He told her that "There was nobody designing children's wear in the industry. They just had cutters, who put on a lace collar or something like that" (Lee 1983: 1). During the early 1930s, she was hired at pioneering firm Joseph Love, Inc.; she stayed there only for a short but edifying time: "I really was in the factory. ... Then I really learned about selecting fabrics and what they would do" (Lee 1983: 8).

Around 1934, Lee joined L. Wohl and Company, a manufacturer whose best-known label was Kate Greenaway Frocks. The company, as Lee recounted, was not classified as "top of the line": "They were volume, and they sold [to] a lot of basement stores too" (Lee 1983: 10). Lee designed there for over a decade, but her name was never featured on the brand's label ("Modern Interpreter" 1946). Craving greater ownership and recognition for her work, Lee eventually decamped, in 1950, to children's wear firm Rosenau Brothers. She did not stay long, however, as the company balked at giving her credit and publicity. Her parting shot: "I'm going to build my name. You built yours; I'm going to build mine" (Lee 1983: 11).

Lee's next position was with the newly established company, Sam Landorf and Company, Inc., and its Youngland brand. Lee brought experience and talent to the young company, and crucially, Landorf allowed her to step into the limelight (Williams 1956: 99). So important was the building of her name that she took a pay cut, initially receiving $5,000 a year, in exchange for the inclusion of her name on the label (Lee 1983: 12). Lee's name was reportedly added to the label almost immediately after she joined the firm, where four times per year, she released sizable children's wear collections (Williams 1956: 99). As talented as she was as a designer, Lee was also quite attuned to the realities of the children's wear business— from manufacturing to sales—and at Youngland, she began to test her business strategies. She felt that her designs must "form an integrated group which tell a story, which can be advertised so effectively that potential buyers will be persuaded to seek out the store where Helen Lee clothes can be bought" (Williams 1956: 91).

Youngland swiftly expanded. According to Lee, within three years the company had generated $8 million dollars. This was a profitable turn for the designer, as she had stipulated in early negotiations that "as your volume goes up, so do I"

(Lee 1983: 12). Sam Landorf told the *New York Times* that Youngland capitalized on price point, namely the "middle price bracket" and style, the two "voids" in the children's market. "Children's dresses," he claimed, "could get recognition as fashion items, if properly designed and exploited" ("Children's Styles" 1954: F7).

In 1953, Helen Lee received a special Coty American Fashion Critics' Award ("Two to Get Coty" 1953). Initially the award was a boon for both Lee and her employer, but Landorf pushed for joint acknowledgment, causing unease in the relationship (Lee 1983: 15). Landorf's reaction may be indicative of the industry's general anxiety as designer names threatened to usurp the prominence of a manufacturer's brand. As fashion historian Caroline Rennolds Milbank asserted, when the press began increasingly "crediting them [the designers] by name" the traditional powerhouses of manufacturing and retail "became less important" (1989: 130).

By 1957, Lee left Youngland for a new opportunity at another comparatively new firm, Alyssa Originals. Lee recalled her apprehension about the move, noting that she was "by then … in the big figures, in income … I was becoming a heavy package" (Lee 1983: 15). Although Alyssa was new, its proprietor, Alfred Flug, was no stranger to the industry, having previously been co-owner of the children's wear firm Alfred Leon. Flug was happy to cash in on Lee's name recognition and featured her name prominently in advertisements. Lee's new partnership also gave her far greater stake in the business than many other children's wear designers possessed. *The Infants' and Children's Review* reported that she was the chief creative talent and an executive: "vice president in charge of designing" ("Helen Lee Joins" 1957: 62).

Even before Lee left Youngland, she had concrete opinions on how to design mass-produced children's clothing: "She knew the kind of clothes that would make little girls happy. … And she also thought she knew how to sell them … and how to promote them" (Williams 1956: 98). At Alyssa, Lee espoused "'conceptual' designing," a more formalized explanation of her previous philosophies: the development of "an overall program" and delivering a complete "package of dresses" ("Alyssa's" 1969: 42).

If by the 1960s Lee had refined her business philosophy, she had likewise established her own personal design style, creating uncomplicated and practical garments in bold, attractive colors (Lee 1960). Lee felt that children's clothing had been subjected to a consistent silhouette of "tight bodice, puff sleeves, sashed or belted fitted waist … and full skirt" for too long. This basic dress, she contended, was plastered with "ruffles, bows, ornaments, and appliques and heaven knows what else" (Lee 1963: 22). Eschewing such details, Lee argued for simplicity as the single most crucial element in a child's garments.

During the 1960s, while she was employed at Alyssa, Lee designed for multiple outlets at varying price points. Lee's work spanned the status hierarchy, from high to low, within the children's wear industry, as she designed Alyssa's "better" goods, in addition to a popular-priced line for Sears (Gantzhorn 1964; Weir 1973; Lee 1983). Helen Lee also added a prestigious Saks Fifth Avenue line to her portfolio, with her name appearing on its label. Saks executive Adam Gimbel was clear on one matter, however, telling her: "I don't want your name to be with Sears. I don't care how much work you do for them" (Lee 1983: 17). In practice, the industry was well aware of Lee's association with multiple labels, but Saks willfully misrepresented the fact that Lee's garments were elsewhere on the market, claiming "Helen Lee's talents . . . available exclusively to customers of Saks Fifth Avenue" (O'Hagan Summer 1961: 1).

Lee's "exclusive" named line for Saks Fifth Avenue debuted in Spring 1961 and was marketed extensively. It was Lee's name, as much as her talent, that Saks coveted ("Children's Designer Joins" 1960: 10). Lee was by this point a veteran designer with decades of experience and maintained, perhaps, the strongest name

FIGURE 7.2 A promotional photograph from Helen Lee's first collection for Saks Fifth Avenue, Spring 1961. Image courtesy of Saks Fifth Avenue Publicity Collection, 1954–1974, The New School Archives and Special Collections, The New School, New York, NY.

recognition of any specialist children's wear designer. During her tenure with Saks, which lasted through at least the early 1970s, the company regularly referred to her as its children's couturière, a deliberate misuse of the term meant to evoke fashionability and status.

The talented Lee had risen to prominence but not without ruffling some feathers. By the 1960s, *Women's Wear Daily* reported that Lee had had "a varied and stormy career with just about every ... leading dress firm in the business" (Gantzhorn 1964: 27). When Alyssa collapsed in 1970, interpersonal conflict and Lee's high wages were cited as two reasons. Lee then set up as a freelance designer (Davis 1971). In 1971, she became a design director at Sears, building on the relationship they had established during the previous decade ("Helen Lee Signs" 1971). Her emphasis at Sears was on basics or "multiples" in a variety of colorways (Weir 1973), a familiar idea to Lee who years earlier stated that "an imaginative designer will recognize a good [dress] body and hold to the shape, achieving variety by making it up in a multiplicity of fabrics" (Lee 1963: 24). Other projects at this time included a line for Danskin as well as designs for an eponymous line (Morris 1977). However, the drop-off in press coverage following her exodus from Alyssa was pronounced, and Lee closed her design business in 1981, around the age of 72 (Lee 1983).

Suzanne Godart

While Lee labored in relative obscurity for years and worked her way up to a place of prominence, Suzanne Godart was something of an upstart. She had little formal training—reportedly doing only a brief stint at Traphagen School of Design ("Designer Yearbook" 1961). Godart spent part of her childhood in France, creating a mystique around the designer. Publications went so far as to claim that Godart was born in Paris, and she even perpetuated that myth, writing in an essay that she was "born and educated in France" (1966: 67). In fact, Godart was born Suzanne Kapa in Chisholm, Minnesota, and ultimately graduated from the town's high school ("Designer Yearbook" 1961; Gantzhorn 1961; "Suzanne Kapa" 2002). Nonetheless, she cultivated a sophisticated European persona emphasizing her French heritage as eagerly as the fashion press reported on it. Essential Parisian chic was the quality emphasized above all in relating the appeal of Godart's designs. Godart made herself "famous for designing the oh-so-French looking clothes for little girls" ("Designing Travelers" 1967: 52). This association began with her debut line in 1949, when the designer self-reported that buyers likened her showings to being at a Paris collection. Her first designs looked decidedly high-end, like "something out of a children's couture collection, yet ... very wearable and becoming" ("Designing Young" 1949: 15).

Godart's meteoric rise astonished the apparel industry. *Women's Wear Daily* asked, "Where did she come from, this designer who with just two seasonal showings has started everybody talking about her... ?" ("Designing Young" 1949: 15). Despite her early successes, and her marital relationship with industry insider, the textile manufacturer Pierre Godart, her first business venture folded ("Suzanne Kapa" 2002). The designer claimed that closing her business was a personal choice, but this may have been a polite fiction to conceal financial embarrassment (Godart 1966: 68). Bankruptcy proceedings at the end of 1950 listed: "Suzanne Godart, housewife, 815 Park Ave.: liabilities $8,671; no assets. She formerly operated a dress manufacturing business at 150 W. 56th St" ("Business Records" 1950: 24). Godart found ready work the following year at children's wear manufacturing firm Suzy Brooks, where she spent over a decade designing stylish clothes for the company's mid-price range ("New Design Character" 1951). Godart's name had been on the Suzy Brooks label from early in their partnership, but in 1963 the company announced its intention to "launch a new advertising and marketing program which will place emphasis on designer Suzanne Godart" ("Rogan" 1963: 35). Regardless of this renewed attention, less than six months later, Godart resigned her post to design for Sam Landorf's Youngland line.

At Youngland, select garments bore her name on the label, while she participated in the design of the company's other products ("Mrs. Godart" 1964). According to the vice-president and son of the company's founder, Howard Landorf, the company devised named or thematic groups within the large seasonal line, similar to what they had done with her predecessor Lee (McDermott 1965: 16).

By Godart's own account, her design style was based on "enduring" classics rather than on cultural or fashion trends. She claimed, "I make it a rule to know fashion trends, but never to be bound by them" (Godart 1966: 69). She advocated a planned, coordinated wardrobe for children. After her first collection, *Women's Wear Daily* described "the Godart formula" as including "ensembles carefully worked out in coat-with-dress, or suit-with-blouse ... and high colors for the fashion-conscious youngster." As Godart stated, "A coat and dress that go together and a hat to match, give a child a well groomed look and teach her good taste as well as wardrobe economy in later life" ("Designing Young" 1949: 15). Polished styling was crucial to Godart's design aesthetic, as she infused her work with classic details, such as pinafores, smocks, shirtwaist silhouettes, pleated skirts, straight lines, and bowed neckties. Many of these elements were likewise present in the French couture designs that Godart admired. Although the American designer industry had come into its own during the Second World War, Paris still reigned supreme in terms of design during this period. Godart drew copious inspiration from the fashion capital and its designers, particularly Gabrielle Chanel, admitting that the designer's effortless, simple chic had "left its imprint on her own designs" ("The Chanel Influence" 1957: 70). Godart was among the many New York–based designers who made the transatlantic trek

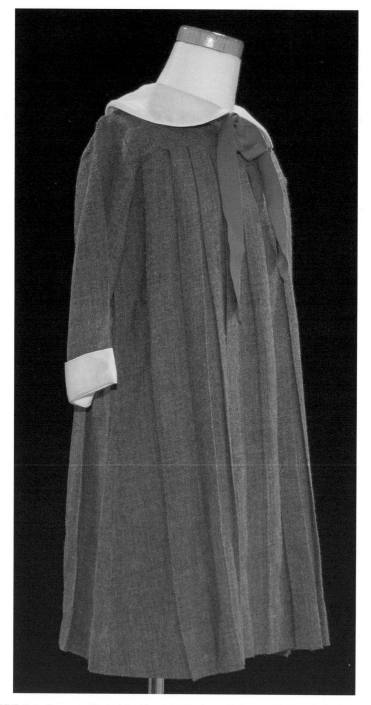

FIGURE 7.3 Suzanne Godart for Youngland, dress, between 1964 and 1969. From the personal collection of the author. Photograph by Minor Gordon.

seeking design ideas, and her long-standing associations with France put her in the unique position to capitalize effectively. She noted, "The designs are not in my field, but I am influenced by the color, the fabrics, and by a certain feeling I get. Construction, fabric, and texture—all interplaying—communicate something to me which I use in my work" (1966: 70).

Journalist Alison Lerrick wrote, "In the Godart design approach, everything... points to Good Taste." By the late 1960s, however, this core value was not always shared by consumers—according to Godart, it was becoming "a vanishing criterion" in children's wear selection (Lerrick 1969: 41). The latter portion of Godart's career saw a number of transitions between manufacturing companies. According to *Women's Wear Daily*, at the end of the 1960s, her employers included coat manufacturer Childcraft as well as Suntogs and Johnston of Dallas (Lerrick 1969: 41). Around 1970 she produced a line called Suzanne Godart Original, although it is unclear how long the enterprise lasted. By the late 1970s, she joined Alfar Imports Ltd. and her name could be found in connection with that company, at least intermittently, until 1990.

Ready-to-wear invasion

During the period of the specialist designer, the industry was increasingly influenced by the entrance of women's ready-to-wear designers into the children's market. *Good Housekeeping*'s 1956 report on children's wear made a point of advising its readers of specialist names under the presumption that these were largely unfamiliar to consumers, suggesting that "you may not recognize them when you see them on labels." On the other hand, there were "names you *will* recognize," and those belonged to women's ready-to-wear designers, such as American clothing creators Claire McCardell and Tom Brigance, who were among the first crossovers ("Report" 1956: 42). Although the children's wear industry promoted its homegrown specialist talent, it also saw the power of more nationally recognized designer names.

By the early 1960s, other prominent designers, such as Arnold Scaasi and Bill Blass, had entered the ring, contracting with familiar children's wear corporations. According to *Women's Wear Daily*, in the early 1960s, "children's clothes by women's apparel designers [were] selling pretty well," including offerings by Scaasi for Little Women, Bill Blass for Love, and Marc Bohan (of Christian Dior) for Sam Landorf, Inc. ("Designer Clothes Click" 1962: 40). *Women's Wear Daily* broached the idea that this "growing phenomenon" could be beneficial for the industry as a whole, but the response of the American children's wear specialists suggested resentment or at least ambivalence ("Name RTW" 1963: 44).

Despite the designers' long careers and fight for acknowledgment, the fashion industry continued to belittle, or perhaps worse ignore, the specialist designer. Writer Susan Black claimed, somewhat erroneously:

> Manufacturers went out looking for designers whose names would command attention and high prices. But no "names" had been developed in the children's field. The manufacturers then looked to the field of adult fashion. (1962: 22)

For specialist children's wear designers, who had struggled to make their names known, these kinds of assertions must have been particularly galling. Suzanne Godart expressed her frustration with these ready-to-wear competitors: "The irony is that top Seventh Avenue names who 'just come piddling around in our field' corner the publicity, advertising and store window displays while the backbone of the industry goes unrecognized" (Lerrick 1969: 41).

Conclusion

Through a combination of circumstance, determination, and talent, Helen Lee and Suzanne Godart emerged from the obscurity under which many of their coworkers labored and became leaders in the children's wear field. Paradoxically, however, the ends of these designers' careers showed a decline in promotion and affiliations as they joined less prestigious brands and companies. Long had the children's wear industry complained of marginalization, using the crude expression "stepchild" to denote its perceived status. The children's wear industry had real difficulty retaining design talent, Godart argued, because "good working conditions and salary, prestige and publicity are all in the junior and women's wear markets" (Lerrick 1969: 41). Furthermore, despite all of the developments in children's wear since the 1920s, Lee wondered whether the specialist had really come so far: "There's tremendous resentment against what they have to pay designers in the children's field. They really feel that grandmother ought to be doing it for free" ("Designer Round Table" 1974: 5).

Meanwhile, ready-to-wear women's designers still loomed large in the industry. *Women's Wear Daily* writer Agnes Clark reported that by the 1970s, Saks Fifth Avenue, which had once so enthusiastically promoted children's wear specialist Helen Lee, placed "too much reliance on imports for 'status,'" preferring European designer names and slighting American specialist designers (Clark 1974: 7). In Lee's opinion, by the 1980s, new and young design talent within the industry was rarely publicized (Lee 1983: 62). Yet the efforts of the specialist designers profiled in this chapter were significant to the 1950s and 1960s children's wear industry.

They contributed to developing the designer and fashion emphasis in children's wear but may have been victims of their own success, as the strength of designer names from the women's wear field surpassed them in perceived prestige. The stories of Lee and Godart provide crucial context for the contemporary children's wear market, in which designer names have become increasingly relevant to the marketing and selling of children's clothing.

Archival Sources

Fashion Group International Records, *c.* 1930–1997, New York Public Library, Humanities and Social Sciences Library, Manuscripts and Archives Division, New York, NY.

Saks Fifth Avenue Publicity Collection, 1954–1974. Kellen Design Archives, Parsons; The New School Libraries and Archives, New York, NY.

Note

1   An earlier version of this biographical account of Helen Lee appeared in the following: J.F. Gordon (August 2016), Helen Lee, and Florence Eiseman: a comparison of mid-twentieth-century children's wear designers, *Berg Encyclopedia of World Dress and Fashion* (online exclusive), ed. Joanne Eicher, Berg Fashion Library, Bloomsbury Publishing, plc.

Bibliography

"About Helen Lee" (1963), *The Infants' and Children's Review*, July: 24.

"Alyssa's 'Conceptual' Plan Spans Price and Style Gap" (1969), *Women's Wear Daily*, December 1: 42.

A.M.S. & C.H. (1966), "Robert Love Takes New Tack: Sportswear," *Women's Wear Daily*, September 26: 27.

Anspach, K. (1967), *The Why of Fashion*, Ames, IA: The Iowa State University Press.

Arnold, R. (2009), *The American Look: Fashion, Sportswear and the Image of Women in 1930s and 1940s New York*, London and New York: I.B. Tauris.

Black, S. (1962), "Haute Mode for Little Girls," *Saturday Evening Post*, September 22: 22–25.

Buckland, S.S. (1996), "Promoting American Fashion 1940 Through 1945: from Understudy to Star," PhD diss., Ohio State University.

"Business Records: Bankruptcy Proceedings" (1950), *New York Times*, December 30: 24.

"The Chanel Influence and How It Grew" (1957), *Women's Wear Daily*, May 1, Section 2: 70.

"'Children's Designer Joins Avenue Store" (1960), *New York Times*, September 5: 10.

"'Children's Styles a Lucrative Field" (1954), *New York Times*, November 7: F7.

Clark, A. (1974), "Kids' Departments: The '74 Report Card," *Women's Wear Daily*, July 8: 6–7.

Cohen, L. (2003), *A Consumer's Republic: The Politics of Mass Consumption in Postwar America*, New York: Vintage Books.

Cook, D.T. (2004), *The Commodification of Childhood: The Children's Clothing Industry and the Rise of the Child Consumer*, Durham & London: Duke University Press.

Davis, D. (1971), "Alyssa's Demise: Future Was Bleak," *Women's Wear Daily*, July 26: 18.

"Designer Clothes Click in N.Y." (1962), *Women's Wear Daily*, October 3: 40.

"Designer Round Table: The State of Children's Wear" (1974), *Women's Wear Daily*, March 25: 4–5.

"Designer Yearbook—1961" (1961), *Women's Wear Daily*, January 4: 56.

"Designing Travelers" (1967), *Women's Wear Daily*, August 25: 52.

"Designing Young" (1949), *Women's Wear Daily*, December 21: 15.

Gantzhorn, E. (1961), "Children's Corner," *Women's Wear Daily*, March 11: 39.

Gantzhorn, E. (1964), "The Best Juggling Act in Town," *Women's Wear Daily*, December 28: 27.

Godart, S. (1966), "Children's Clothes," in R. Warfield (ed.), *Your Future in Fashion Design*, 67–72, New York: Richard Rosen Press, Inc.

Gordon, J.F. (2016), "Helen Lee and Florence Eiseman: A Comparison of Mid-Twentieth Century Children's Wear Designers," in J. Eicher (ed.), *Berg Encyclopedia of World Dress and Fashion* [Online exclusive], Berg Fashion Library: Bloomsbury Publishing plc.

Hawes, E. (1942), *Why Is a Dress?* New York: The Viking Press.

Heal, E. (1966), *Fashion as a Career*, New York: Julian Messner.

"Helen Lee Joins Alyssa Originals as Vice President" (1957), *The Infants' and Children's Review*, April: 62.

"Helen Lee Signs with Sears as Design Director" (1971), *Women's Wear Daily*, March 1: 6.

Lambert, E. (*c*.1960s), *Helen Lee: Biography*. [Press release] At New York Public Library, Humanities and Social Sciences Library, Manuscripts and Archives Division. Fashion Group International Records, *c*. 1930–1997. Box 67, folder 23.

Lee, H. (1960), "Designing for Children," in O.P. Gately (ed.), *Your Future in the Fashion World*, 22–28, New York: The Richards Rosen Press, Inc.

Lee, H., as told to Spritzler, M. (1963), "Girls' Dress Industry on Brink of a New Era," *Infants' and Children's Review*, July: 22–24.

Lee, H. (1983), Interview by Finger, M. Oral history collection, F.I.T.: The Fashion Industry Leaders: Helen Lee: Designer, Specialist in Children's Wear. [Transcript]. At Gladys Marcus Library, Department of Special Collections and College Archives, The Fashion Institute of Technology, New York, NY.

Lerrick, A. (1969), "The Godart Gamble," *Women's Wear Daily*, May 26: 41.

Manlow, V. (2007), *Designing Clothes: Culture and Organization of the Fashion Industry*, New Brunswick, NJ and London: Transaction Publishers.

Matheson, R.J. (2015), *Young Originals: Emily Wilkens and the Teen Sophisticate*, Lubbock, TX: Texas Tech University Press.

May, E.T. (1999), "The Commodity Gap: Consumerism and the Modern Home," in L.B. Glickman (ed.), *Consumer Society in American History: A Reader*, 298–315, Ithaca & London: Cornell University Press.

McDermott, T. (1965), "Children's Fall Look Not Mere Kid's Stuff: Retailers Reap Rewards of Children's Fashion Look," *Women's Wear Daily*, July 19: 1, 16.

Milbank, C.R. (1989), *New York Fashion: The Evolution of American Style*, New York: Harry N. Abrams, Inc.

"Modern Interpreter of Kate Greenaway," (1946), *Women's Wear Daily*, July 24: 13.

Morris, B. (1977), "Child's World," *New York Times*, July 13: C9.

"Mrs. Godart Leaves Suzy Brooks to Join Sam Landorf" (1964), *Women's Wear Daily*, January 2: 67.

"Name RTW Designers Pass Test on Children's Lines," (1963), *Women's Wear Daily*, October 9: 1, 44.

"New Design Character in Holiday Group," (1951), *Women's Wear Daily*, July 11: 47.

O'Hagan, H. (Summer 1961), *Helen Lee Summer Collection at Saks Fifth Avenue*. [Press release] at Kellen Design Archives, Parsons the New School Libraries and Archives. Saks Fifth Avenue Publicity Collection, 1954–1974. Series 2, binder 25.

Olian, J. (2012), "From Division Street to Seventh Avenue: The Coming of Age of American Fashion," in G.M. Goldstein and E.E. Greenberg (eds.), *A Perfect Fit: The Garment Industry and American Jewry, 1860–1960*, 114–128, Lubbock, TX: Texas Tech University Press.

"The Queen Bees" (1963), *Women's Wear Daily*, October 30: 22.

"Report to Mothers of Little Girls" (1956), *Good Housekeeping*, August: 42.

"Rogan Heading to Suzy Brooks" (1963), *Women's Wear Daily*, August 21: 35.

"Suzanne Kapa Godart Cella" (2002), *Hibbing Daily Tribune*, May 12. Available online: http://www.hibbingmn.com/obituaries/suzanne-kapa-godart-cella/article_b2fa1dc2 -37f8-59e2-b740-191b4440c023.html.

"Two to Get Coty Special Awards" (1953), *Women's Wear Daily*, September 24: 6.

Webber-Hanchett, T. (2003), "Dorothy Shaver: Promoter of 'the American Look,'" *Dress*, 30: 83–87.

Weir, J. (1973), "Helen Lee: Be Colorful & Multiply!," *Women's Wear Daily*, October 29: 1, 26.

Williams, B. (1956), *Young Faces in Fashion*, Philadelphia and New York: J.B. Lippincott Company.

Yohannan, K. and Nolf, N. (1998), *Claire McCardell: Redefining Modernism*, New York: Harry N. Abrams, Inc.

8 NICKI "CATHERINE SCOTT" LADANY: CHICAGO'S EMPRESS OF FASHION

ADAM MACPHARLAIN

From the early days of American fashion, Chicago has been an important hub, with style-conscious customers, renowned department stores, and design talent. One such talent who made a name for herself in the high-end ready-to-wear market was Nicki Ladany, the designer of "Catherine Scott." Her label became known for quality women's wear that reflected sophistication and refinement. Throughout her career, her designs received positive reviews in major publications including the *Chicago Tribune*, *Vogue*, and *Women's Wear Daily*. Well-respected fashion writer Peg Zwecker, who promoted designers with Chicago connections the likes of Halston and Charles James, called her a "nationally acclaimed couture designer" (1976) and "a name familiar to fashion pros in every part of the country ... always ... Chicago's only genuine couture designer" (1968). A few years earlier, Zwecker even went so far as to write that Ladany was "Chicago's empress of fashion whose niche is couture" (1963).

The designer was born on June 12, 1922 as Naomi Patricia Hodes.[1] She grew up in Great Neck on New York's Long Island. From an early age, she had a love and an aptitude for fashion, studying fashion at the young age of 8 at the Pratt Institute, and she finished her studies at the Chicago Fashion Academy. It's unclear when she started using the name Nicki, but it appears to be around the same time that she moved to Chicago, sometime in the 1940s. She married William Ladany, vice-president of the Vienna Sausage Manufacturing Company, and son of its co-founder Samuel Ladany.

Throughout her career, Ladany was admired for her beauty and stature. Several articles refer to her "tawny hair," strong bone structure, and her "petite" size 8 figure. Zwecker even called her "mannequin-like" (1976). In another article,

Zwecker adds (conflating Ladany with the name of her label): "Strikingly chic, Miss Scott is often described as 'her own best model.' Sophisticated, self-possessed and a dedicated individualist, she creates for the woman who understands the beauty of simplicity" (1963). Ladany's personal flair won her the title of "best tressed" as part of the eighth annual Ten Best Coiffured Women of 1964 by a Guild of Professional Beauticians. The women were chosen because they could "balance career obligations with home, family and fashion in truly impressive style" ("Ten Best" 1964: 11). Other winners that year included Queen Farah of Iran, modeling agent Eileen Ford, fellow designer Anne Klein, and famed actress Debbie Reynolds. According to one writer, the woman behind Catherine Scott was able to fit a "busy designing career into a schedule that includes caring for her home, husband and two [children]" ("Ten Best" 1964). Financially comfortable through her marriage, she was able to pursue varied interests. She collected lusterware and Impressionist paintings, and her hobbies included skiing and needlepoint. Her passion for fashion and history made her a frequent museum visitor, and she became involved with the Chicago Historical Society. She was also a member of Chicago's Fashion Group costume committee.

Through her own busy schedule, Ladany recognized a space in the market for clothes that suited the life that she and many other women led. After eight years as a suburban Chicago housewife with a monotonous wardrobe of "sweaters and skirts; starched shirts and slacks," her design studio opened. Scott sought to break this monotony, stating, "There was nothing in between those casual outfits and dressy cocktail outfits" (Kachan 1957: 13). In another interview, Scott cleverly added, "I either looked overdressed in the morning and right at night, or tweedy in the morning and seedy at night" (Luther 1957). Ladany created her label in 1955, combining the first names of her daughter and son to fashion a new moniker. It didn't take long for the name Catherine Scott to become Ladany's public persona, and she was almost exclusively referred to as "Miss Scott" in media. Her looks sold primarily at department stores like Marshall Field and I. Magnin, which would later play an important role in her career. Garments were priced between $135 and $225 in 1957. By 1975 pieces were from $350 to $695, approximately $1,160–1,930 and $1,570–3,110, respectively, in 2016 dollars.[2] Ladany designed for women of means who wanted to look polished and put-together, whether they were at home, on the town, or working.

Early work from Catherine Scott focused on separates that were foundations for a solid wardrobe in silk, tweed, and cashmere with classic styling. These were meant as mix-and-match ensembles for a "carefully planned-for-the-occasion look" (Livingstone 1957). Evelyn Livingstone of the *Chicago Tribune* continued, "All of these 'separates' avoid the hastily put together appearance of some of today's mix or match fashions." One *New York Times* author called her style the "understated dressmaker look" ("The American Collections" 1961: 40), and another noted her "ladylike designs" (Baldwin 1963: 13). Ladany believed that "the same feeling of elegance can be achieved in executing sportswear as in designing late day clothes" (Zwecker 1956). She achieved this with custom tailoring, classic colors, and contrasting textures. Her garments featured hand-worked buttonholes, French seams, and other key touches. She provided readymade clothes up to size 14 and opted for made-to-order for larger women.

FIGURE 8.1 I. Magnin advertised exclusive Catherine Scott styles in *Vogue* (March 15, 1963). Ladany promoted the shirtwaist dress and mix-and-match ensembles. Image courtesy of Fashion Institute of Technology.

One of her first collections provided "unusually smart and popular" (Zwecker 1956) looks such as a cashmere jacket lined with printed silk. She preferred to pair these tops with full skirts: "All you have to do is glance at my collection and you can tell I love full skirts … they are more flattering and more comfortable. And they adjust themselves to the body as you move" (Zwecker 1957). This silhouette was in line with the New Look style first introduced in 1947 and popularized by noted designers like Christian Dior and Norman Norell. It remained the epitome of haute couture style until the mid-1950s. Ladany's love of cinched waists and full skirts certainly represented iterations of the New Look, but she continued to promote the style well into the 1960s, after many mainstream designers had moved on.

Another of Ladany's design influences was the shirtwaist, saying it was a piece she personally favored and that it was the basis for many of her looks. She also incorporated sheath dresses and other simple styles, always carefully tailored. Catherine Scott designs appeared in *Vogue* with descriptions that exemplified her style: a belted dress called "summer in-town costume," (1959) a worsted crepe "new lease on suit-life," (1960), and a suit with a "showing a little, or a lot" blouse (1957). There was one common thread among editorial coverage: adaptability. A *Vogue* feature on in-home evening wear includes a classic Catherine Scott ensemble with a caption that promotes the look as a "good idea for little dinners at-home—in someone else's house: the look's casual but not offhand" ("Fashion: New Ideas" 1956: 142). An advertisement for Lord & Taylor in 1961 perhaps summed it up best as a "simple approach to perfection." Her style was so "perfect" that it was ripe to be pirated. Among the favorable press Ladany received, journalist Jean Sprain Wilson wrote that Catherine Scott had "invaded New York long enough to capture a wide audience for her most copyable princess line dresses with seams that break into pleats" (1964: 4B).

Ladany's target consumers were women like her—affluent suburban housewives and businesswomen—who spent much of their time in the city and traveled the world. This was a growing segment of the population as the move to the suburbs became the new normal after the Second World War; women returned to being housewives as their husbands returned from war efforts. Economic growth also meant a larger highway system leading to expanded suburban sprawl and easier routes for road trips with the family. With a decrease in domestic help and an increase in leisure time for America's middle class, fashion naturally moved toward a more casual daytime dress. Other designers of the time that catered to this burgeoning market were Anne Fogarty, Hattie Carnegie, and Claire McCardell.

An *Omnibus Magazine* in 1963 noted that Catherine Scott "pioneered with the widely acclaimed sportive look in quietly chic leather bound, cashmere and tweed separates" (Zwecker 1963: 21). This pioneering look and her target market are remarkably similar to another American female designer: Bonnie Cashin. This is not the only comparison to a notable fashion designer garnered by Catherine

FIGURE 8.2 Dress and belt, Catherine Scott by Nicki Ladany (1922–2013), *c.* 1959; Gift of Mrs. Thomas E. Kluczynski; 1986.772.15a-c; Chicago History Museum, ICHi-89260.

Scott—in 1957, Peg Zwecker mentioned that Scott "has been called the James Galanos of the sportswear field" (1957). This comparison isn't surprising as she was "creating clothes comparable in price to those of top designers in New York and California" (Baldwin 1963: 13).

It wasn't only the fashionable suburban woman who sought out Catherine Scott. In 1964, Ladany designed a new nun's habit for the Sisters of Mercy, presented at a luncheon at St. Xavier College in Chicago. The habit was meant to reflect a more modern style while maintaining monastic modesty. According to one article, a spokeswoman at the luncheon was "quick to point out that the habit design had not been approved, but it is 'very much' the sort of updated fashions she believes nuns would welcome" ("Fashion Changes" 1964: 25).

Important to the Catherine Scott look were coordinating ensembles that were mix-and-match. She believed in casual daywear with an air of sophistication, and while she preferred these daytime ensembles she did offer some evening wear. Some of her elegant designs were inspired by history. One example is her autumn-winter 1963 collection, which used elements from the inaugural dress worn by first lady Helen Herron Taft in 1909, which Scott saw in an exhibition at the Chicago Historical Society entitled "One Hundred Years of Great Lady Gowns." Nevertheless, her heart and soul were simply chic. *Women's Wear Daily* wrote in 1966 that "Catherine Scott believes in the easy look for spring. As she says, 'Women like the ease of culottes for entertaining at home'" ("New York Spring" 1966).

Scott did move away from separates for a time. In 1963, the designer noticed that her separates were often too expensive for the sportswear departments of some stores and, therefore, her garments were only being sold at smaller specialty stores. To remedy this and expand her brand, Catherine Scott began primarily producing single-piece dresses and coats, though still made as coordinating ensembles. Her separates during this time focused more on at-home attire such as an ensemble made of a paisley shawl-turned-skirt paired with a fuchsia silk shirt. By 1973, she had returned to separates as the staple of her collections. No matter the type of garment, the message stayed the same. In her own words, Scott stated, "I've never liked very fancy clothes. And I don't believe that clothes should ever be more important than the woman who wears them" (Baldwin 1963: 13).

In addition to I. Magnin, other stores to carry Catherine Scott clothing included Marshall Field and Stanley Korshak in Chicago and Bergdorf Goodman and Henri Bendel in New York. To increase her profile and stay current in the 1960s, Scott traveled to New York several times a year. These trips included "meet and greets" with clientele. She was also presenting her collections in New York alongside other notable American designers, such as Bill Blass, who became known for his women's wear inspired by men's clothing. While such mentions were not frequent, Catherine Scott pieces did make it periodically into fashion magazines like *Vogue*, both in advertisements and style features.[3] The designer was recognized for her contributions to the industry, receiving *Chicago Magazine*'s Designer Award, their "first salute to the fashion industry" (Zwecker 1968). She was also an invited member of the New York Council of Fashion Designers, the only Chicago designer to receive the honor, joining the ranks of contemporaries like Pauline Trigère, Geoffrey Beene, and Bill Blass. These were not her only honors. Scott participated in the 1965 Gold Coast Fashion Award luncheon, presenting alongside prominent names like those listed above and others like Teal Traina, Norman Norell, and

Ferdinando Sarmi, a group that was described as "about as close to a Who's Who in high fashion as you can get" (Livingstone 1965).

One of the most notable features of Catherine Scott garments was the fabrics Ladany favored. Her self-proclaimed credo was "fabric makes fashion" (Zwecker 1963: 21), and this philosophy showed in the pieces she produced. During the 1950s, a boom in the creation of synthetic fibers allowed the general public to wear clothes that were easier to care for than natural fibers like cotton, wool, and silk. Catherine Scott's almost exclusive use of traditional fibers and leather, a tenet of couture design, meant her "casual separates" were not so casual. She often found inspiration from fabrics first, then sketched out her designs. From the beginning, Scott sourced her fabrics from high-end firms including Staron, Scalamandre, Lesur, Bianchini, Abraham, and Rodier. The desired effect of these pieces: exclusivity. She also commissioned special fabrics domestically and, notably, maintained a long partnership with the handweaving firm of Churchill Weavers out of Berea, Kentucky.[4] How the fabrics fit the body, whether in a tailored suit or a softly draped blouse, was vitally important to the quality of a finished Catherine Scott piece. In addition to tweeds and silk, Scott liked to use jersey and even used handwoven, European-made paisley shawls in garments for a collection in 1963.

Ladany originally had a workshop on Franklin Street in Chicago, but she also created workspace at home. She and her husband and children lived in a multilevel house in Highland Park designed by Milton Schwartz set around a ravine, trees, and gardens. This house included two areas for Scott to work: a larger main space in the basement and a "portable" space in the family den. The basement space was reported to house one of the first pattern-making machines in the world (Zwecker 1968); the portable space included a table hidden behind folding doors that held a sewing machine and could shift to form a desk.

Chicago wasn't always Catherine Scott's headquarters. In 1965, Ladany opened a showroom in New York City. Having been raised in nearby Great Neck on Long Island as a "displaced New Yorker … like a homing pigeon, she return[ed] at least six times a year" (Baldwin 1963: 13). Her Midtown showroom was just as sophisticated as the designer herself. Located at 550 7th Avenue on the sixth floor, with "Catherine Scott, Inc." emblazoned on the door, the room was decorated with beige and white wallpaper and drapes. On the walls were two-foot-tall brass scissors and needle and a composition made of pattern forms. Furnishings included a c. 1750 French armoire, flowers in wooden buckets, and other French pieces.

Ladany's first public collection viewing[5] in her Seventh Avenue showroom in 1965 exemplified her ethos of understated quality. The ensembles were announced by number, with no descriptions, allowing the clothes to speak for themselves. Reporters and buyers in attendance saw Catherine Scott's classic style and luxurious fabrics. Mannequins with true-to-the-day aloofness walked around the room wearing pieces made of sequined point d'esprit and dresses trimmed with sable. One mannequin that day was the renowned model Ellen Harth (Nangle 1965).

The buyers were impressed, including powerful men such as Russell Carpenter, president of I. Magnin in California. Eleanor Nangle of the *Chicago Tribune* was there and reported: "[Buyers] never ooh and aah and rarely applaud … When they do applaud, a designer knows he has a smash on his hands. Applause tells Catherine Scott she has one in this first collection … in more ways than one" (1965). But the

FIGURE 8.3 Ladany's designs featured luxurious European fabrics and sophisticated tailoring, as seen in an advertisement from *Vogue* (December 1, 1965). Image courtesy of Fashion Institute of Technology.

show wasn't over after the fashion walked. Ladany hired Dione Lucas, head of New York's Au Petit Cordon Bleu school of cookery, to provide lunch for the showing, where attendees enjoyed made-to-order cheese or mushroom omelets.

The following year, the "former Chicagoan … who has moved 'lock, stock and barrel' to NYC" presented an Indian-inspired collection, departing from her usual subdued palette. Despite success, Ladany did not stay in New York City long. She was there to explore as a speculation, investigating her prospects in a new city. However, the rough-and-tumble fashion world of New York didn't suit her, and she returned to Chicago two years later, not in defeat, but simply to pursue her passion in an environment she dominated.

Into the 1970s, Ladany was still going strong. One *Chicago Tribune* author writes, "If Chicago designer Catherine Scott feels a little smug these days, she's justified … So what's the big news in the '70s? Quality separates designed with sweater ease and layered at will" (Livingstone 1975). While Ladany had sold her line in I. Magnin stores since the 1950s, it wasn't until a chance encounter at a Chicago Historical Society Function in 1972 that she became formally associated as an exclusive designer for I. Magnin. This lucrative deal meant she was featured prominently in the store's advertisements in major magazines and newspapers. She also opened a new shop at 49 East Oak Street in Chicago in 1973, still producing lines apart from her retail connection. It was a salon on the first floor of a brownstone. For the opening, her husband gifted her with a doorstop, a brick from new building he was opening. Her business partner in this venture, Nanette L. Laitman, was a sculptor and daughter of a New York executive.

However, by the mid- to late 1970s, American life had changed drastically from the world in which the Catherine Scott label began. Her target suburban housewife was becoming a rarity, both with the increase in women in the workforce and with the increase in divorce and delayed marriage. From 1955 when Ladany began her career to her retirement in 1977, the number of women in the U.S. civilian labor force doubled, from about twenty million to over forty million, and labor force participations jumped from 35.7 percent to 48.4 percent.[6] The divorce rate more than doubled from 1960 to 1975, from a rate of 2.2 to 4.9, while the marriage rate only moved from 8.5 to 10.1 in the same time frame.[7]

The 1960s and 1970s saw several subcultures influence mainstream fashion. Designers like Mary Quant and Rudi Gernreich produced wild mod fashion and introduced the world to new pieces, including the miniskirt and the thong bathing suit. Hippies eschewed high-end wear for purposefully distressed-looking fabrics and Eastern influences. André Courrèges and Pierre Cardin created space-age fashion with new materials and silhouettes that moved away from form-fitting to A-line looks. Jeans went from the uniform of cowboys, workers, and rebellion to a staple of the American wardrobe.

Nicki Ladany retired in 1977. She moved from fashion design to interior design, staying in Chicago and joining the firm of Daniel DuBay & Associates. She started there at the recommendation of a mutual friend who wanted Ladany to decorate her penthouse. She used the same concepts in interiors as in her fashion, including starting from a monochromatic or neutral scheme and adding color, sophistication, and flair with furniture and accessories. A *Chicago Tribune* feature in 1981 noted that the firm's projects that year included varied and high-profile jobs such as a co-op on Washington's Embassy Row for former Chicago Bonwit Teller fashion coordinator Barbara West Waters, an apartment in the Joseph Pulitzer mansion in the Upper East Side of New York City, and store design for Handy Andy Home Center in Chicago.

Conclusion

The name Catherine Scott has largely disappeared from the chronicles of American fashion. There could be multiple reasons for this. Ladany's designs were consistently praised for their beauty and elegance, but she was not known as a trendsetter. This was not an unusual scenario in the American industry. As one article noted, "One fashion authority who recently viewed Miss Scott's collection called the clothes beautiful, the kind that most women want to wear, but probably not the kind to make fashion news headlines" (Baldwin 1963: 13). However, according to Tortora and Eubank (1998: 430), "in higher-priced lines, innovative and creative American designers also originated new styles, and their work was regularly reported by the fashion press." One such "new style" that became prevalent in the 1970s and 1980s was the inclusion of product logos as an important visual cue of status. High-end brands, once marked by luxurious fabrics and superb tailoring, were now marked, quite literally, with logos on ready-to-wear lines. Products proudly included labels in prominent places or as repeated pattern, even covering the entirety of a garment or accessory, a practice Ladany and others eschewed.

Another likely reason for her ultimate move out of the fashion industry was her choice to be based in Chicago. While she had a large Midwest following and sold nationwide, she was aware of the hardships of working outside of New York or California in the high-end fashion market. It was difficult for her to source luxury fabrics as representatives from these firms often did not travel to middle America, leaving Ladany to seek them out herself. Because her garments were at a higher price point than much of what other Chicago-based companies were producing, she limited her production volume. French haute couture designers often did not profit from their highest-priced originals but rather resorted to side businesses such as perfumes, accessories, and lower-end brands or licensing. This business model perhaps could have been useful for Catherine Scott, which was limited to the production of garments.

As suburbs expanded, so did a new form of shopping: the mall. With large numbers of specialty stores and ample parking, men and women were no longer confined to the downtown department store. This may have been one factor in Ladany's decision to move out of the fashion world—her high-priced designs were more suited to the now-dying department store and less appealing in most shopping malls across the country. According to author Vicki Howard, "Facing rising prices and stagnating wages, many chose convenience over service, low prices and mass consumption over luxury and amenity" (Howard 2015: 191). Her target suburban housewives and businesswomen were no longer loyal to their local department store, instead seeking easy access and affordability.

Nicki "Catherine Scott" Ladany passed away at the age of 90 on March 2, 2013. She actively supported the Chicago History Museum up to her final years, including donating financially.[8] The museum holds a large collection of Catherine Scott ensembles ranging from the label's early years to the 1970s, all worn by their donors. These donors were among Chicago's elite, who, in addition to being married to notable men, were recognized for their sophistication and influence. Some include Julie Ann Wrigley, wife of chewing gum and Major League Baseball magnate Philip Knight Wrigley; Dorothy Fuller, wife of marketing executive William Englehaupt; Melanie Kluczynski, wife of Illinois Supreme Court Justice

FIGURE 8.4 The Catherine Scott label (detail of dress), Gift of Mrs. Thomas E. Kluczynski; 1986.772.15a-c; Chicago History Museum, ICHi-89261.

Thomas E. Kluczynski; and Marilynn Bruder Alsdorf, wife of business executive James Alsdorf. That these women chose Catherine Scott, and valued the clothes enough to donate them to the museum, stands as a testament to the importance of the Catherine Scott line.

Notes

1 Genealogy information obtained from ancestry.com, 1930 U.S. Federal Census.

2 Based on inflation calculations from http://www.bls.gov/data/inflation_calculator.htm (accessed July 26, 2016).

3 Advertisements in *Vogue* were often for I. Magnin, touting Catherine Scott as their exclusive designer, but also included an ad for Hampton Greeting Card Company that featured a model in a Catherine Scott ensemble (November 1, 1957: 163).

4 The Kentucky Historical Society holds the Churchill Weavers archive, which includes business records, fabric samples and products, and more. This archive holds correspondence, fabrics, weaving records, and a sample skirt for Catherine Scott.

5 Scott had already held semi-private viewings for her "hometown" Chicago buyers from stores like Marshall Field and Stanley Korshak.

6 Statistics from the U.S. Department of Labor.

7 Statistics from the Centers for Disease Control (CDC), National Center for Health Statistics (NCHS).

8 As noted in the Chicago History Museum's 2010 Annual Report.

Bibliography

"'65 Ebony Fashion Fair, was Complete Sell-Out" (1965), *The Chicago Defender*, November 20: 23.

Advertisement: Bergdorf Goodman (1959), *New York Times*, April 12: 97.

Advertisement: Hampton Greeting Card Company (1957), *Vogue*, 130(8): 163.

Advertisement: I. Magnin & Co. (1963), *Vogue*, 141(6): 21.

Advertisement: I. Magnin & Co. (1963), *Vogue*, 142(5): 2.

Advertisement: I. Magnin & Co. (1963), *Vogue*, 146(10): 17.

Advertisement: Lord and Taylor (1961), *New York Times*, May 2: 3.

Albert, C. (1975), "Catherine Scott Skirts the Waistline," *Chicago Daily News*, September 5.

"The American Collections" (1961), *New York Times*, October 24: 40.

Baldwin, M.B. (1963), "Chicagoan Designs for World Traveler," *New York Times*, June 22: 13.

"Changes 1960" (1960), *Vogue*, 135(1): 90–103.

"'The Chicago Look' Gets Many Retakes" (1975), *Chicago Defender*, June 21: A6.

"Chicago Well Represented in Orbiting Fashion Fair" (1965), *Chicago Daily Defender*, November 8: 17.

Death Notice: Nicki H. Ladany (2013), *Chicago Tribune*, March 4: 7.

"Fashion: at Home—Fashions Men Adore" (1965) *Vogue*, 149(9): 102–103.

"Fashion Changes" (1964), *Ottawa Citizen*, February 1: 25.

"Fashion: Check-Dot Printing Plus Jacket" (1959), *Vogue*, 133(9): 142–143.

"Fashion: in a Lighter Vein: Warm-Weather Suits" (1957), *Vogue*, 129(7): 164–165.

"Fashion: New Ideas About in-for-the-evening Clothes" (1956), *Vogue*, 128(10): 138–143.

[Fashion sketches] (1973), *Chicago Daily News*, February 14: 18.

Hill, J. (1981), "Design: From Apparel to Interiors," *Chicago Tribune*, May 3: W A1.

Hooks, T.F. (1966), "Spring Ushers in Colorful, Tone-Rich Shades, Prints," *Chicago Daily Defender*, January 10: 16.

Hooks, T.F. (1975a), "Teesee's Town," *Chicago Defender*, May 17: 12.

Hooks, T.F. (1975b), "Teesee's Town," *Chicago Defender*, June 24: 12.

Howard, V. (2015), *American Business, Politics, and Society: From Main Street to Mall: The Rise and Fall of American Department Stores*, Philadelphia: University of Pennsylvania Press.

Kachan, V. (1957), "Suburban Wife Too Often Drab, Says Fashion Expert," *Daily Defender*, March 3: 13.

Livingstone, E. (1957), "She Designs Separates Made for Each Other," *Chicago Sunday Tribune*, August 18: 2.

Livingstone, E. (1965), "Designs of a Dozen Stars Will Point the Way to Fashion Styles for the Summer," *Chicago Tribune*, April 25: G3.

Livingstone, E. (1975), "The Name Designers in Chicago, Tho Small in Number, Are Big on Talent," *Chicago Tribune*, August 11: C7.

Luther, M. (1957), "Chicago's Designing Woman," *Chicago Sunday Tribune*, January 20: E1.

Morris, B. (1965), "Go Is the Signal from 7th Ave. for Spring Green," *New York Times*, December 25: 8.

Nangle, E. (1965), "We Go to a Fashion Opening…," *Chicago Tribune*, July 15: D1.

"New York Spring" (1966), *Women's Wear Daily*, November 15: 27.

Odom, K. (1975), "Back to the Traditional," *Chicago Defender*, July 2: 13.

"Ten Best Coiffured Women Are Named" (1964), *The Tuscaloosa News*, December 30: 11.

Tortora, P. and Eubank, K. (1998), *Survey of Historic Costume*, 3rd ed, New York: Fairchild Publications.

Wilson, J.S. (1964), "Style Pirates Find Treasures," *St. Petersburg Times*, July 4: 4–B.

Zwecker, P. (1956), "Sportswear Goes Elegant," *Chicago Daily News*, March 3.

Zwecker, P. (1957), "Sport in the Fashion World," *Chicago Daily News*, August 15.

Zwecker, P. (1963), "Women's Fashions: 'First Lady' Collection Inspires Fall, Winter Designs," *Omnibus*, November: 20–21.

Zwecker, P. (1968), "A Designing Woman," *Chicago Daily News*, October 15.

Zwecker, P. (1973), "Separates Only for Catherine Scott," *Chicago Daily News*.

Zwecker, P. (1976), "Our Designers Have Become Fashion Stars," *Chicago Daily News*, January 17–18.

9 JEAN WRIGHT: THE "REAL" LILLI ANN

HANNAH SCHIFF

During the 1930s as Hollywood's motion picture industry boomed, popularizing American sportswear, America sought a stronger position in the global fashion economy, and California played host to a stream of upstart clothing companies.[1] Names such as Bonnie Cashin and Edith Head are familiar in discussions of the early years of design and fashion in California, but one of the most influential designers of the day, Jean Wright, is all but unknown. Although Wright's name has not stood the test of time, her designs have endured, under the desirable label "Lilli Ann."

In 1933 after years of work in the garment industry, aspiring entrepreneur Adolph Schuman partnered with Rudolf Kutche, his financial backer, and Jean Wright, his designer, to establish Lilli Ann Fashions, a San Francisco–based manufacturer of women's coats and suits (Steinberg 1956). Named after Schuman's first wife, Lillian, the company steadily grew, and in the mid- to late 1940s it hit its stride, advertising liberally in national publications and undertaking significant expansions on the existing small business. By the 1950s, Lilli Ann was known as "one of the nation's largest producers of high-fashion coats and suits for women" (Steinberg 1956: A10).

A savvy businessman, Schuman combined American business practices with an emphasis on quality and traditional European textile production. Rather than simply competing with the Parisian market, he found a previously little explored niche in blending French and American fashions. In addition, Schuman, Wright, and the designs emanating from the Lilli Ann factory reflected the dynamic international influences in postwar fashion, and comparisons with names such as Balenciaga and Dior peppered the Lilli Ann history.

illi Ann

san francisco

fabric-of-France iridescent worsted

about one hundred dollars at fine stores

or write Lilli Ann, 973 Market Street, San Francisco

or 512 Seventh Avenue, New York.

Vogue
July, 1952

VOGUE incorporating Vanity Fair is published semi-monthly except for the months of January, June, July and December, when it is published monthly by The Condé Nast Publications Inc., Boston Post Road, Greenwich, Connecticut. Entered as second-class matter at the Post Office at Greenwich, Connecticut, under the act of March 3rd, 1879. Subscriptions $7.50 a year in U. S. A.

Vol. 120, No.
Whole No. 11

FIGURE 9.1 The elegance and drama of Lilli Ann suits were captured by noted photographer Richard Avedon, as exemplified in this advertisement featured in *Vogue* in 1952. © The Richard Avedon Foundation. Image courtesy of Fashion Institute of Technology.

Although the company hit hard times as planned obsolescence became the mainstay of the American ready-to-wear industry, ultimately closing after a steady unraveling brought on by Schuman's death in 1985, the label has seen a resurgence in popularity in the twenty-first century. Vintage enthusiasts praise the brand for its quality materials and designs, and garments bearing the Lilli Ann labels from the 1930s through the 1950s are passionately collected, often fetching prices rarely seen for mid-twentieth-century mass-produced clothing. Designers and costumers also laud and collect the label, and its influence can be seen everywhere from the 1940s-inspired power suits of the 1980s catwalks to the silver screen. As recently as 2016, two Lilli Ann reproductions even found their way to Tilda Swinton's wardrobe in the Coen Brothers' film *Hail, Caesar!*, costumed by Mary Zophres.

While the Lilli Ann name has not been forgotten, Jean Wright, the company's primary designer through the mid-1950s, has faded into relative obscurity. In large part Wright's lack of name recognition was a side effect of postwar marketing techniques used by the company which presented "Lilli Ann" as more than a name: as a real designer. Through clever advertising copy and a keen awareness of what American women expected of a designer and fashion authority, Jean Wright was relegated to the workroom while Lilli Ann took center stage.

Though little published information exists about Wright and her decades working for Lilli Ann Fashions, extensive research has allowed a more detailed portrait to emerge of the talented young woman who kept pace with notable couturiers, designers, and costumers of the 1930s through 1950s. Wright's high-end ready-to-wear designs in many ways embody the ethos of quality mid-century American design, and it is the intention of this chapter to argue for Jean Wright's reinstatement in the company of the notable American designers who were in fact her peers.

Much of Jean Wright's life outside of her tenure with Lilli Ann remains unknown. She was born July 17, 1915 in Everett, Washington; her family appears to have relocated to Atascadero, California, by 1930 (United States Census 1930), where, according to the census, Wright was enrolled in school. Beyond a record of her death on May 26, 1967 at the young age of 52, and burial in Golden Gate National Cemetery where she is now beside her husband Lieutenant Colonel Galen V. Miller, there are no known records of her life that don't also pertain to her career (National Cemetery Administration 2006).

Her career in fashion had an interesting start, with a failed modeling attempt for the fledgling Lilli Ann company unexpectedly launching her into the design sphere. According to a 1946 account in *Women's Wear Daily*, "If Jean Wright hadn't been just a little bit too thin, and a lot too scared at being a professional model when she was 16, the chances are she wouldn't be one of San Francisco's foremost apparel designers today" ("California" 1946: 22).

Wright had no design aspirations, and her initial success appears to have been born more through opportunity and skill than drive. Speaking about becoming a designer in the 1946 article, which focused on California designers, Wright stated, "I was literally shoved into it, and besides, I wasn't a very good model. I just needed a job!" (22). In many respects, Wright's modesty and self-deprecation were antithetical to the image of confidence and charisma consistently projected in her own designs and through the company's advertising.

Prior to taking on a more technical role for Schuman, Wright's experience was limited to "dressmaking for friends in a small suburban town," but his confidence in her abilities along with some brief instruction at a local design school provided sufficient-enough credentials for her to get her start as a designer ("California" 1946). In describing her earliest experiences as the designer for Lilli Ann, Wright's characteristic modesty is on full display. "'Everyone I met gave me all the help they could,' she stated. 'The information and guidance I've received from Mr. Shuman [*sic*] and my coworkers, plus practical experience, has enabled me to learn every step in the production of our lines, and this, I believe, is vital knowledge for a designer'" ("California" 1946). Although Wright credited others for her initial progress, when the training wheels rapidly came off she emerged as the creative mastermind behind suits and coats that frequently graced the pages of notable publications such as *Vogue, Harper's Bazaar, Mademoiselle, Glamour*, and *Women's Wear Daily*.

One of the earliest known documents referencing Wright as the company's designer is a 1945 issue of *California Stylist* that displays a spread of photographs of fashion show attendees under the headline "Lilli Ann Goes To Ciro's" (174). Ciro's was one of the trendiest nightclubs in Los Angeles in the 1940s, and the venue staged fashion shows for many prominent brands of the era, including Lilli Ann. The publication includes a picture of the three founding members of the company, captioned "Adolph P. Schuman (Lilli Ann) discusses gowns which will be on parade with his designer Jean Wright and Rudolph Kutsche" (California Stylist 1945: 174). The exclusive and upscale environment was indicative of the fashion-conscious clientele Lilli Ann maintained.

A rare text produced by Lilli Ann and donated to the Thomas J. Watson Library at the Metropolitan Museum of Art contains a slightly earlier mention of Jean Wright. This small book, *Adolph Schuman for Lilli Ann: Celebrating Fifty Years 1933–1983*, features some early press materials and articles about the corporation. The article entitled "Design for a Decade" commemorates ten years in business and discusses the origins of the company: "'We owe our success to the gods, and to Jean Wright, our designer,' Schuman admits with characteristic honesty" (Adolph Schuman *c.* 1983: 5). As the article continues, Wright's design prowess is further lauded:

Today, Lilli Ann stands for costumes in the de luxe sense of the word. Dressmaker suits and combinations of suits and coats comprise their exciting line. "And Jean is responsible," Schuman insists, although he does not point out that he had the daring and the intuition to develop her ideas. "She came to us nine years ago, and was overpaid at $14 a week. Today she gets, and earns, one of the highest salaries in the industry, and we wouldn't take a quarter of a million for her contract!" Right there you have the nucleus of Lilli Ann's success: a designing genius, a production wizard! Sounds a bit on the superlative side, but then … that's Lilli Ann. (5)

Schuman readily acknowledged Wright's merit as a designer, and it was evident that she was valued and recognized within the company.

"We design our clothes based on the psychology of a woman. Our job is to interpret what a woman wants and project it forward one year," Schuman said, expressing the ethos driving the Lilli Ann label (Adolph Schuman *c*. 1983: 1). In Jean Wright, Schuman succeeded in finding a designer who was adept at such fashion forecasting. One of the clear calling cards of Wright's design tenure was variety. By the mid-1940s, Lilli Ann collections were impressively large and packed with diverse selections. A 1945 *Women's Wear Daily* article highlighted some of the innovations offered by Wright in her collection of twenty-five fall suits. "Fur sleeves on tunic suits were featured by designer Jean Wright, whose work is further characterized by ingenuity in combining black and white, unique ornamentations, side-wrapped jackets, and wing tip collars. Cut-away jackets, both short and hip length, were also prominently featured" ("Sportswear" 1945: 20).

As indicated through the 1945 fall suit line, options abounded to satisfy a range of tastes and silhouettes. From flashy fur sleeves to clean and classic black and white, from long tunic-length jackets to cropped options, Wright made sure that Lilli Ann suits maintained their high quality while creating an abundance of styles. Her astuteness in forecasting, coupled with Schuman's thorough use of modern methods of manufacture, allowed the brand to maximize its market and stay on the cutting edge of modern American women's wear.

The marketability and distinction of Wright's designs was crucial to the rapid growth and success of Lilli Ann Fashions. According to the book celebrating the corporation's fifty years in business, in eighteen years it grew "from a two-man operation to one of the country's most successful coat and suit manufacturers" (Adolph Schuman *c*. 1983: 20). A photograph from the 1940s pictured Wright in her studio "with a gleam of satisfaction in her eyes at a job well planned and well done," indicating her expertise in both the technical and aesthetic aspects of her job (Adolph Schuman *c*. 1983: 12). Wright attributed the popularity of the label to "the Lilli Ann policy of providing a couture-type garment which the consumer can buy in the volume market" ("California" 1946: 22). Wright stated:

We don't feel that we design only a dressmaker suit. It is true that in our two-piece ensembles we include complete details of suit type tailoring. However, it is our aim to produce designs in ensembles of skirt and coat or jacket that can give the effect of a two-piece dress or a suit, depending on how the outfit is accessorized. We feel the needs of the average American business woman or housewife call for one basic costume that can be dressed up or down for the

FIGURE 9.2 A Lilli Ann suit (*c*. 1945) designed by Jean Wright. Author's collection. Photo by Leticia Valdez.

particular occasion, but which must always be distinctively hers in line. This is the thought behind our interpretation of design. ("California" 1946: 22)

Wright's description focuses on versatility and notes how Lilli Ann designs sought to cater to most women by providing them with smart options. The critical acclaim and ever-increasing profits the company received offered proof that Wright's intentions were met with success.

While Wright was not the only designer working for Lilli Ann Fashions throughout the company's existence, she was by and large the designer responsible for bringing the Lilli Ann name into the forefront of America's mid-century ready-to-wear market. Unlike later designers for the company, Wright was mentioned in early advertising and received recognition in the press. A 1947 *Women's Wear Daily* article entitled "Sun Spots," which focused on the California climate's role in inspiring designers, even cheekily noted her leisure activities, "Take Jean Wright, designer for Lilli Ann Co., San Francisco coat and suit house. Last week Kay Jamison, Fairchild's San Francisco reporter, found her sunning and swimming at Sonoma Mission Inn" (Martin 1947: 27).

After Wright's marriage to Lieutenant Colonel Galen V. Miller (at which point she was known as Jean Miller), she stepped down from her position as the head designer for Lilli Ann, but assurances were made in the press that she was hardly gone for good, a testament to her design clout ("Miss Wright Retires" 1955: 15). A 1956 *Women's Wear Daily* article announced significant changes at the company, including placing Miss Billie Jean Eberhart into the roles of head dress designer, head stylist for the company, and a company director. The article also informed readers that "Mrs. Jean Miller, in the business with him [Schuman] 21 years, remains as fashion coordinator and executive vice president" ("Good Prospects" 1956: 44). A respected designer, and the technical design mastermind behind the Lilli Ann look, Wright's impact on American fashion can be measured by her foundational role in a company that became one of America's mid-century triumphs.

In the early years of Lilli Ann's existence, before the company had a national following and extensive advertising campaigns in prominent publications, Wright was acknowledged as the design genius behind the Lilli Ann brand. In fact, through the early 1940s Wright even had her own labels—"Originals by Jean"—featured in the garments the company produced ("Fashion Empire Builders" 1944). Despite public recognition and her success at one of the largest American ready-to-wear companies of the time, Wright's slide into obscurity was in fact largely caused by a "rival" within the corporation: Lilli Ann. In the first decade of its existence the company advertised using a variety of names, including "Lilli Ann Fashions" and "The Lilli Ann Company," but the one constant was "Lilli Ann." Even when Wright's own labels appeared in garments, the Lilli Ann label was there as well. Because of this continuity, Lilli Ann, though nothing more than a name, became the perfect vehicle for the designer name recognition the company needed to bolster the "couture" image it sought to construct.

In addition to providing a figurehead (if fictional) designer for the company, the name "Lilli Ann" had a French ring to it, and called to mind many of the great female Parisian designers, such as Chanel, Paquin, and Lanvin. France had long been revered as the ultimate source of high fashion, and in naming his company Schuman not only honored his wife but also imbued his business with a trace of that French authority. While it is unclear if this was his intention, the decision shaped the trajectory of his company more than anyone could have anticipated.

The influence of French authority was at play in a 1947 *Women's Wear Daily* article: "Adolph Schuman, president of the Lilli Ann Co., introduced the spring collection of seven coats, 11 suits and four costume suits, explaining that it was planned and conceived when he and the company's designer, Miss Jean Wright, made a trip to Paris in August" ("Paris-Inspired" 1947: 3). Schuman's comment, capitalizing on France's long-standing command of the fashion industry, in a decade that had seen the Parisian fashion empire temporarily silenced by the Nazi occupation, revealed his awareness of the value of an association with European fashion.

In the mid-1940s Lilli Ann's success was cemented when Schuman created valuable contracts with European (particularly French and Italian) textile mills ("Foreign Mills" 1953). His business dealings radically reshaped much of the traditional textile production industry in Western Europe, but not at the expense of quality, something Schuman and the Lilli Ann Corporation advocated for relentlessly during their years in business. The postwar contracts were mutually beneficial, launching Lilli Ann into the 1950s with greater prominence than ever while simultaneously supporting textile industries hard-hit by the war ("Schuman" 1954). This move also gave credence to the French allusions the Lilli Ann name presented.

At the zenith of the mid-twentieth century Lilli Ann flourished; the late 1940s through the mid-1950s were the peak years of the label's design, quality, and notoriety. With record profits achieved annually, Lilli Ann placed advertisements in high-end publications featuring prominent models and shot by noted photographers. Jean Wright's designs adapted easily to the stylistic features of the New Look with its emphasis on lavish use of luxurious materials. The top-quality woolens produced in the European textile mills for Schuman were well suited to the construction of highly tailored and structural silhouettes. It is during this period in which the most memorable Lilli Ann looks were conceptualized and created, spurred along in part by increases in both advertising and production to complement a postwar economy.

It is also at this time, however, that a major shift occurred in the brand's marketing, which ultimately led to Jean Wright's name being erased from ad copy. While news articles made it clear that the company was a corporation run by a singular, male

FIGURE 9.3 A 1947 advertisement placed by Lilli Ann in *Vogue* features the popular illustrative style of fashion images of the day, as well as a glimpse at the design of their rare early black labels. Image courtesy of Fashion Institute of Technology.

FIGURE 9.4 Lilli Ann used the distinctive black label with white text until approximately 1950. Photo by Leticia Valdez.

entrepreneur, advertising began to present a different depiction of just who was behind the Lilli Ann label. As the business gained momentum, ads often presented "Lilli Ann" as if it were the name of the design genius behind the whole operation. An advertisement featured in the January 1945 issue of *California Stylist* asserts: "Inspired by the creative imagination of this clever California designer, salón suits have become the fashion forte of smartly-dressed women. From coast to coast, they have enthusiastically accepted this Lilli Ann interpretation of the 'return to feminine elegance'" (Advertisement 1945). Bolstered by quality design, materials, and construction, this method of marketing imparted an air of exclusivity further enhanced by the notion of a brilliant woman behind each creation.

One year later an advertisement in the January 1946 issue of *California Stylist* shows the evolution of this marketing technique. In 1945 the fictitious Lilli Ann had been given a degree of agency, but by 1946 she developed into a more fully fleshed out figure behind the designs. "Jungle Allure by Lilli Ann," the text boldly begins, "No one but a famous designer—with flaming imagination—could have dared to combine the natural beauty of the skins of jungle creatures with the finest loomed fabrics of the weaver's art … bringing forth exotic styling—so new, so alluring, so unique that every woman's heart cries out, 'I MUST POSSESS ONE!'" (Advertisement 1946). The copy continues by stating "Lilli Ann has created five distinctly different collections of suits for Spring" (Advertisement 1946). While the name "Lilli Ann" was emphasized throughout the early advertising produced by the company, it was primarily used in reference to the company itself, indicating a shift in the public image of the brand. During the mid-1940s the name accrued an identity, eventually crystallizing into the notion of Lilli Ann as a real designer.

By the mid-1950s, this advertising practice was fully established with ads making claims such as "That talented Lilli Ann creates a collection of suits in beautiful fabrics, imported from France" (Advertisement 1954: B3), and "From the hands of the expert, Lilli Ann" (Advertisement 1957: A1). In the latter example, the fictitious Lilli Ann is not merely dubbed an expert, she is praised as "one of America's foremost couturiers" (A1). While the assertion of Lilli Ann's talent and creativity was simply a marketing strategy, the claims were supported by the quality of the product, unusually high for an American manufacturer. The woman behind the company may have only been a conceptual persona, but it was a well-executed tactic to model the company on traditional Parisian couture in which houses were named for the designers behind them and often capitalized on their inventive, artistic, and even extravagant personalities.

While "Lilli Ann" rose to prominence as a designer, Jean Wright continued to produce the actual designs for the company. Though "Lilli Ann" was praised in *Vogue* and *Harper's Bazaar* for creating remarkable suits and coats, the real credit belonged to Wright. The transition from a small San Franciscan business with a unique young designer to a multimillion dollar national company with the elusive "Lilli Ann" at the drawing board happened along with Schuman's increased advertising in such renowned publications. In earlier years the fine-quality garments had been an accessible luxury, sold in better department stores and via mail order. By the time the New Look became the mode, however, and "Lilli Ann" had been established as a "designer," the cost of a Lilli Ann garment had increased, and the clientele had become more elite. A 1953 *Vogue* ad prices a new suit at "about one hundred dollars at fine stores or write Lilli Ann" (Advertisement 1953). Although the clothes were still sold via mail order and department store, economic shifts after the Second World War and the higher pricing turned Lilli Ann into a company for the upper middle class.

The use of the Lilli Ann name was artful, and it may be easily argued that without it the corporation would never have achieved the success it enjoyed. However, the peculiarities of the usage of "Lilli Ann" in many ways collapsed the notoriety Wright had begun to achieve as a young, creative designer. Although the name "Lilli Ann" may have provided the Parisian panache and air of authority that helped propel the company to success in a more refined market, without Wright's designs and ability to trend forecast, there would have been no Lilli Ann.

As time has passed, the legacy of the brand has sustained, and even enjoyed a return to popularity. The desirability of the garments among vintage enthusiasts and designers has made Lilli Ann a hotly discussed label, one that many still believe was created by an actual woman bearing the same name. Although the success of Schuman's marketing enabled Jean Wright to have an extensive and lucrative career with the company prior to her retirement, it also cast a looming shadow over her achievements. The influence of her designs is seen to this day, but her name is never credited.

It is not particularly unusual for a designer's name to be forgotten or overshadowed by the company they worked for, especially at large ready-to-wear monoliths. What makes the case of Jean Wright unusual is that a fictitious woman, a marketing creation, subsumed her potential for lasting renown. Although mentions of the company and designer from their earliest years have thus far not been uncovered, the earliest records found from the 1940s point to a potential for another narrative. With her own feature in *Women's Wear Daily* and a number of mentions in the pages of influential publications, Jean Wright seemed poised for enduring prominence. Had Lilli Ann Fashions stayed with its original marketing method, its true designer may not have spent decades in anonymity.

In many respects the fictional Lilli Ann was born out of a perceived necessity. Wright's name had already appeared in news articles and advertising and the information was already familiar to industry insiders. A young American model turned demure designer by happenstance, Wright perhaps lacked the personal glamour that was synonymous with fashion, especially as expected of a California designer during the Golden Age of Hollywood. As the company began to reach new audiences and unpredictable levels of success, it seemed logical to re-brand, and what better way to do so than to exploit the name of the company itself?

While Wright's astute trend-forecasting and design sensibilities allowed the company to grow each year, it also cannot be denied that the promotion of a "designer" named Lilli Ann propelled Lilli Ann Fashions into new markets and heightened success. The character alluded to in mid-century advertising possessed the spark and larger-than-life persona that Jean Wright, with all her modesty, lacked. Lilli Ann was brilliant, magnetic, and brought a hefty dose of Parisian chic to the label. She was mysterious and unpredictable, the epitome of an artistic yet eccentric designer. The women who read the name "Lilli Ann" in *Vogue* and *Harper's Bazaar* in the 1950s had grown up hearing about Coco Chanel and Elsa Schiaparelli, designers who had larger-than-life personalities and designs to match. Lilli Ann was a more accessible version of this, especially when it came to cost, and stylish women across the United States came to regard the label as their chance to have the couture experience while staying within their means.

Through a transformative use of language in the mid- to late 1940s, the name "Lilli Ann" took on a dual meaning, that of brand and designer. In many respects, however, she was more than a mere invention. The designer who existed solely in name can be viewed as the public persona of Wright, an unintentional counterpart of the real woman who conceptualized suits with python sleeves and bejeweled buttons. The two effectively worked in tandem—Lilli Ann as the star on a stage of glossy magazine pages and Jean Wright behind the scenes choreographing the show.

Just as Wright's years of creative and influential designing deserve acknowledgment, "Lilli Ann" merits recognition as an archetype of the mid-century American designer. When the company name was personified, it was because fashion industry insiders perceived Lilli Ann to be a figure that American women would both trust and aspire to. The phenomenal success of the label in the years after "Lilli Ann" began receiving design credit demonstrates the accuracy of that perception. It also speaks volumes about the expectations of fashionable women at the time, their notions of French fashion authority, and the desire for drama in a postwar environment.

Ultimately, the Lilli Ann story is one of two women, the designer Jean Wright, and her fictional counterpart, both essential to Lilli Ann Fashions' trajectory of success. Wright left behind a powerful design legacy, creating some of the most iconic silhouettes and styles of the 1940s and 1950s. Her work has since inspired legions of designers and costumers, but though her creations are often instantly recognizable, it's more likely than not they will be identified as designs by Lilli Ann.

Note

1   For more on the connections between the film industry and American sportswear, see Warner, "The Americanization of Fashion."

Bibliography

Adolph Schuman for Lilli Ann: Celebrating Fifty Years 1933–1983 (c. 1983). Publication details unknown.
Advertisement: Lilli Ann (1945), *California Stylist*, 9(1): 22.
Advertisement: Lilli Ann (1946), *California Stylist*, 10(1): 24.
Advertisement: Lilli Ann (1953), *Vogue*, 122(2): 2.
Advertisement: May Co. (1954), *Los Angeles Times*, January 1: B3.
Advertisement: May Co. (1957), *Los Angeles Times*, February 17: A1.
Buckland, S.S. (2005), "Promoting American Designers, 1940-44: Building Our Own House," in L. Welters and P.A. Cunningham (eds.), *Twentieth-Century American Fashion*. Oxford: Berg, 99–121.
California, Death Index, 1940–1997. Available online from: Ancestry.com
"California: Economic Need in Earlier Years Guided Steps of Stylists to Designing Careers" (1946), *Women's Wear Daily*, 73(46): 22.
Engle, F. (1947), "Coats and Suits: Says Greatest Competition Is from Woman's Wardrobe," *Women's Wear Daily*, 74(29): 46.
"Fashion Empire Builders" (1944), *Women's Wear Daily*, 68(5): 33.
"Foreign Mills Find New Home Market," (1953), *New York Times*, June 12: 35.
"Good Prospects Are Forecast for Fashion Business" (1956), *Women's Wear Daily*, 92(11): 44.

Martin, A. (1947), "California: Sun Spots," *Women's Wear Daily*, 74(79): 27.

"Miss Wright Retires from Lilli Ann Post" (1955), *Women's Wear Daily* 109(91): 15.

National Cemetery Administration (2006), U.S. Veterans Gravesites, *c.*1775–2006. Available online from: Ancestry.com

"Paris-Inspired Coats and Suits Made in San Francisco Shown: Joint Presentation by the Emporium and H. C. Capwell Stores of Lilli Ann Suits and Costumes Emphasizes Belted Waistlines and Padded Hips" (1947), *Women's Wear Daily*, 75(107): 3.

"Schuman Is Honored for Aiding French Textile Industries" (1954), *Women's Wear Daily*, 89(43): 34.

"Sportswear: Tunic Suits with Fur Sleeves Featured in Lilli Ann Showing" (1945), *Women's Wear Daily*, 70(97): 20.

Steinberg, D. (1956), "Lilli Ann Turns Out Chic on Coast Assembly Line," *New York Herald Tribune*, September 23: A10.

United States Federal Census. 1930. Available online from: Ancestry.com.

Untitled photo feature, *California Stylist* (1945), 9 (1): 174.

Warner, P.C. (2005), "The Americanization of Fashion: Sportswear, the Movies and the 1930s," in L. Welters and P.A. Cunningham (eds.), *Twentieth-Century American Fashion*. Oxford: Berg, 79–98.

10 MOLLIE PARNIS: TASTEMAKER

ANNETTE BECKER

In 1966, *LIFE* magazine declared, "When Mollie Parnis Thinks It Will Sell, It Goes" (Lurie: 43).[1] A collage of conversation and remarks from Parnis, the article highlighted the "extraordinary run of virtuosity" that allowed a designer with no sewing skills and a Park Avenue apartment to achieve fame and fortune. By 1966, Parnis was several decades into a career as a manufacturer, editor, and designer. The public knew her for dressing First Ladies in flattering, feminine dresses and ensembles with beautiful fabrics, and well-off, mature women who patronized her multimillion-dollars-a-year business appreciated her conservative interpretations of trends.

In spite of her wide commercial success and name recognition at the height of her career, Parnis is rarely included in the canon of fashion history. Many collections of dress include her garments, yet these have largely been unrecorded in the digitization efforts and omitted from exhibitions. Textbooks and survey courses of fashion studies instead favor the designers with legacies in active fashion houses, designers whose work sold at higher price points, and those who received critical acclaim during their careers. Nonetheless, Parnis embodies a complex and critical point in the history of American fashion. Writers during her time—from Eugenia Sheppard at the *Herald Tribune* to Marilyn Bender in *The Beautiful People*—framed her as an important social figure and designer whose life and career existed in a liminal space, percolating between the Seventh Avenue world of fashion creation and the Park Avenue world of fashion consumption. Balancing between these spaces earned her more dinner invitations than industry awards, but it also brought greater profits and a higher profile for the developing American fashion industry.

This chapter explores the unconventional and transformative career of Mollie Parnis. In her words, she found success through "knowing what people want to wear" and by casting herself as one of those people (Parnis 1982). Blurring the lines between designer, editor, and socialite, Parnis forged a path of commercial success through her role as a tastemaker. Through highly public associations with political and media figures—as both a social companion and clothier—Parnis worked between the worlds of designer and consumer, everywoman and star. This model, though not recognized in most fashion histories, has been practiced by designers since; many twenty-first-century successes draw their credibility as much from their carefully managed relationship with celebrities and the media as from recognizing the fashion needs of their clientele.

As Mollie Parnis told it, her career's inception was semi-mythical, the serendipity of chance steering her toward fashion. In her first encounters with dressmaking, success came through taste and instinct rather than training or skill. While attending Wadleigh High in the Upper West Side of Manhattan in the early 1920s, a classmate invited her to a party following the homecoming football game. With limited time and resources, she remade her only dress by altering the neckline and adding lace and an artificial flower. This portentous occasion—and its frequent retelling later in her career—offers anecdotal evidence of her ingenuity and practicality as a designer.

Though she enrolled in Hunter College to study law, in the summer of 1923 she took a job as an associate saleswoman with a blouse manufacturer in New York's bustling Seventh Avenue. Her instinct in changing necklines, sleeves, and hems led to her promotion within the firm and the addition of her name to the building directory. This work—altering dressmaker details and adapting designs—led many to later characterize her as "more of an editor than a designer," both a credit to and dismissal of her work (Milbank 1989: 125).

Parnis's next advancement came through Leon Livingston, a textiles salesman whom she met while working as a stylist for the dress house of David Westheim in 1929. After they married in 1930, Leon continued his career, Mollie raised their son Robert, and in 1933 the couple opened Parnis-Livingston, Inc. Their business partnership played off their respective strengths, with Mollie's skills with design and client relations working symbiotically with Leon's business acumen. Their prices were accessible to those of means—between $79.50 and $195—and were sold with department store labels at many of the best retail spaces in the United States (Milbank 1989: 125). While many businesses closed during the economic depression of the 1930s, Parnis-Livingston held strong.

Throughout her career, Parnis repeated a concise biography of her early years, reinforcing two key points: her lack of business and manufacturing skills and her faultless creative instinct. In many ways, this message was a boon to her business; it positioned her not as a fashion expert but as a fellow consumer who leveraged her keen eye into a successful career. Rather than drawing inspiration from places removed from her clients' lives, Parnis reminded them that she merely adapted what was familiar into something more aesthetically pleasing. She cast her talent as vernacular rather than high-style while still producing garments that were desirable.

In the 1940s, both Parnis's career and the status of American fashion advanced. Parnis-Livingston moved to Seventh Avenue. Though many designers had worked for decades both creating original designs and producing in-demand copies of French garments, changes in promotion and sale of American fashion pushed the names and creative efforts of Seventh Avenue designers into the minds and onto the bodies of consumers. After a decade of designing in anonymity, Parnis began selling her clothing with the label "Mollie Parnis/New York."

Many mid-century changes in the industry are credited to Eleanor Lambert, a visionary publicist who made a career of forging paths for recognition of American fashion ingenuity. Beginning in 1943, she administered the prestigious Coty American Fashion Critics' Awards, an honor reserved for American designers, and coordinated New York fashion showings to occur during the same week, setting a point from which New York Fashion Week developed. Lambert and a cohort of fashion industry leaders founded the Council of Fashion Designers of America in 1962. As "one of American fashion's key personalities" and a designer with "a following of smart conservative women throughout the world," Parnis was a founding member and served on the Board of Directors of the CFDA (Lambert 1976: 242).

Adapting to the industry's changing landscape, Parnis embraced the liminality of designer-manufacturer. She benefited from the industry's streamlined organization—better press coverage, more organized seasonal showings—but remained comfortably conservative rather than pushing toward the innovation rewarded by Lambert's initiatives. Her continued success and professional affiliations, however, caused tension within the industry. For example, the CFDA followed an inclusive model, admitting both designers and designer-manufacturers. Jacques Tiffeau, a designer twenty years Parnis's junior with experience in French houses, admonished the group to limit its membership. In the October 10, 1966 issue of *Women's Wear Daily*, he said, "If they don't get rid of some of those people, I'm going to quit ... Non-creators like Mollie Parnis and Vincent Monte-Sano should get out. They weaken the prestige and authority of a group that should just include this country's top creative designers" (Kosover: 1). To Tiffeau, Parnis's success diluted the credibility and success of the quickly advancing American fashion scene.

Parnis also found herself outside the growing ranks of American fashion school alumni. Young faces from newly created fashion programs throughout New York City fed the steadily professionalizing Seventh Avenue. In 1904, the Chase School—now part of The New School—established the first fashion design program in the United States. This inaugural "costume design" program was held on equal level with other arts taught at the school. In 1924, the Pratt Institute's Department of Household Arts held its first fashion show. The Fashion Institute of Technology was founded in 1944 and accredited in 1957. These programs provided professional credentials, networks, and more standardized industry and design framework. Parnis and her business functioned tangentially to this system, sharing a geography but finding alternative paths to success. Today Parnis's legacy exists as a shadow within these educational frameworks, with no institutional home to collect her garments, house her archives, display her work in exhibitions, or advocate for her history in classrooms. Rather than aligning herself with the world of high fashion and seeking alliances with design program graduates, Mollie Parnis developed her client base and developed social networks. Because of this, her personal and professional histories have found less conventional homes, often archives and museums dedicated to fashion patrons rather than designers.

Parnis existed as both a social and professional player, creating a brand that extended further than her garments. She intertwined these two major roles, self-fashioning an image that capitalized on polished personality and professionalism. Her dinner parties were featured in newspapers, and the next day readers and party guests alike purchased her garments. She dressed herself, high-profile figures, and middle- and upper-class American women in the same dresses and suits, creating a desire for her lifestyle and taste.

Many successful designers have followed similar models of business, creating celebrity for themselves by closely associating their business or style with a public figure. For example, Charles Frederick Worth grew his business by capitalizing on his chief patron, Empress Eugénie, the wife of French emperor Napoleon III. Other designers, such as Coco Chanel, conflated their personal style with their garments, blurring the boundary between designer and consumer. One of Parnis's contemporaries, Anne Fogarty, made a name for herself designing and writing for middle-class women navigating mid-century respectability.

Parnis, however, is unique for drawing from these models of success, crafting a more demotic approach to design, self-fashioning, and celebrity. Though she did take notes from the French fashion houses and frequently copied their designs, Parnis did not set her sights on those women who would or could exclusively wear Balenciaga or Dior. Her mainstay client was not an empress or even necessarily a member of the ultra-moneyed elite. As she said, "I think the essence of a designer's work is in the designer's own personality... I make dresses for people who live the kind of life that I live and understand" (Diamonstein 1985: 67). She settled into the ranks of women with aspirations beyond—but evidenced by—their clothing.

Like Parnis, many of her clients—either through their own work or that of their spouses—gained their power, prestige, and income through routes characterized by highly visible lifestyles. Often associated with the media or the political world, these women relied on their public images. Their self-presentation—and therefore their clothing—needed to do work for them. As Parnis said, "Fashion is not molded by designers as much as it is by everyday living" (Lurie 1966: 47). Parnis understood that the women who wore her garments defined her business and created her success, a tenet that shaped much of her career.

Parnis's most public proponents were American First Ladies, women who embodied Parnis's ethos. Historically, First Ladies are often ordinary women who, once their husbands are elected to high office, are swept into the vortexes of the public eye and popular history. This unique role pushes less high-profile women forward, allowing those who read about them in the media to analyze their own lives through a more relatable model. When Parnis dressed the First Ladies, she created an attainable material manifestation of the fantasies of women who wished to be thrust into the spotlight. While clothing First Ladies and women of their ilk created moving models of her designs, Parnis's visibility as their stylist and spokesperson reinforced the infallibility of her fashion and social sense.

Though Parnis designs were worn by Jacqueline Kennedy, Pat Nixon, Betty Ford, and Rosalynn Carter, Mamie Eisenhower and Claudia "Lady Bird" Johnson were most closely associated with her in the public imagination and reflect the taste and clientele of the designer. Both women were actively advised by Parnis, who polished their public images through garments, styling, and media interviews. These symbiotic relationships provided Parnis with leverage for other social relationships, inspired desire among her mainstream customers, and gave the First Ladies much-needed coaching through a period when the media was increasingly critical of these women as fashion figures.

Mamie Eisenhower was one of the first high-profile clients associated with Parnis. Already a member of influential social circles, Parnis met the Eisenhowers in the early 1950s while they resided in New York City and Dwight served as the president of Columbia University. With an increased public profile, Mamie felt the need to adapt her wardrobe to her new lifestyle. She mentioned to a friend that she liked Parnis's clothing, an introduction was made, and the two developed a long-term relationship (Levin 1965).

When her husband was elected to the presidency, Mamie's lifestyle and status as a fashionable woman changed dramatically. She received many unsolicited letters from well-known designers—including Oleg Cassini, who later rose to fame through his connection with Jackie Kennedy—and she developed relationships with designer Nettie Rosenstein and milliner Sally Victor.

Archival records from Mamie's time as the First Lady suggest a remarkably strong and affectionate relationship with Parnis. Ever the promoter of her own taste, Parnis recounts the formative role she played in shaping Mamie's self-presentation. In a 1985 interview, Parnis was asked if Mamie had a sense of fashion. Parnis responded:

No, she didn't. How could she have had? She had spent all of her life on army bases and bought her clothes from post exchanges. I had to work very hard to lead her away from that synthetic world into that which her position demanded. Pure silk and pure wool were the only answers to her social and travel schedules. (Diamonstein 1985: 165)

Rather than discussing specific styles or garments, Parnis steers into the more abstract but still tangible ways in which she assisted Mamie. Chatty letters between the two suggest that Parnis also gave the First Lady gifts—pearl earrings and necklaces, shoes dyed to wear with a specific chiffon dress, a pink birthday sweater embroidered with pearls—and supervised fittings and gave other styling suggestions (Eisenhower 1954, 1955, 1956). However, it was not only garments that Parnis provided. She elevated Mamie's taste, serving as counselor in her new lifestyle.

However, rather than refining Mamie's wardrobe to merely reflect the taste of the elite, Parnis cast her as a respectable and relatable figure. Though made from fine fabrics and tailored to fit well, Mamie's Parnis garments were available

FIGURE 10.1 As part of the 1959 opening ceremony for the St. Lawrence Seaway, Mamie Eisenhower greeted Queen Elizabeth while wearing a favorite Mollie Parnis dress, styled with pearls, gloves, a handbag, and matching Sally Victor hat. This ensemble can be found in the collection of the Eisenhower Presidential Museum in Abilene, Kansas. Hulton Royals Collection/Getty Images. Photo: Central Press/Stringer.

to any woman with a budget that could accommodate her price tags. Admired but accessible, the clothes worn by the First Lady reinforced her position as a demotic figure, elevated but still of the American people.

The popularity and wide appeal of Parnis's clothing is best demonstrated through an event in early 1955, when Mamie attended a small event hosted by wives of the U.S. senators and greeted each woman in a receiving line. Parnis's Model 448, a full shirtwaist dress in a blue and green print, made two appearances that day, on the First Lady and on Mrs. Durries Crane, who reportedly tried to hide the dress with a mink cape. The two women reacted to the "excruciating juxtaposition" with good humor, each commenting on the attractiveness of the other's dress ("Blue-Green" 1955: 118). Hearing of the incident later, Parnis was mortified by the faux pas but "finding what consolation she could in a flurry of business the incident brought" ("Blue-Green").

LIFE magazine reported the incident with a typical patriotic spin, celebrating the good American fashion sense of Mamie, Parnis, and respectable women from "Washington DC to the State of Washington" who sported Model 448 ("Blue-Green"). In the article, photos of women from across the country illustrate a variety of lifestyles and life stages, each tagged with descriptions that include the woman's city and a short description of her role or the situations in which her dress has been appropriate. One woman mentions that she's "glad the President's wife buys U.S. clothes," while another notes its special appeal because it is like the First Lady's. Another notes that she calls hers the "Mamie dress," delightfully conflating Parnis's work with Mamie's.

This shirtwaist dress bolstered each woman's public image. A departure from her less glamorous former life as a mail-order shopper and Army wife, Model 448 was a material and metaphorical manifestation of Mamie's social progress. And for Parnis, this garment indelibly tied her to women of good taste and respectability, a client base that she continued to build.

Parnis continued her ascent as a fashion figure through her relationship with Claudia "Lady Bird" Johnson. Even more than Mamie Eisenhower, Lady Bird was scrutinized for her dress. Through her time as the wife of the vice-president, the press unfavorably compared her to the then–First Lady Jacqueline Kennedy. Following John Kennedy's assassination in 1963 and Lady Bird's subsequent "promotion" to First Lady, the criticism of her self-presentation was even more severe. An August 1964 *Time* article titled "White House: The First Lady" provided a widely read (though rather superficial) biography of Lady Bird, highlighting her less-than-polished dress and country mannerisms. The article declares her "not outstanding at clotheshorse-manship ... playing the role of the politician's perfect wife, the possessor of flawless mediocrity that generates warm admiration but no scorching envy" (20). Though active in her husband's presidential campaign and a successful businesswoman in her own right, Lady Bird failed to meet the press's expectations for fashionability.

FIGURE 10.2 Mollie Parnis, ensemble of green silk brocade and mink, *c.* 1959. Texas Fashion Collection, College of Visual Arts and Design, University of North Texas. Lady Bird Johnson wore this ensemble while her husband was U.S. Vice-President.

Although Lady Bird met Parnis while shopping at the Dallas-based department store Neiman-Marcus earlier in Lyndon Johnson's political career and owned several of her garments before becoming the First Lady, the two women reconnected and formalized their relationship in late 1963. Parnis's husband had passed away one year earlier, leading her to briefly pause her career and refocus on developing her business and social life. In Lady Bird lay the opportunity to groom a high-profile woman and to re-energize her connection with the White House. Parnis wrote a letter offering her services to the First Lady, and from that point forward Lady Bird consulted the designer regularly.

Working together, the two women reinvented the First Lady's public image. Once Lady Bird revitalized her wardrobe with Parnis's assistance, articles in newspapers and magazines favorably described Lady Bird's clothing and recast her as a member of the social aristocracy. Rather than being omitted from style columns—as was previously the case—Lady Bird's (and Parnis's) garments at state dinners and high-profile events were described in careful detail. Whether she was "looking elegant in a Mollie Parnis scoop-necked gold and white brocade evening dress" at a 1966 event at the National Art Gallery or reporting on "a lovely gold dress that Mollie Parnis had made for me" in her widely read White House diary, Lady Bird indelibly tied her image and fashionability to Parnis ("Mrs. Johnson" 1966; Johnson 1966). And through this, Parnis refocused her relationship with the public. As she said, "When I see Mrs. Johnson dressed in my clothes I feel I am part of history" (Lurie 1966: 47).

Toward the end of her time as First Lady, Lady Bird—like Parnis—found herself at the height of her fashion celebrity. Both women appeared on "best dressed" lists, illustrating the media exposure that came from their fashionability. A 1967 Associated Press article named Lady Bird among the twelve best-dressed women in the United States, as selected by American fashion editors. Rather than placing agency for this win in the hands of the First Lady, credit was given to the fashion designers "who worked closely with the First Lady in polishing her image" (Wilson 1967a). Parnis, whose comments composed the majority of the article, was cited as "one of Mrs. Johnson's favorite designers." Even *Women's Wear Daily*, who remained highly critical of her dress, begrudgingly added, "although she is more interested in politics and business than fashion, the fashion world hopefully wishes her well" (ibid.). The article closed with comments about Lady Bird's shopping style that "contributed to her simple and appropriate wardrobe."

Interestingly, that same year Parnis was inducted to the Hall of Fame for the International Best Dressed List, marking a parallel rise in social status for the designer. This list, managed by fashion publicist Eleanor Lambert, recognized both designers and non-industry individuals who showed particular sartorial accomplishment. After being listed on the 1964–1966 "women fashion professionals" roll, Parnis advanced to the Hall of Fame, marking her name alongside many of her other high-profile clients.

Parnis adroitly managed the feedback loop of social and fashion industry reporting, casting herself in every role that could advance her public image and her career. She embedded herself in the world of her more "aspirational" clients, reinforcing her business and social acumen through self-styling as a member of the same elite that she dressed. This blurring of boundaries made her both more accessible through press exposure and less attainable through her social status, creating an even more ravenous appetite for her garments.

Parnis's success and legacy owe much to the symbiotic relationships she developed with the burgeoning and increasingly formalized platforms that promoted, publicized, and reported on American fashion. While her ties with publicist Eleanor Lambert through the CFDA and International Best Dressed List gave her the professional credentials necessary to capitalize on the rising profile of American fashion, her relationship with the media provided regular interest in her as a public personality.

One of her closest allies was Eugenia Sheppard, best known as the "Inside Fashion" columnist for the *New York Herald Tribune* in the 1950s and 1960s. Sheppard reported on industry news, designers' collections, and the wardrobes and social schedules of socialites. Her penchant for witty, entertaining prose gained readers through her tenure at the *Tribune*. Her column was published with increased frequency, and buzz surrounding her friends on Seventh Avenue grew.

Parnis regularly appeared in Sheppard's writing, providing the reporter with access to all angles of fashion production and consumption. Sheppard wrote about Parnis's new collections, included descriptions of her garments as worn by well-known women, and devoted column space to the fashionable parties at her well-appointed home. In this coverage, Parnis seamlessly moves between her industry and society roles, providing a charismatic presence rather than a clearly identified position. As Marilyn Bender wrote in her fashion and society tell-all *The Beautiful People*, "It can be argued that Miss Parnis is entitled to behave like a prima donna. Isn't she, after all, a celebrity?" (1967: 85).

Parnis leveraged her lifestyle to cast herself as a tastemaker beyond the boundaries of the fashion industry. Throughout her career, when she purchased garments from French couture houses to copy for her own business (which was common in the industry), she ordered them in her size and wore them to social functions. When her husband passed away in 1962, she sold their home outside of the city, moved to a fashionable duplex on Park Avenue, and had it fabulously furnished by society decorator Billy Baldwin. Her living room, which served as the "backdrop to her stimulated and stimulating life," featured a small but impressive collection of Impressionist and modern art (Sotheby's 1992).

The artwork that Parnis was most associated with—both through interviews and in photographs—is *L'Asie*, an early-twentieth-century oil painting by Henri Matisse. This bold and expressive painting with an orientalist theme features a

FIGURE 10.3 Accompanying a *LIFE* magazine article, this photo included the caption, "Miss Parnis sits before her prized Matisse during a party at her Park Avenue home. Although she owns dresses by other couturiers, this is her own." This image and text highlight her career as a high-level designer, her social and hostessing skills, and her wealth and taste through her ownership of Henri Matisse's *L'Asie*. Photo by Bob Peterson, May 1, 1966. The LIFE Images Collection, Getty Images.

woman in brightly colored textiles, the patterns emphasized through the flatness with which they are rendered. Parnis was particularly attracted to the "divine colors and shapes on the canvas" rather than technique, echoing the ways in which she approached her career as a designer (Diamonstein 1985: 169). When she moved it to her New York apartment, she requested that Baldwin arrange the space around it, and many photographs of her parties include her sitting casually, surrounded by stars and underneath this jewel of her collection. The few times it left her quarters were for exhibitions, at major museums in New York, and the Grand Palais in Paris, further endorsing her good taste (Sotheby's 1992).

In the late 1960s and 1970s, her Park Avenue apartment functioned as an exclusive salon. Building on the relationships she made in the White House, Parnis's Sunday evening parties included politicians, media and entertainment luminaries, and others of high public status—Henry Kissinger, Mike Wallace, Frank Sinatra, Walter Cronkite, Barbara Walters, Dan Rather, Kirk and Ann Douglas, Johnny Carson, and other "people who interest her" (Walz and Morris 1978: 170; Sotheby's 1992: Preface). Many of the women who attended these parties were already, or shortly thereafter became, her clients. And any reader of the society columns could buy a Parnis dress to feel like part of that crowd.

Like many of those who attended her salons, Parnis extended her public profile and earned good will through named philanthropic activity. Through her foundation, in 1971 she began the "Mollie Parnis Dress Up Your Neighborhood" project, which allocated $50,000 annually for prizes to New Yorkers in less developed or blighted areas to beautify their neighborhoods. The project functioned as a localized, urban parallel to the national beautification efforts initiated by Lady Bird Johnson during her husband's presidency and related to gardening and landscaping projects many ladies' clubs sponsored in civic spaces. The social justice implied in the "Dress Up" project, however, elevated the work above mere society activity. Parnis also established the Livingston Award for Young Journalists in memory of her son Robert Livingston after he passed in 1979, which gave her the opportunity to network with the high-profile judges for the yearly contest and reaffirmed her appreciation of the media (Sotheby's 1992).

These components of her lifestyle, when considered in conjunction with the tasteful clothing she created, developed a social practice and reputation that was intrinsic to her success. To the public, Mollie Parnis was a person before she was a designer, and her clothing allowed them to become more like the person she was. Though her designs were not necessarily innovative and her work was not critically acclaimed, her mass appeal and the commercial success that accompanied it offered an alternative path for American designers.

Today, in the first decades of the twenty-first century, an increasing number of commercially successful—and even critically recognized—fashion collections are created by people with little or no design experience. With new media offering designers exposure to new audiences and a strong market for moderately priced clothing, celebrities and public personalities no longer need to follow traditional fashion industry routes to find success in fashion. Retailers welcome the paths and contributions of less traditional creators within the fashion system, expanding upon the example offered by Parnis.

For example, Mary-Kate and Ashley Olsen have refashioned their careers and identities through celebrity intervention in the fashion world. The former child stars had lines of merchandise early in the early 2000s, including a girl's clothing line at Wal-Mart. As they matured and their images became less "wholesome," their editorial viewpoint evolved; many described Mary-Kate's high-low style as "bohemian-bourgeois" or "homeless." Through this style evolution, the twins were hired as the faces of Badgley Mishka in 2006, and later founded high-end fashion label The Row, launched the Olsenboye for J.C. Penney, and started a line in Olso, Norway. Marking a departure from the narrower perspective of Mollie Parnis's era, the CFDA named the Olsen twins Womenswear Designer of the Year in both 2012 and 2015 and Accessories Designer of the Year in 2014.

The career of Michael Kors, a well-known and successful designer celebrity, also aligns with Mollie Parnis's. Though Kors found critical acclaim early and served as the creative director for Céline, his modest namesake label's success was bolstered by his friendly relationship with the press and work outside traditional fashion industry roles, including serving as a judge on the television show *Project Runway*. Though he continues to show collections, his frequent public appearances and the booming success of his mass market and peripheral merchandising enterprises suggest the importance of celebrity branding as much as designing. As fashion writer Teri Agins writes of Kors and others, "The job of a fashion designer used to be about designing clothes. But lately, it's no longer enough for a designer to push high-toned intellectual looks to get the attention of critics. Instead, the most successful designers are those who are telegenic, media savvy—in short, celebrities in their own right" (2007). In that statement, Agins sees boundary-crossing as a recent development, now expected activities through which Parnis built a decades-long career.

That is the quiet brilliance of Mollie Parnis and her status as designer-celebrity. Through that hyphen, she created a career as a socialite and tastemaker. Her quiet but lasting mark on fashion lies in the commonplace paths to success that have allowed a greater diversity of perspectives in the fashion industry to be heard by a wider range of the public.

Archival Sources

Carpenter, L. (1969), Interview with Joe B. Franz, August 27.
Eisenhower, M. (1954), Letter to Mollie Parnis, November 19.
Eisenhower, M. (1955), Letter to Mollie Parnis, November 20.

Eisenhower, M. (1956), Letter to Mollie Parnis, October 26.

Johnson, C. (1966), Unpublished White House Diary manuscript.

Marcus, S. (1969), Interview with Joe B. Frantz, November 3.

Parnis, M. (1982), Interview with M. Finger, June 2.

Parnis, M. (1983), Interview with Michael L. Gillette, October 13.

Note

1   I would like to thank University of North Texas Professor Denise Baxter and costume historian Kimberly Chrisman-Campbell for encouraging me to pursue this line of research. Additional thanks to Texas Fashion Collection Director Emeritus Myra Walker for her support.

Bibliography

Agins, T. (2007),"TV, Parties—and Designing, Too," *The Wall Street Journal*, September 8. Available online: http://www.wsj.com/articles/SB118920157111120975

Agins, T. (2014), *Hijacking the Runway: How Celebrities Are Stealing the Spotlight from Fashion Designers*, New York: Gotham Books.

Bender, M. (1967), *The Beautiful People*, New York: Coward-McCann, Inc.

Berger, M. (1992), "Mollie Parnis, Designer, Dies in her 90s," *New York Times*, July 19. Available from: http://www.nytimes.com/1992/07/19/nyregion/mollie-parnis -designer-dies-in-her-90-s.html

"Blue-Green on the National Scene" (1955), *LIFE*, April 25: 118–124.

Carpenter, L. (1970), *Ruffles and Flourishes*, Garden City, NY: Doubleday.

Diamonstein-Spielvogel, B. (1985), *Fashion: The Inside Story*, New York: Rizzoli.

Kosover, T. (1966), "Tiffeau Blasts the CFDA," *Women's Wear Daily*, October 10: 1.

Lambert, E. (1976), *World of Fashion: People, Places, Resources*, London and New York: R.R. Bowker Company.

Levin, P.L. (1965), *The Wheels of Fashion*, Garden City, NY: Doubleday.

Lurie, D. (1966), "When Mollie Parnis Thinks It Will Sell, It Goes," *LIFE*, June 17: 43–49.

Milbank, C.R. (1989), *New York Fashion: The Evolution of American Style*, New York: Abrams.

"Mrs. Johnson's the 'Masterpiece' as Art Preview Attracts 8,000" (1966), *Long Beach California Press Telegram*, March 18: A3.

Russell, J.J. (1999), *Lady Bird: A Biography of Mrs. Johnson*, New York: Scribner.

Sotheby's. (1992), *Personal Collections: Property from the Estate of Mollie Parnis Livingston*, New York: Sotheby's.

Tiffany, J. (2011), *Eleanor Lambert: Still Here*, New York: Pointed Leaf Press.

Walz, B. and Morris, B. (1978), *The Fashion Makers*, New York: Random House.

"The White House: The First Lady" (1964), *Time*, August 28: 20–23.

Wilson, J.S. (1967a), "Lady Bird Johnson Joins List of Best Dressed," *Eugene Register-Gard*, January 2: 2B.

Wilson, J.S. (1967b), "These Were the Best Dressed," *Birmingham News*, January 3: 9B.

11 ELIZABETH "LIBBY" PAYNE: DESIGNING FOR MRS. MAIN STREET AMERICA

CAROLINE A. SURRARRER AND CATHERINE AMOROSO LESLIE

The history of the American ready-to-wear industry is filled with unknown fashion designers who worked "behind the labels" for apparel manufacturers. This was especially true in the mid-twentieth century between the advent of readily available manufactured women's clothing and the rise of the "celebrity" fashion designer. In downtown department stores and boutiques all over the country, consumers purchased moderately priced styles created by names that never appeared on a retail-selling floor. One of those was Elizabeth "Libby" Miller Payne (1917–1997), a prolific designer whose career spanned fifty years in the Midwest and New York ready-to-wear industry. Payne designed hundreds of garments for "Mrs. Main Street America" under well-recognized moderate price-point labels such as Bobbie Brooks, Jonathan Logan, Beau Baker, David Warren, and John Henry. Her creations "sold like hotcakes" (Payne 1995, Vol. 4: 67).

Like other unknown ready-to-wear designers, Libby Payne could have been lost to history. But she made sure that this was not the case. In the eight years after her retirement in 1987, Payne carefully documented her life and career, creating four volumes of memoir notebooks titled "Things I Remember." The notebooks encompass 456 pages and 153 images of personal and professional remembrances in the form of stories, diary entries, images of designs and sketches, advertisements, fabric swatches, and family photographs (Payne 1995). Beginning with her family history and chronicling her fifty-year fashion design career, Libby Payne's memoirs encapsulate experiences and memories, including the particular designs that made her especially proud or brought incredible success to the companies whose labels they carried. Although customers did not know her name, Libby Payne considered her story worth telling, worth noting, and worth archiving.

The oldest of four children, Elizabeth Miller was born in Havana, Cuba in 1917 to well-educated American missionary parents, and the family immigrated to the United States in 1923. Because of her father's work as a Baptist minister, the Millers moved frequently and were often dependent on the meager donations of parishioners. By the age of 16, Libby had lived in eight different locations and interacted with a wide variety of Americans. She was a "product of her parents" and, through these foundational experiences, felt a strong connection to "the everybody," a need to employ her talents in a positive manner, and a mission to be successful in life. Simply put, Libby Payne wanted to make her family and herself proud (Payne 2016).

Libby Payne came of age in the Great Depression, which was amplified by her family situation, and acutely felt the pain of the times. She devised creative solutions for entertainment, including designing and making clothing, which she first learned from her mother. The two frequently went to movies where they would find fashion inspiration and sewing ideas from Hollywood's leading ladies. Libby then put her inventiveness to work. For example, she cleverly draped plain muslin fabric over a rusty, iron fence to get an imprint, which she made into a patterned dress. She often utilized small pinecones, acorns, and other found objects to construct buttons for the savvy designs she made for herself, family members, and friends. It was this cost-aware and innovative mindset developed in her early life that translated so well into the designs she created throughout her long career targeting consumers who preferred moderate-price garments. Payne thrived when creative problem-solving was the name of the game. She saw possibilities in materials that others did not, a valuable asset for the numerous manufacturers for whom she worked. This was especially important during the Second World War when wartime restrictions regulated design details, including hem width and length and collar and cuff size. In the early 1980s, a dress made of three colors of trimmings fabrics was so successful at market that competitors attempted to copy it, only to find the exact colors unavailable in bulk.

By 1933, Libby was 16 and on her own, attending Virginia Intermont Women's College in Bristol, Virginia, where she first gained attention for her talent, resourcefulness, and design skills. Friday evening dinners required more formal attire, and one week she decided to update a dress by repurposing her dorm room curtains. Her memoirs recall the many compliments on her "new" dress as well as the originality of her creation. Upon graduation in the summer of 1935, Libby Payne joined her family in West Virginia and first experienced fashion-related employment, selling dresses part-time at Telford's Dress Shop and working at the Diamond Department Store as a sales associate. That fall, she went to Northwestern School of Speech to major in stage costume on a scholarship. While in Chicago, she worked at Cooley's Cupboard Tea Room and in the costume crew or on stagecraft as extracurricular activities. Payne's memoir notebooks include letters to family describing experiences at school and work, along with details of how she garnered attention for personal design accomplishments.

March 28, 1936

Another unusual thing happened tonight at work. I went into the "powder room" to straighten up and a very attractive young woman followed me. She said, "Pardon me, but I have been noticing you all evening as you walked about (hostessing) and I have admired your dress so very much. Please don't think me impertinent, but where ever did you find it?" I told her that I had designed and made it, which surprised her very much. She later introduced me to her father. They seem very genteel and aristocratic.

The dress she was admiring is the new one I made of very sheer "Kelly green" wool. It has a yoke with shirring on the bodice, very full sleeves, and a multi-gored very full flared skirt that swings as I walk. The most unusual thing is the belt, exceptionally wide, about 3½" with multi-rows of stitching and a very large buckle. After I made the belt, I couldn't find a buckle to fit, so I had to make one. I took three or four layers of cardboard, cut out a buckle with a razor blade, used fine piano wire to wrap the layers of cardboard to hold the buckle together, then cut long bias 1" strips of the green fabric and wrapped the buckle around and around till I got the look I wanted. The belt pulled through and snapped, since I had no prong. I get compliments every time I wear it. Many, including the young woman I met tonight, tell me I should go into designing clothes. (Payne 1995, Vol. 3: 50)

In another letter while at Northwestern, Payne told of how she ushered at the annual Shakespeare's Birthday production of "Henry IV" at the University Theatre. Expressing her savviness in material utilization as well as revealing future ambitions, she wrote:

At the last minute, I discovered that the ushers for this informal occasion were supposed to wear long dresses with sleeves. Since I had nothing I thought appropriate, I'd have to make one.

Since I figured that everyone else would be in white or spring pastels, I decided I would like to wear black net, but I would have to get done by 8:00 pm. Perhaps I could wear it over my red taffeta slip. So at noon, I ran down to Lord's Dept. Store to look for the net. It was Evanston's "Dollar Day" and to my amazement, just inside the front door I saw a sign—"Pure Silk French Net—72" wide— $1.00/yd." There were flat bolts of about ten colors including black! I bought five yards and ran the six or eight blocks home.

When I got home at 2:00 I discovered the black net over red didn't look right, so I decided to chase back to town and buy some black material for a slip and some colored trimming to offset the black. At 3:30 pm I started sewing and at

8:00 I had on and wore a perfect dream of a dress, believe it or not! (Payne 1995, Vol. 3: 51–52)

She went on to describe the dress and included a small sketch to illustrate.

Well, believe it or not, and I hope I don't sound too braggy, I was as much of a show as the play itself and received almost the same amount of attention. When I walked into the lobby of the theatre, where everyone was talking, a hush came over everything & people said in whispers to their neighbors, "Isn't that a gorgeous dress! Who is that girl? Oohhoooh! Lovely! Devine [sic]! etc. etc."

All the cast and crew members (& there were about 100 in it) raved and came up and asked if this was the dress people said I made, teachers commented in extremely complimentary terms. I was in my seventh heaven! You know how I thrive on things like that. And I did look striking and attractive! One girl is begging me to make her one. I may try to get an order for one like mine at some exclusive store—just for fun. People would evidently like it and I've certainly never seen anything like it. If I can make things people like, why can't I sell them? I shall! I shall! (Payne 1995, Vol. 3: 51–52)

While attending Northwestern, Payne audited a Fashion Merchandising class taught by Helen Sisson, the Fashion Director of Marshall Field and Company. She recalled, "this gave me the know-how I have used ever since" (Vol. 3: 61). She not only set her sights on being a fashion designer but also stated her goal was to be "the great American designer" (Vol. 3: 99).

To support herself after graduation from Northwestern in 1937, Payne pursued positions in retailing, working in the College Shop at Marshall Field's and Saks Fifth Avenue as well as Carson Pirie Scott and Co. in Chicago. Friendship with a Junior dress designer, Virginia Spears, led to her first paid fashion design job. Spears was the "first real live designer" Libby met, describing their initial meeting as "what really set me on my way" (Vol. 3: 63). Spears provided advice on how to break into fashion.

If you have good taste, a good sense of color, know how to make your own clothes, sketch a little, bluff a lot, and have "half a brain" you can bluff your way into the business. You have to be able to *act* like you do have the experience and that you know what you're doing. (Payne 1995, Vol. 3: 63)

In November 1937, Payne "bluffed" her way into the fashion industry and so began a fifty-year career. With formal schooling at an end, an entry in her diary revealed great ambition for becoming a fashion designer. "I thought to myself, if *they* can do it, I can do it! I will! I have to be a success! I have to!" (Vol. 3: 63).

Her first design position (under her maiden name, Betty Miller) was with Franklin Dress Company, the only job she acquired through a classified newspaper advertisement. Her claim of "extensive experience" was quickly dismantled, and after less than a month she was onto her next position, eventually working for thirteen different Chicago manufacturers in just under a year. These lasted anywhere from two weeks to three months; however long the firm needed a designer or her skill level kept her employed. Table 11.1 outlines Libby Payne's career as documented in her memoir notebooks. Out of a total of thirty jobs in her long career, the first nineteen were within two years (1937–1939), sixteen of those within a six-month period (Vol. 3: 132). Though not as knowledgeable as other trained fashion designers when she started, Libby Payne admitted that inexperience served her well; she was eager, ambitious, and learned something from each job she had.

Table 11.1: The Career of Elizabeth "Libby" Miller Payne

Location	Job #	Company	Years Active
Chicago, IL	#1	Marshall Field's—The College Shop	Summer 1937
	#2	Saks Fifth Avenue—The College Shop	Summer-Early Fall 1937
	#3	Carson Pirie Scott & Co.	Fall 1937
	#4	Franklin Dress Co.	November 1937
	#5	Helena Dress Co.	November 29–December 17, 1937
	#6	Barney Wolk Dress Co.	December 28, 1937–January 18, 1938
	#7	Gilbert Ribback/ "Gilbert Originals" Blouses	January 18–February 11, 1938
	#8	Michel, Inc. Coats and Suits	February 16–March 1, 1938
	#9	Abert Sportswear	March 1–13, 1938
	#10	Joyce Frocks Eveningwear	March 17–20, 1938
	#11	David Roth & Co. Dresses and Gowns	March 26–April 17, 1938
	#12	Nick Kovler Coats and Suits	May 1–17, 1938
	#13	London Dress and Suit	May 25–June 2, 1938

Location	Job #	Company	Years Active
	#14	Debutante Frocks	June 3–17, 1938
	#15	Lorraine Frocks	June 18, 1938–August 27, 1938
	#16	Reich Dress Co.	September 1–16, 1938
St. Louis, MO			
	#17	Bernard's	September 16–October 7, 1938
	#18	Schickman and Frager	October 7, 1938–October 20, 1939
Chicago, IL			
	#19	Johara, Inc.	October 22, 1939–February 11, 1945
New York, NY			
	#20	Dartford Deb	February 1, 1945–December 10, 1950
	#21	Peggy Caswell	Spring 1951
	#22	Bobbie Brooks	July 20, 1951–January 20, 1956
	#23	Toni Edwards	January 30, 1956–November 1, 1958
	#24	Parade Dress	November 1, 1958–January 1, 1960
	#25	Jonathan Logan	January 1, 1960–July 1979
	#26	Kay Windsor	July 1979–December 1980
	#27	Tracy!/St. Barths	December 1980–April 1984
	#28	David Warren	April 1984–April 1985
	#29	Freelance	April 1985–May 1985
	#30	John Henry	May 1985–August 1986
		Private Label Design Services: Libby Payne, Inc.	1986–1987

Developed from Payne (1995, Vols. 1–4).

In her memoir notebooks, Payne credited Chicago designer Louise Mulligan with being the creator of the Junior dress market in the Midwest ("Louise Mulligan" 1935). Once again, Payne took Virginia Spears' advice about "bluffing" coupled with her Northwestern University major and stated, "I hadn't been studying acting 'for nothing!'" (Payne, 1995, Vol. 3: 65). Although no longer in college, she called Louise Mulligan posing as a journalism student interested in an interview for the *Daily Northwestern*. Mulligan agreed, and Payne wasted no time asking exactly how she began in the Junior dress business. Not only was she able to interview Louise Mulligan, she was also given a tour of the factory, witnessing production first-hand and gaining knowledge of the different functions at a manufacturing firm. This experience solidified her interest in designing and fueled her aspiration to succeed in the Junior market. Junior dresses were in demand, and the Midwest was their birthplace. This was a perfect fit for Libby Payne; she said, "the Midwest is the everybody" (Payne 2016).

Libby Payne was quite strategic, and after hearing St. Louis was *the* place for Junior dresses, she relocated in 1938. Although she was only with the Bernard's company for three weeks, it was here that Libby (as Betty Miller) encountered her first "real" success as a moderate-price Junior designer. Buyers from department stores such as Famous-Barr, the biggest in that city at the time, enthusiastically placed orders for her designs because they knew they would be "big sellers" (Vol. 3: 113). Her next position, with Schickman and Frager, who specialized in the emerging Junior category, was an important turning point in her career. A friend who had previously worked for the firm advised Payne to take the job, encouraging her that it would not be exciting but she would really learn the foundations. She considered this a "post graduate" experience—learning the "tricks of the trade" from Mr. Schickman, a kind manager who took time to train designers (Payne 1995, Vol. 3: 113). She also increased her salary from $50 to $60 per week (the equivalent of $1,050 in 2017).

A year later when Libby's younger brother was accepted into Northwestern, she pursued a position at Johara, Inc., to watch over him and help her father with college expenses. On a visit to Chicago, Payne dropped in at the firm, spoke with the owners, and told them she "intended" to be their designer (Vol. 3: 121). A week later, she was hired. Over the next five years, Libby (Betty Miller) created numerous styles of Junior dresses that sold well and built Johara's reputation among moderate consumers. The first line she designed for the company turned out to be very successful, of which she remembered, "I knew they would sell, and they did!" (Vol. 3: 125). Payne credits Johara's pattern-maker, Harry Alaynick, as someone who imparted useful information about the fashion industry saying, "It would have taken me weeks or months to learn the things he taught me immediately" (Vol. 3: 124). Libby Payne was with Johara for six years, from October 22, 1939 until February 11, 1945, the longest design job she held up to that point.

While working for Johara, "Betty Miller" married Frank Payne, on December 13, 1941, just one week after Pearl Harbor. When Frank was sent overseas six weeks later, the newlywed Mrs. Payne continued to design Junior dresses with Johara in Chicago. Shortly after Frank's return in 1945, he was assigned to the Signal Corps Photographic Center (Army Pictorial Center) in Long Island City, New York, and Libby made her way to the center of the American fashion industry. A new city brought a new professional name. Frank told her, "You don't look much like a Betty, you look more like a Libby" and so, Midwest designer Betty Miller became New York designer Libby Payne (Payne 2016).

Although the move was precipitated by Frank's assignment, Libby Payne's experience designing Junior dresses gave her an advantage and her career really took off. Tapping into her network, Payne called Virginia Spears to say she had just relocated and was job hunting. Virginia secured her an interview with Ed London of Dartford Deb who was looking for a "Midwestern designer." Just two days after arriving in New York, Payne landed the position which she held for five years ("Youth" 1946).

Many family moves in her early life meant Libby acquired an ability to quickly make friends. As her daughter pointed out, she could make anyone feel instantly at home just by saying, "You look like you do something interesting!" (Payne 2016). Throughout her career, Libby Payne maintained relationships and expanded her network through friendships made in her personal and professional life, including regular attendance at Fashion Group luncheons with designer friend Mary Tettreault.

> Each month we went to The Fashion Group, usually in the Grand Ballroom of the Waldorf-Astoria during my early years in New York. This is an organization for women in the fields of Fashion and Advertising, and their guests. It was always interesting to meet the other people at the table, as we introduced ourselves and identified our field of interest, actually the reason for being an invited member of the Fashion Group. There were always interesting speakers or a great fashion show. When I went to the first Fashion Group Luncheon, I sat at the same round table with two famous designers, Claire McCardell and Adele Simpson. (Payne 1995, Vol. 4: 15)

Payne's remembrances, including interactions with designers whose names are well known, demonstrate the importance of networking for women in American ready-to-wear. Although working in different situations, they shared many elements of similar lived experiences.

As a career woman in the mid-twentieth century, Libby Payne encountered societal tensions over expected female roles. She was fired from Dartford Deb in December 1950 after having her second child. Manager Ed London came to Libby's home to inform her that he and his partners felt she would be too busy

Libby Payne   *Wedding Day - Dec 13, 1941*

Eugene L. Ray

FIGURE 11.1 Elizabeth "Libby" Payne on her wedding day, December 13, 1941. Image courtesy of Penny Payne.

and business was not very good, anyway. Payne responded tactfully by telling Mr. London that she understood perfectly but she was not about to stay at home. She would find another job and continue her designing career. Payne's next position was with Peggy Caswell, a woman's name on a label managed by men. At Caswell, the line that she designed was presented to buyers with management taking credit for her ideas.

From 1951 to 1956, Libby Payne worked for Bobbie Brooks, a sportswear firm based in Cleveland, Ohio, with designers and a showroom in New York. When she interviewed with owner Maury Saltzman, Payne asked for $500 a week, which was a hefty salary in the 1950s, almost $5,000 in 2017. Initially, Saltzman said he would start her at $400 a week and reevaluate in six months. What Payne did not know was that prior to her hiring, Bobbie Brooks had found success by knocking off her designs for Johara, Inc. Once Saltzman became aware that "Libby Payne" and "Betty Miller" were the same designer, her salary was raised accordingly (Vol. 4). At Bobbie Brooks, Libby Payne created several dresses that were well received by her best customer, "Mrs. Main Street America" ("Libby Payne" 1998: 1). One of her most successful, Bobbie Brooks Style #862, sold 100,000 in its first two months on the market in 1951. Department store buyers all over the country continued to place orders for this in-demand denim shirtwaist dress. It remained on the market until 1953 (Payne 1995: 51).

Payne's Junior designs included simple lines with an emphasis on details, like trimmings; she prolifically presented uncomplicated, innovative, and saleable garments ("Cotton Dresses" 1951). This creative strategy was especially valuable for success in the moderate consumer market, as she could keep costs low and make a profit. Between 1951 and 1956, Bobbie Brooks' annual gross sales grew from $12 million to $19.5 million (Payne 1995: 48). Despite the company's success, Payne was fired from Bobbie Brooks and replaced by a male fashion director.

Searching for a job after Bobbie Brooks, Payne went to see Ed London who was now at Toni Edwards, letting him know that she was on the market and had used him as a reference. London jokingly told her that he would give her a "terrible recommendation" because he would like to have her for himself (after previously firing her when she had a second child). Confident in her track record, she responded, "Oh Mr. London, working for a large volume company, I've learned to make a lot of money. With your volume, you couldn't possibly pay me that much!" London's accountant chimed in to say, "Ed, you'd better pay her what she's asking. She's the only designer you've ever had who made money for you" (Payne 1995, Vol. 4: 67). Payne designed dresses under the Toni Edwards label for the next two years ("Buyers" 1958).

From early on, Libby Payne realized the importance of maintaining good relationships with the right people in the industry. Her network was a tremendous resource in finding and securing jobs, an experience all too common for moderate price-point fashion designers. Despite being let go from many positions, she was

FIGURE 11.2 Bobbie Brooks Style #862, designed by Libby Payne in 1951. Image out of copyright.

never without work for more than two months throughout her long career. Of the ten different jobs she held in New York City, all were in the Garment District, and sometimes she only relocated to different floors in the same building; Libby Payne worked at 1400 and 1407 Broadway for the majority of her design career.

She landed all but one of those positions through co-workers and friends, ex-bosses, and especially fabrics and trimmings salesmen who were the "backbone" of the industry. In her memoir notebooks, Payne (1995) admitted, "the fabric or trimming salesman with whom a designer works is extremely important to the designer's success. They must become the designer's friend and confidant" (Vol. 4: 101). Despite the advice of fabric salesman Mr. Messner, she took a job at Parade Dress after Toni Edwards because of a good base salary. Her talents, showcased in a *Women's Wear Daily* article ("Parade" 1956), resulted in $3 million worth of business. However, Parade "gypped" Payne out of her bonus, and she realized they were, in fact, "untrustworthy scoundrels" (Vol. 4: 71).

One of the most prominent moderate labels for which Payne designed was Jonathan Logan, Inc., a large firm with twelve sub-divisions who sold at retailers such as B. Altman, Bloomingdale's, and Gimbels (Hanenberg 1969). She worked for Jonathan Logan, Inc., for eighteen years and first experienced trips to Europe, gathering new inspiration for her marketable designs. She started in the Betty Barclay division, Logan's Junior and Petite line, and was also asked to be responsible for 25 percent of the Bleeker Street line because she ran a "fast and prolific" design room. In a short amount of time, Bleeker Street's annual sales reached $62 million and they "practically owned Bloomie's Misses dress department" in the mid-1960s (Vol. 4: 89–91). Payne's 25 percent responsibility carried 90 percent of the orders. Although she enjoyed designing for Betty Barclay, she permanently moved to the Bleeker Street division as she wanted to "go with the new" (Vol. 4: 91).

Payne's natural gravitation toward "newness" made her a very innovative designer. She liked to use unexpected color combinations, prints, or fabrics just introduced to the market. One of her most successful Bleeker Street designs in the 1970s was a cream-colored group featuring the new "Raschel knits" with alternating pastel colors in a scalloped pattern. This collection—a jacket with scallop detail, a solid cream-colored collar, and matching solid cream colored dress—earned a full-color page in the *Sunday New York Times Magazine* from March 16, 1975. Similar to Bobbie Brooks Style #862, 100,000 units of the Bleeker Street group sold and shipped in two months. Payne later learned that Merry-Go-Round, the fabric manufacturer, distributed 3,000,000 yards of the same pattern to other manufacturers who copied her jacket dress all over the world (Payne 1995: 103).

As the designer, Payne was responsible for presenting her line to a range of department store buyers at the manufacturer's showroom. She said, "I always knew when I was doing well by the reaction of the 'nodders,'" referring to people in the audience who nodded approval (Vol. 4: 53). Despite the warm reception to her creations, she left Jonathan Logan in 1979 after being told she was "too old" to be designing young dresses (Vol. 4: 155).

One of her favorite fabric salesmen, Nat Marcus, knew this was not the case and referred Payne to Jack Baker of Tracy!/St. Barths who reassured her, "once a good

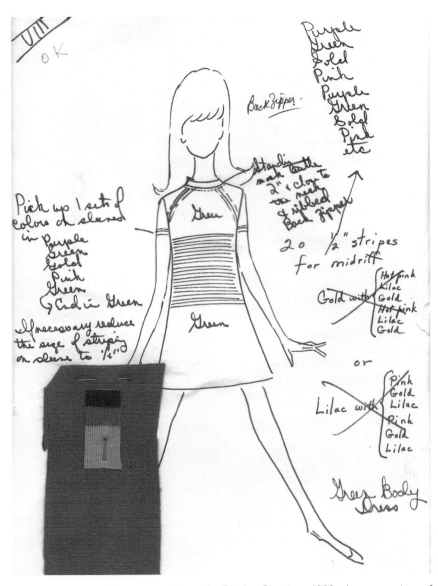

FIGURE 11.3 Sketch by Libby Payne for Bleeker Street, *c.* 1960s. Image courtesy of Penny Payne.

designer, always a good designer" (Vol. 4: 155). Although in her sixties, Libby Payne's fertile imagination never let her feel old or out of place. When visiting one of her fabric suppliers, she spotted a group of gray, white, and pink trimmings fabrics in a corner. With these bolts, she designed a dropped waist dress for Tracy! that sold out in one day. Buyers told Payne the reason sales were so exceptional was because the style of the dress and color combination were "new"; it was "rare to find newness" in the American ready-to-wear market at the time (Vol. 4: 160). Knockoffs in this color combination were soon seen on selling floors "all over the place." Payne believed this dress "made" her reputation, stating, "I have always been very much pleased when I see someone wearing the fabrics or clothes which I designed" (Vol. 4: 160).

It was with Jack Baker's son, Beau, that Libby learned to shop the SoHo stores for inspiration that would appeal to contemporary young consumers. Payne helped to turn Tracy! around; buyers said the line had not looked so good in years, assuming the styles were created by a young "swinging" designer. It was also with Beau Baker that Libby Payne finally accomplished the one thing that she had not originally set out to do but many American moderate-price-zone designers wish for: their own name on a label. "Baker-Payne" was added as a secondary label to St. Barths' clothing in the early 1980s. Her label-bearing success was short-lived. When Baker's business partner broke off and business slowed down, she parted ways with St. Barths in 1985.

By this time the industry had changed. The shift to offshore manufacturing was underway. Moderate-price-zone fashion designers no longer created styles in close proximity with production. The days where a network of different supply chain stakeholders—designers, manufacturers, pattern-makers, fabrics and trimmings salesmen, and so on—were all located in the Garment District, sometimes in the same building, were gone. Libby Payne began freelance designing, working for three different houses over a two-month period, an activity she did not enjoy. She concluded, "freelance was definitely for beginners" (Vol. 4: 175), and it is clear from her memoirs, at that point in her career, Payne was far from a beginner.

> After "running the whole show," working side by side with my bosses on an executive level, making presentations to the top fashion directors and buyers, setting trends or interpreting them, designing fabrics and trims as well as choosing them, running large design rooms, putting on fashion shows, making judgments that brought millions of dollars to the large firms whom I had helped build, this was "penny-ante" stuff. Frank said, "it's like asking Michelangelo to 'paint by numbers.'" (Vol. 4: 176)

After fifty years in the industry, working behind more than thirty labels, Libby Payne's daughter remembered, "I think she was ready to retire. The business just wasn't the same anymore" (Payne 2016). Payne left the fashion industry in 1987. In addition to spending more time on their boat, she and Frank became interested in genealogy. What began as a hobby grew into an eight-year legacy project. After carefully recording her life and career experiences as a moderate ready-to-wear designer, Libby Payne died of breast cancer at the age of 80 in 1997.

Throughout her long career, Elizabeth "Libby" Miller Payne experienced the evolution of the American fashion industry first-hand, from "bluffing"

FIGURE 11.4 "Baker Payne" label for St. Barths *c.* 1982/83. Image courtesy of Penny Payne.

her way into a Midwest manufacturer's workroom in the 1930s to concluding as a sometimes freelance designer with a New York showroom and offsite production in the 1980s. Her story provides insights to the business behind accessible moderately priced ready-to-wear clothing, the evolution of the fashion designer, and secrets to success in this role. Libby Payne's accomplishments were grounded by her background and foundational experiences, furthered by her personal characteristics, expanded by her career aptitude, powered by her network, and resulted in considerable personal influence, although the only evidence of her name on a retail selling floor was shared billing on a short-lived secondary label.

Contemporary fashion designers often come to the career path with aspirations of becoming a "celebrity," highlighted in the media when their latest collection creates a buzz. That was not the case with Libby Payne. In comparison to her contributions, press coverage of Payne was limited. Two local newspaper articles have been located; in one she announced, "everybody deserves quality fashion" (Castleberry 1968; Manley 1968). She did not set out to be famous. She set out to work hard, be successful, and make her family proud, all of which she achieved. Libby Payne was connected with "the everybody," and they gladly purchased her moderately priced creations. Her talent was designing clothing with "newness" that filled retail selling floors and appealed to "Mrs. Main Street America." Payne's experience can be viewed as a lens that reflects the American moderate fashion industry's growth and change. The value of her legacy and foresight in carefully documenting her accomplishment cannot be overstated. The career of Libby Payne helps us understand American fashion.

Archival Source

Payne, E.M. (1995) "Things I Remember," Volumes 1–4. Unpublished manuscript in collection of Penny Payne.

Bibliography

"Buyers Order Free Translations of Trapeze" (1958), *Women's Wear Daily*, April 15: 38.
Castleberry, V. (1968), "Dreams Style Fabric of Life," *The Dallas Times Herald*, March 5, n.p.
Cotton Dresses; Rayon Suits; Separates in Cleveland Spring Group for Juniors" (1951), *Women's Wear Daily*, November 7: 67.
Hanenberg, P. (1969), "Jonathan Logan to Build Within," *Women's Wear Daily*, April 24: 1–3.
"Libby Payne, Fashion Designer" (1998), *Roslyn News*, January 16: 1.
"Louise Mulligan, Inc., New Chicago Firm" (1935), *Women's Wear Daily*, May 14: 17.
Manley, F. (1968), "Fashion Story Tells of Good Taste," *Dallas Morning News*, March 5: n.p.
"Parade Dress Co. Is New Firm" (1959), *Women's Wear Daily*, October 6: 37.
Payne, P. (2016), Interviewed by Caroline Surrarrer, January 15.
"Youth Carrying on in the Dress Business" (1946), *Women's Wear Daily*, March 29: 9.

12 RUTH FINLEY'S "FASHION CALENDAR"

NATALIE NUDELL

Although listings are repeated until the scheduled date of each event, they frequently incorporate IMPORTANT CHANGES. A CAREFUL CHECK OF EVERY ISSUE will yield maximum use of Fashion Calendar to the reader. (Ruth Finley, Publisher)[1]

Immediately recognizable by its red or pink cover and pink pages, *Fashion Calendar*, founded and published by Ruth Finley, established and maintained the American fashion schedule as well as the official timetable of New York Fashion Week (NYFW) for approximately seventy years.[2] Widely known by those working within the fashion industry in the United States and abroad, *Fashion Calendar* was at first run from Finley's home office with a very small team and quickly became the standard industry publication for fashion dates at a time when there was little cohesion or structure among the manufacturers of Seventh Avenue. *Fashion Calendar*, therefore, served as the consolidator of information for people working within the fashion industry, and was designed as a tool to navigate the increasingly large American fashion business. *Fashion Calendar*, and by extension Finley, occupied a central role in the development and evolution of the fashion industry and provided an essential service.

In the development of the postwar American fashion industry, as in other industries, networks of power, spheres of influence, and networks of information helped form conduits and systems in which organizations and individuals could operate. Within the pages of the *Calendar* we can track the careers, initiatives, collections, and trajectories of the majority of the designers discussed in this collection of chapters.[3] There were numerous practices that denoted participation

FIGURE 12.1 Ruth Finley's *Fashion Calendar* featured a boldly graphic red or pink cover, as seen in this example from 1947. Image courtesy of Fashion Institute of Technology| SUNY, Gladys Marcus Library Special Collections and FIT Archives.

within the commercial community of the fashion business in the United States, and to some degree they remain present today. This includes seasonal fashion shows, showroom events and openings, and the regular promotion of all of these information vehicles through public relations representation and media coverage. It is standard practice for a designer or brand to list the dates of their fashion show and showroom openings in the *Fashion Calendar*, as it is the site where all of the information about the goings on of the entire industry is concentrated. The

Fashion Calendar served as a tool for the professionalization of the American fashion industry. All of the designers discussed here used *Fashion Calendar* as a means to engage with and fit within the American fashion system, which was open and democratic in nature, but already had embedded power networks and structures to denote influence. I wish to frame the *Fashion Calendar* as not only a logistical tool, but as a site of engagement and exchange of information about the networks of the fashion community.

As a female fashion executive, Finley not only acted as the centripetal organizing force and provided the forum for this engagement, but she and her publication are an example of how affiliations within the spheres of influence can determine one's career trajectory. Finley, who hails from Haverhill, Massachusetts, began thinking of starting a clearinghouse for fashion events while still attending Simmons College in Boston between 1937 and 1941. Her studies toward a major in journalism and minor in nutrition led her to a summer internship in New York at the Food Section of the *New York Herald Tribune*. There, Finley met Eugenia Sheppard, the publication's fashion writer. Sheppard introduced Finley to fashion and Eleanor Lambert.[4] Lambert is understood to have been a key force in the development of the American fashion industry during the Second World War. The German occupation of Paris significantly reduced the production of the French fashion industry. In 1941, the entry of America into the war interrupted the movement of fashion from Europe. Lambert organized an event called "Press-Week," a precursor to today's Fashion Week. Press-Week would bring together domestic fashion writers and editors twice a year to show the work of American designers and manufacturers.

During Finley's final summer at college, she worked as a "girl Friday," what would today be described as an intern, for a Red Cross fashion show organized by Lambert. While in New York, Finley met with two fashion editors who were family acquaintances. The editors expressed their frustrations over conflictingly scheduled fashion events, making it impossible to attend both. This conversation prompted Finley to strategize how she would carve out a place for herself within the growing American fashion industry.

While living in New York during college and after she graduated, Finley often worked in the evenings as a theater usher to supplement her income. New York's theaters had a central schedule of theater dates and events. Finley surmised that the fashion industry was in need of a clearinghouse, a publication that could bring together the people and organizations involved in American fashion. At the time, the American fashion industry was unstructured, and considered to be focused on commercial garments rather than participating in driving the evolution of design. With the blessing of her mentor, Eleanor Lambert, Finley began *Fashion Calendar* as a subscription-based, weekly publication in 1945, before the end of the Second World War.[5]

In Paris, London, and Italy (Rome, Florence, and later Milan) the governing bodies that organize the respective European fashion industries are tied to government ministries and are organized by centralized institutions. The Chambre Syndicale de la Haute-Couture Parisienne, most notably, set the model for governing its national industry, with a top-down approach and very strict rules limiting participation. Such governing bodies continue to schedule the semi-annual fashion shows. The disjointed nature of the mid-twentieth-century American fashion industry enabled an independent outsider to provide the service of initiating and maintaining the "official" schedule. From its foundation and within its pages, the innumerable stories the *Calendar* provides evince the richness of this publication as a resource for understanding the evolution and inner dynamics of the American fashion industry.

The *Fashion Calendar* debuted as a clearinghouse for fashion information; however, over time the publication became the authority on the scheduling of fashion and social events in New York. The *Calendar* listed all domestic fashion shows, department store and retail openings, market weeks, promotional presentations for press and buyers, and the dates and schedules for continuous showings in showrooms. Much of the same audience that attended fashion shows and fashion events also attended the various social and promotional events; thus, it became important for Finley to understand the audience for each event and advise event organizers on the ideal date and time, and often location, for hosting an event in order to maximize attendance and exposure. The *Calendar*, therefore, listed all types of events, which worked as conduits to navigate the optics and promotion of a company, including fundraisers, charity fashion shows, the sponsorship of designers by large companies, and collaborations between companies. An exploration into the listings of some designers discussed in earlier chapters of this book demonstrates varying degrees of engagement with the American fashion system and its power networks.

Some regular subscribers, including Fira Benenson, Mollie Parnis (at first as Parnis-Livingston), Kiviette, and Tina Leser, listed their showroom openings and fashion show dates and locations throughout the periods their businesses were in operation as well as engaged within the established system of promotional conduits.

The benefit fashion show was an established way of participating within the community of the fashion industry, promoting designs to the press and directly to clients, while aligning the company with a charitable cause. On January 26, 1949, Fira Benenson presented her spring 1949 collection at a fashion show luncheon sponsored by the New York Heart Association, held at the Cotillion Room at the Hotel Pierre. The show also featured accessories, such as "hats from Germaine Vittu, furs from John Dragonette, jewels from Cartier ... Press by invitation, public by reservation" (Finley 1949a: 6). Along the same lines, Kiviette, with another

```
DATE          WHAT'S GOING ON            GIVEN BY                WHERE

┌──── AMERICAN DESIGNER SHOWINGS - SPRING 1969 - FOR VISITING PRESS (January 5-10) ────┐

Unless otherwise noted, all showings will be held in the GRAND BALLROOM, DELMONICO'S,
59th Street and Park Avenue. By invitation.  Publicity: Eleanor Lambert, MU. 8-2130.

Sun., Jan. 5:  2:00 P.M.  SCAASI KNITS for TANNEL
               3:00 P.M.  HELEN LEE and ALYSSA
               4:00 P.M.  FASHION FORECAST - Eleanor Lambert
               7:30 P.M.  MEET THE PARTICIPATING DESIGNERS(cocktail-buffet)CRYSTAL ROOM
                            Guests of Mr. & Mrs. S. Joseph Tankoos, Jr. of Delmonico's

Mon., Jan. 6:  8:00 A.M.  Breakfast
               8:30 A.M.  ANNE KLEIN AND COMPANY
               9:00 A.M.  JACQUES TIFFEAU
               9:45 A.M.  BILL BLASS for MAURICE RENTNER
              10:30 A.M.  MOLLIE PARNIS
              11:15 A.M.  MALLORY
              12:00 Noon  Writing Period
               1:00 P.M.  JERRY SILVERMAN by SHANNON RODGERS (luncheon)
               2:30 P.M.  TRIGERE
               3:15 P.M.  GEOFFREY BEENE
               4:00 P.M.  ANNE FOGARTY
               4:45 P.M.  SARMI
               5:30 P.M.  Writing Period
               6:15 P.M.  NATIONAL FOOTWEAR INSTITUTE (cocktails) CRYSTAL ROOM
               7:45 P.M.  HYSTRON FIBERS (dinner)           PARKE-BERNET GALLERIES
                            (buses leave Delmonico's 7:15 P.M.)

Tues., Jan. 7:  8:00 A.M.  MEN'S FASHIONS (breakfast)
                             Bill Blass, Oleg Cassini, John Weitz
                9:00 A.M.  ADELE SIMPSON
                9:45 A.M.  JERRY FEDER of ANNE KLEIN for HADLEY
               10:30 A.M.  GINO CHARLES (Beverly Moyer and Bill Denatale)
               11:15 A.M.  HERBERT & BETH LEVINE; ADOLFO (aperitif)-COLONNADE SUITE
               12:00 Noon  Writing Period
                1:00 P.M.  WARNER SLIMWEAR (luncheon)
                2:30 P.M.  CHESTER WEINBERG
                3:15 P.M.  MR. MORT (Stan Herman)
                4:00 P.M.  STAVROPOULOS
                4:45 P.M.  MR. JOHN (champagne)              24 WEST 57TH STREET
                5:45 P.M.  NATIONAL COTTON COUNCIL (cocktails)
                7:30 P.M.  LENTHERIC (dinner)                L'ETOILE
                             "Tweed" Designer Award          1 EAST 59TH STREET

Wed., Jan. 8:  8:00 A.M.  MISTER PANTS, LYNN STUART, PANTSVILLE, GHIA (breakfast)
               9:00 A.M.  KASPER for JOAN LESLIE
               9:45 A.M.  KIMBERLY
              10:30 A.M.  CHRISTIAN DIOR-NEW YORK
              11:15 A.M.  Writing Period
              12:30 P.M.  DU PONT COMPANY (luncheon)         PLAZA - BALLROOM
               2:30 P.M.  FLORENCE EISEMAN
               3:15 P.M.  VICTOR JORIS for CUDDLECOAT
               4:00 P.M.  OLGA UNDERFASHIONS (cocktails)     CRYSTAL BALLROOM
               5:30 P.M.  LA BANQUE CONTINENTALE             785 FIFTH AVENUE (60TH)
                            "The New World of Pushbutton Money"
               7:30 P.M.  BURLINGTON INDUSTRIES (dinner)     PLAZA - BALLROOM
           ──────────────── (continued on following page) ──────────────── .2.
```

FIGURE 12.2 *Fashion Calendar*, January 6, 1969, p. 2. Schedule for the Spring 1969 "American Designer Showings" organized by Eleanor Lambert. Included in the listing are the showings for Helen Lee and Mollie Parnis, among some of the most noted American fashion designers of the twentieth century, such as Bill Blass, Geoffrey Beene, Anne Fogarty, and Anne Klein. This listing demonstrates the shift in how design attribution was promoted within the fashion industry, where the designer's name is associated with the manufacturer although perhaps not yet included on the label. Image courtesy of Fashion Institute of Technology|SUNY, Gladys Marcus Library Special Collections and FIT Archives.

group of designers, in March 1950, participated in a charity fashion show for the Israel Orphan Asylum (Finley 1950b: 1).

Lambert's influence was unmatched, and she regularly organized fundraising events for charitable organizations and the industry associations that she directed, such as the New York Dress Institute (NYDI), the New York Couture Group (NYCG)—and after 1962 for the Council of Fashion Designers of America (CFDA). These were important occasions where the community that formed the industry gathered. The 1949 NYDI annual "March of Dimes" fashion show luncheon organized by Lambert and held in the Grand Ballroom of the Waldorf Astoria, benefited the National Foundation for Infantile Paralysis and included designs from over forty of the most important American designers and department stores of the era, including Mollie Parnis, Tina Leser, and Fira Benenson (Finley 1949b: 3).

Thematic fashion shows sponsored by large textile and chemical firms were another established means to engage with the fashion industry; their popularity provides insight into broader shifts in material culture toward synthetics in the postwar period. The "Fashion Accents Crisp" cocktail-party fashion show took place on February 2, 1949. The show organized by Linit Starch of The Linit Division of Corn Products presented "advance 1949 summer cotton fashions by lead designers," and among the long list of participants in this sponsored show were Claire McCardell, Pauline Trigère, and Tina Leser (Finley 1949a: 8). A similar fashion show in 1949 promoted the Kee Zipper Company and included designs by Leser that utilized the sponsor's product (Finley 1949c: 4). The following year, Fira Benenson participated in a sponsored fashion show with the Crompton Richmond Textile Corporation, which featured designs made with the company's velvet, corduroy, and velveteen fabrics (Finley 1950b: 3).

Finley's democratic approach enhanced the openness of the American fashion industry, which was largely based in New York City, to outside forces and represents a continuity of that participation. The publication not only printed listings advertised by subscribers for subscribers but also allowed outsiders and newcomers, domestic and foreign, to place single listings aimed at accessing the *Calendar*'s readership and networks. Although there is no mention of Jean Wright, the company's head designer, Lilli-Ann of San Francisco held a breakfast press showing of fall suits at the Park Lane Hotel's Tapestry Room in the Spring of 1949 (Finley 1949e: 7). American design firms and manufacturers that were based in other metropolitan centers throughout the United States would often hold press events in New York to give the company exposure to the New York and foreign press.

The commercial and professional networks of the American fashion industry prior to the founding of the CFDA shifted over time in relation to Lambert's "Press-Week" and its participants. Eleanor Lambert started Press-Week, the precursor to New York Fashion Week in 1943, bringing together the seasonal presentations of the domestic American designers who were part of the NYDI promotional organization, which later became the NYCG. Other groups also organized shows, such as the Fashion Originators Guild of America (FOGA), that Finley describes as the "volume people." We can track that in the early 1950s the group of designers who had previously been showing under the NYDI promotional organization were re-organized as the NYCG, and showed during Press-Week as the "Couture Group," represented by Lambert. By the end of the 1950s, Kittie Campbell and later Mildred Sullivan took over as directors of the Couture Group and continued using the "NYCG Press-Week" name and opened it to mass market brands. Lambert thus reoriented her group of American designers away from the "couture" label to the decidedly American ready-to-wear connotations of "American Designer Showings," made up of design houses her public relations company represented. The most notable American designers of the twentieth century, such as Anne Klein, Ralph Lauren, Calvin Klein, Bill Blass, Oleg Cassini, Oscar de la Renta, and many more, were affiliated or worked with Lambert as their publicist.

Both Suzanne Godart and Helen Lee, the children's-wear designers, worked with Lambert for publicity.[6] Helen Lee's collections were part of the American Designer Showings fashion show schedule, and regularly grouped with other children's-wear companies. Godart on the other hand did not show during fashion week, but hired Lambert for publicity for a showing she did on November 22, 1949, for her "spring collection of children's clothes sizes 2-12" for press and buyers at the Hampshire House Cottage (Finley 1949g: 3).

Mollie Parnis went from running the Parnis-Livington Company, a member of FOGA, to becoming the face of the reconceptualized "Mollie Parnis" label. The company began working with Lambert for publicity after it was renamed for its female founder. Mollie Parnis was included in the American Designer Showings schedule, pivoting the company away from its manufacturing origins to a fashion house headed by a named designer (Finley 1950a: 1). Thus, aligning with Lambert and her group of designers enabled the movement into a different network of influence within the commercial community of the fashion industry.

Alternatively, Catherine Scott Ltd., which was established in Chicago, took the plunge in the summer of 1965, opening a showroom in New York City (Finley 1965a: 6). We can see from the listings found in the *Fashion Calendar* of that year that the company opened its showroom in one of the most prestigious addresses in the Garment District—550 Seventh Avenue—with a cocktail reception and press preview of their fall 1965 collection. The company run by Nicky Ladany hired Lambert for publicity and held fashion shows for two seasons on the American Designer Showings schedule with the likes of Mollie Parnis and Helen Lee, among others (Finley 1965b: 14–15). In the spring of 1966, the Catherine Scott label held a showing of its collection in their showroom but opted out of holding a formal fashion show during fashion week. Perhaps due to related costs or not enough traction with their New York showroom, by the end of 1966 the company was no longer listing in *Fashion Calendar*.

The May 19, 1969, issue included a listing that utilized the *Fashion Calendar* as a means to announce a new fashion label to the scene and used established conduits such as a sponsored event, name recognition, and foreign prestige for promotion. The launch of Mia-Vicky for Youthquake was held at the MGM Theater in cooperation with Metro-Goldwyn Mayer, where "Mia Fonssagrives and Vicky Tiel of Paris, present[ed] a preview of their first junior dress collection for Youthquake" (Finley 1969: 13). Fonssagrives, daughter of the famous model Lisa Fonssagrives and stepdaughter of photographer Irving Penn, partnered with Vicky Tiel, an American who had been working in Paris, on a youth-driven fashion line, and launched the label in cooperation with a Hollywood film studio. Over time, the *Calendar* helped form a community for the American industry where established members intermingled with newcomers, vying for publicity and a larger market.

The *Calendar* also included the schedule for the European showings and other various fashion market and promotional events throughout Europe. With the consistent aim of remaining neutral to the machinations of the fashion industry, the publication never included image-based advertisements, sold ad space, or used any other promotional methods to increase profitability, relying on its subscription-based model. Each listing denoted who was putting on the event, its purpose, and intended audience. Listings often included a short blurb taken from the press release. Logistical information was also included, such as time, location, and contact information, for how to request an invitation or book an appointment. The creation of informational networks is another key component of the *Fashion Calendar*. One could access the direct telephone numbers, contact information, and addresses of almost all subscribers, enabling readers a means of direct engagement with the fashion community in New York.

Ruth Finley was one of the few people in the American fashion industry who interacted and worked with virtually all the designers, manufacturers, PR houses, and fashion show producers and dealt with many more elements of the supply chain that make up the American fashion system. It was necessary for all these actors to go through *Fashion Calendar* in order to find the right time to present their event. It was not only crucial to be listed in the *Calendar*; what was equally important was to consult and work with Finley and her small team to ensure that all elements of a show come together. The *Calendar* perpetuated networks of information and influence, and represented the growing establishment of industry foundations, organizations, professional associations, informational forums, and events held to allow for the exchange of ideas and the broadening of professional networks in the ever-growing American fashion business.

As early as 1949, an important industry group, the Advertising Women of New York (ADWNY), was holding monthly luncheon workshops and discussions on opportunities for women in fashion (Finley 1949d: 3). Even at a glance, it is clear from reading through *Fashion Calendar* that women were working at all levels in the fashion industry, despite the prevailing assumption that in the postwar period women were expected to return to working exclusively in the home. Finley and other women executives were shaping the industry we see today. The meeting, held as a "clinic" by ADWNY in March 1949, is particularly interesting because it aimed to educate attendees about public relations and how it related to the fashion industry and represents a space where women already established in fashion and advertising were encouraging others to participate. This further enabled a socially acceptable entrée into working in the fashion business through established networks that did not involve working in the manufacturers on Seventh Avenue, reflecting Finley's experiences with Eugenia Sheppard and Eleanor Lambert early in her career.

Without a fashion show or presentation a designer's collection will likely never enter the public sphere. This need for exposure and exchange makes *Fashion Calendar* a central point where information about events and initiatives in the fashion world coexists and is exchanged. Ruth Finley's *Fashion Calendar* was a constant independent organizing force for the American fashion industry from its earliest years until it was acquired by the CFDA in 2014. The personal tone of Finley's interactions with her subscribers and her propensity to be the industry's consummate problem-solver made her a key figure in the American fashion system, reflecting the important impact of female fashion executives in its evolution. In 1993 the CFDA formalized NYFW with the organization of Seventh on Sixth at Bryant Park, and further entrusted Finley with her role as the keeper of the timetable. *Fashion Calendar* became the "official" calendar—the publication of record— further solidifying its value as a historical document as it is reflective of established informational and power networks. The *Fashion Calendar* is therefore also a record of the importance of the participation of women fashion executives in the growth of the American fashion industry from the Second World War to the present day.

Finley was instrumental in the logistical maneuvering that enabled maximum attendance for fashion shows, by endeavoring to eliminate conflicts. This allowed Finley to pivot into the position of the arbiter of the "official" fashion calendar of NYFW. The *Fashion Calendar* therefore is not just a service to the fashion industry; it quickly became an important element in the development of the industry as well as representational of its commercial culture and networks.

Despite its long lifespan, the publication remained a guide for insiders. Although she was awarded the CFDA Board of Director's Tribute Award in 2014 and the Fashion Institute of Technology's President's Lifetime Achievement Award in 2016, Ruth Finley and her contribution to American fashion are largely unknown outside the industry. Finley and her story remain one of a kind; however, the *Fashion Calendars* themselves are an invaluable resource and are also a key to unlocking more of the hidden history of American fashion.

Archival Source

The Ruth Finley Collection, Special Collections at the Fashion Institute of
Technology, New York, NY.

Notes

1   These two sentences (and a similar earlier version) constitute the only message
delivered to the readers of *Fashion Calendar* directly from publisher Ruth Finley.

2   Finley herself cannot pinpoint the date the first issue of *Fashion Calendar* was
published. There are only a handful of surviving *Calendars* that predate 1949.
Interestingly, in 1950, a note appeared on the cover asserting that the *Calendar* was in
its "tenth year of publication." The note subsisted throughout almost the entire run.
Clearly, the implication is that the first issue came out sometime in 1940. However,
Finley has admitted to stretching the truth in order to present the *Calendar* as more
established than it truly was. Her best estimate is that the first issue was printed in
1945, a few years after she graduated from college. The American fashion industry
has evolved since the first print of *Fashion Calendar* in relation to shifting commercial
culture, technological advancements, and the globalization of markets. In recent years
the Council of Fashion Designers of America (CFDA) has grown exponentially and
aims to exert more authority over American fashion and its schedule, culminating
with its acquisition of *Fashion Calendar* from Finley in 2014. The subscription-based
service is currently exclusively online and has instituted an application process for
designers or firms to be listed, but continues to support emerging talent through the
CFDA Fashion Incubator.

3   All of the designers discussed in this book and whose businesses were in operation
after 1945 are represented with listings in the *Fashion Calendar*, except for Zelda
Wynn Valdes, Libby Payne, and Sandra Garratt.

4   Lambert was the press director for the New York Dress Institute, which was an early
promotional organization of women's garment manufacturers in New York.

5   *Fashion Calendar* was originally a weekly publication. In 1989 it became biweekly.

6   The November 21, 1949 issue of *Fashion Calendar* has a listing for "Suzanne Godert"
[*sic*].

Bibliography

Blanks, T. (2016), "How to Fix the Fashion System," *The Business of Fashion*. [Online],
February 8. Available from: https://www.businessoffashion.com/articles/opinion/the
-roundtable-fixing-the-fashion-system
Evans, C. (2001), "The Enchanted Spectacle," *Fashion Theory*, 5(3): 271–310. August 1.
Available from: http://www.tandfonline.com/doi/abs/10.2752/136270401778960865

Finley, R. (1949a), *Fashion Calendar*, January 17.

Finley, R. (1949b), *Fashion Calendar*, January 24.

Finley, R. (1949c), *Fashion Calendar*, February 2.

Finley, R. (1949d), *Fashion Calendar*, March 7.

Finley, R. (1949e), *Fashion Calendar*, April 18.

Finley, R. (1949f), *Fashion Calendar*, October 31.

Finley, R. (1949g), *Fashion Calendar*, November 21.

Finley, R. (1950a), *Fashion Calendar*, February 27.

Finley, R. (1950b), *Fashion Calendar*, March 20.

Finley, R. (1965a), *Fashion Calendar*, May 10.

Finley, R. (1965b), *Fashion Calendar*, June 14.

Finley, R. (1966), *Fashion Calendar*, July 4.

Finley, R. (1967), *Fashion Calendar*, January 9.

Finley, R. (1969), *Fashion Calendar*, May 19.

Gregg Duggan, G. (2001), "The Greatest Show on Earth: A Look at Contemporary Fashion Shows and Their Relationship to Performance Art," *Fashion Theory*, 5(3): 243–270. August 1. Available from: http://www.tandfonline.com/doi /abs/10.2752/136270401778960883

Interviews

Finley, R. (2015), Interview with Natalie Nudell. January 13, 2015, New York.

Herman, S. (2015), Interview with Natalie Nudell. January 10, 2015, New York.

Koda, H. (2015), Interview with Natalie Nudell. May 20, 2015, New York.

Mallis, F. (2015), Interview with Natalie Nudell. January 10, 2015, New York.

Trivette, K. (2016), Interview with Natalie Nudell. April 7, 2016, New York.

PART THREE

HOLLYWOOD, BROADWAY, AND SEVENTH AVENUE

13 VIOLA DIMMITT: LOS ANGELES ENTREPRENEUR

SHELLY FOOTE

Viola S. Dimmitt was one of the pioneers in the California ready-to-wear industry, and one of the earliest name-recognized designing manufacturers in Los Angeles. She was one of the first Los Angeles–based fashion designers to create dresses, particularly evening and wedding dresses, for a national market. An examination of her business and her designs provides an intriguing glimpse into the development of the Los Angeles fashion industry; it also points out the complicated relationship between the Hollywood film industry, local fashion designers, and the marketing of the concept of Hollywood glamour through fashion to the American public.

Viola Smith was a native Californian, having been born in San Bernardino County in 1893. In later life she sometimes altered that date to 1898 and occasionally to 1901, the latter after she married Alan C. Morgan, a man who was about fifteen years her junior. However, by the time she was 17, she is listed in the 1910 Census as living in a rooming house in Los Angeles and working as a telephone operator. Within a few short years, she married Frederick Dimmitt, a bookkeeper for an iron works. They resided in Pasadena, not too distant from downtown Los Angeles. Soon she was the mother of two children, although the daughter passed away as a toddler. Her husband became ill, dying in 1920, leaving her with a young son to support. These circumstances forced her to seek regular employment in the workforce. In a syndicated article published in 1930 (NEA Service), she stated,

> I had never thought of working until my husband became ill. Even then I merely made children's aprons and other gifts that I sold through the women's exchange. It took me a few years to graduate to making dresses.

She was being modest, because within two years of her husband's death she was listed in the 1922 Los Angeles City Directory as a designer at Polly Smart, a housedress manufacturer in Los Angeles. She became dissatisfied with working for the company, believing she had used her creative ability but was receiving a modest salary. In the same 1930 interview she recounted how, one day in 1924, as she shopped for fabric to make a dress for someone (which might imply that she already had a small custom dressmaking business in addition to her job at Polly Smart), she noticed a vacant building and considered opening her own business. She only had $250 available to invest but received credit. She had one employee when she opened, but within three months she had added an additional nineteen workers. She moved several times within the first five years, each into larger facilities; by 1930 she employed 100 people.

Her business operated under the name Viola S. Dimmitt, the same name that appeared on all her labels and later advertisements. When columnist Tamara Andreeva wrote about Dimmitt in 1943 she noted that Dimmitt "went into design and custom-made clothes as a matter of necessity," further describing Dimmitt bringing bold color and imaginative line to her designs (Andreeva 1943). While her business may have started out as a custom one, its rapid expansion in space and numbers of employees indicates that at some point she also produced ready-to-wear. In all probability her business was a combination of the two—a ready-to-wear one with some custom designs for local residents and the film industry.

The California fashion industry was emerging in the 1920s. Its development had lagged behind the East Coast, where a plentiful immigrant labor force—often skilled in the needle trades—combined with technological developments in manufacturing and a transportation system that provided delivery allowed the ready-to-wear industry to grow. By the 1920s Americans could purchase stylish readymade clothing in a wide range of price points (Kidwell and Christman 1974).

As Los Angeles clothing manufactories opened in the early twentieth century, many of them specialized in sport clothing or casual clothes. While the *California Stylist* ("The Dream" 1945) claimed that the first dresses were made in Los Angeles in 1923, that information may not be correct since Dimmitt herself was working for Polly Smart in 1922. Nevertheless, this information indicates that her business was at the forefront of dress manufacturing in Los Angeles. That same trade magazine claimed that she was also the first to offer evening dresses ("Who Are the Real Designers???" 1941).

The growth of advertising, label recognition, and the plethora of fashion information available to the public through magazines and newspapers in the 1920s and 1930s were essential ingredients to bring the ready-to-wear industry to maturity. California was aided in its entry into clothing production by the popularity of movies and the coverage of movie stars and the clothes they wore on and off the screen and featured in movie magazines such as *Photoplay* and *Movie Mirror*. Initially both San Francisco and Los Angeles were impeded in establishing a national market by the distance between California and the more populated East Coast. As a result, they developed a local market and tended to encourage the development of distinctive local styles (Leventon 2011).

Dimmitt's business was located in downtown Los Angeles, but she used Hollywood in her early labels. While in later years she changed them to say California rather than Hollywood, it was important for advertising and promotional purposes for her to be associated with Hollywood in her early years. As Hollywood gossip columnist Louella Parsons once wrote, "By Hollywood, I mean Los Angeles, Beverly Hills, Culver City and everything that movies touch and which we curiously enough call Hollywood" (Parsons 1944: 41). In other words, Hollywood was used as a synonym for all the Los Angeles area and Dimmitt used that fact in her advertising and labels.

While scholars have discussed the development of costume shops in movie studios, the role of theater designers, and the local costume rental businesses in movie costume design (Landis 2012), the contributions of local fashion manufacturers have been largely overlooked. Contemporary references to Dimmitt are rare before 1930, but it is clear that by that date she is associated, in part, with the film industry. When interviewed for that syndicated column in 1930, she claimed that she "had a windfall" in the early years of her business when movie studios ordered "dozens and dozens of individually designed gowns." A few years later, she stated she had created designs for RKO, Warner Brothers, Tiffany, and MGM ("Style Leader" 1936). Just what she was supplying is unknown.

There is, however, one well-documented example of her providing garments for a supporting actress in a film. Dimmitt flatly stated that she had created the clothing for Gail Patrick in *Getting Smart* (released as *Smart Girl*) ("Style Leader" 1936). Travis Banton, as the head of the costume studio, is credited with the movie. He most likely designed the garments for the leading lady, Ida Lupino, as was the custom (Bailey 1982). Credit for Gail Patrick's wardrobe is complicated by a publicity photograph issued by Paramount showing Patrick wearing a silver lamé evening gown. The caption states that this gown "was designed by Edith Head, assistant to Travis Banton, Paramount's noted style expert." It would be easy to dismiss Dimmitt's claims, except for the fact that several ready-to-wear garments based on clothing worn by Gail Patrick in *Smart Girl* and manufactured by Dimmitt, appeared in Texas department store advertisements. One of these garments, a black crepe dinner dress with draped neckline with attached double string of pearls, was billed as an original Hollywood fashion with Dimmitt's and Patrick's names prominently displayed (Advertisement 1935). In reality, film credits for costume design were often lacking or just credited to the head of design at the studio until an award for costume design was established by the Academy of Motion Picture Arts and Designs in 1948. For *Smart Girl*, perhaps Edith Head actually did design the silver lamé dress and Dimmitt contributed

FIGURE 13.1 Actress Gail Patrick wearing an evening dress in *Smart Girl* (1935), credited to Edith Head as Paramount studio designer but most likely designed by Viola Dimmitt. Courtesy of Universal Studios Licensing LLC.

others, or, more likely, all credit was given to Head as a designer employed by the studio. From this one small instance, it is clear that movie studios used local designing manufacturers as suppliers for at least some of their costumes. In addition, Paramount allowed the designer to use the title of the movie and the star's name in their advertising.

Dimmitt was not shy about dropping the names of Hollywood stars who were her customers. Dimmitt mentioned she had designed a black tulle gown, cut on form-fitting lines and with a flaring train for actress Norma Shearer (Alden 1930). Dimmitt went on to claim that Shearer was the best-dressed woman in Hollywood. Ann Sothern was cited as another customer, having been provided by Dimmitt with a dress containing eleven yards of lace ("Dressy Dress" 1936).

Movie studios and fashion designers also used each other for publicity through fashion photographs that featured full-length portraits of stars or starlets from the studio. If the clothing was from an upcoming movie, the costume designer was usually credited. At other times, when the actress was simply wearing fashionable clothing that had nothing to do with a studio production, the source of these garments is often uncredited. But some were released to the press with captions citing American manufacturers or department stores, particularly those in California. The photographs were intended to be published in newspapers with the attached caption. A 1937 fashion photograph in the author's collection of Jean Rogers of Universal Studios explains that Rogers was soon to be seen in "Reported Missing," but here is wearing a full-length blue dress in what appears to be a damask fabric. Credit for the design is given to Viola Dimmitt. One of these fashion photographs, this time of actress Kay Francis, appeared in the *San Antonio Light* (March 22, 1932). The accompanying information describes Francis as a "charming" screen star wearing a full-length eggshell chiffon dress, further mentioning that Dimmitt's designs can be had at the local store, implying that Dimmitt designed this particular gown.

In the early 1930s, J. W. Robinson, a Los Angeles department store, hosted a number of fashion shows and special events featuring movie and local designers. In the spring of 1933 their fashion exposition and fashion show included notable film designers such as Adrian, Travis Banton, and Walter Plunket as well as Dimmitt and a few others (Advertisement 1933a). That same year, their fall exhibition received extensive coverage in the *Los Angeles Times* (Advertisement 1933b; Gray 1933). Dimmitt's offering, a soft gray corded silk coat dress with a shoulder cape, ornamented with elbow-length cuffs made of novelty velvet shirred to imitate fur, was pictured alongside a red wool coat by Degnan and two evening outfits by Andre-Ani.

In tandem with advertising and interviews promoting her association with the film industry, Dimmitt was increasing her business by expanding her sales across the country. Initially her sales were local and then she expanded to twelve of the Western states ("Viola Dimmitt" 1948). This included Texas where she appears to have had a strong market, evidenced by the amount of publicity she received in the San Antonio, El Paso, and Corpus Christi newspapers. Later, she had permanent sales representatives in San Antonio as well as in New York, San Francisco, and Alaska (Advertisement 1948).

By the mid-1930s Dimmitt was placing advertisements in *Women's Wear Daily*, indicating that by that date she was selling nationwide. Each of these advertisements featured a sketch, either of a young woman in a crinoline type dress or a shield. Each included text about her line of designs. The text varied, but all her advertisements included the tag line "California for the Unusual." A series of advertisements published in 1936 illustrate the depth of her line and reflect the tone of her business. On June 12, 1936 she indicated that she made "Clothes for a Discriminating Clientele." She mentions dinner suits and evening gowns along with lingerie top dresses (February 14, 1936), classic sports costumes, dinner suits and evening gowns (January 17, 1936), pastel and dark sheer suits with self-colored lace (February 28, 1936), and gowns for the bride and the bridesmaids (May 3, 1936).

In fact, bridal attire was an important part of her business. Some of the earliest references to her by name, aside from syndicated newspaper interviews, are in the social columns reporting on weddings. When Alva Daniel married William Glassock in Austin, Texas, in 1930, the wedding announcement ("Valley Girl" 1930) proclaimed, "The bride wore a Viola Dimmitt model of old ivory Viennese lace over shell pink chiffon. The fitted bodice in the new style was very plain, but the bouffant skirt, extremely full, was elaborately trimmed with delicate blue ribbon bow-knots caught through the lace with pastel French rosebuds. The skirt touched the floor and a train was formed by ivory tulle which edged a cape of ivory Viennese lace." A few years later, Grace Clarke of Beverly Hills wore "a Viola Dimmitt gown of nude velvet with close fitting matching hat" ("Beverly Hills Girl Marries" 1933). Another dress, this time worn in Greenville, Mississippi, "was an original Viola Dimmitt made of antique white tulle. The dress was made along empire lines. The long shirred sleeves corresponded with the shirring in the fitted bodice" ("Vera Field" 1938).

The extent of her identification with bridal attire is evident in the coverage of the dress Dimmitt made for Nancy Bumpas when she served as Queen of the Tournament of Roses parade in Pasadena, California, on New Year's Day in 1937. The dress was a heavy white satin evening dress covered by a trained lace coat that buttoned part way down the front. A sketch and a description of the outfit appeared in *Women's Wear Daily* ("Lace Coat" 1937). The writer commented that this outfit was an excellent idea for a spring wedding. In fact, the accompanying drawing included a veil and wedding bouquet.

Besides wedding dresses, it was the evening and dinner dresses that garnered the most attention from the press. Lace embellishment or strong color contrasts were the hallmarks of these dresses. In addition to Bumpas' dress, *Women's Wear Daily* also featured a black crush-resistant velvet dress with Venise lace for the bodice and sleeves the following year ("Velvet" 1938). A photograph of Mrs. Alexander Spencer, Jr. of the San Antonio Junior League appeared in the *San Antonio Light* in a Kilarney green and gold satin backless blouse with a black Canton silk skirt (March 20, 1934). Advertisements and published photographs of the period do not convey the dramatic colors or color contrasts Dimmitt considered an important part of her designs.

At the same time that Dimmitt was expanding her business, so was the Los Angeles industry growing—from the couture house of Howard Greer to sportswear manufacturers such as the Bettermade Garment Company and swimwear manufacturers such as Catalina and Cole of California. Among the manufacturers was a small group of women who called themselves designing manufacturers because they designed most of their garments as well as had their own factories. All these women were members of the Associated Apparel Manufacturers of Los Angeles and participated in the market week held in Los Angeles in January of every year. However, in 1938 when meeting socially, they expressed their concern over the fact that the California market was not getting as much publicity as they would like (Andreeva 1943). They decided it would be in their best interests to band together to promote their products as a group. They called themselves The Affiliated Fashionists of California. The original six members were Irene Bury, Jean Carol, Marjorie Montgomery, Patricia Perkins, Violet Tatum, and, of course, Viola Dimmitt. This loose association lasted until the 1960s with membership changing over the years as members dropped out or joined. The group was unusual. They did not maintain formal offices. They rotated the office of secretary. They presented joint fashion shows. They included their membership in their advertisements, either identifying themselves as member of the Affiliated Fashionists of California or just using the initials AF.

While these women did not copy designs from each other, they definitely influenced each other. For a few years they even selected a palette of colors that each would use in their designs for the upcoming season ("The Complete Costume" 1939). Dimmitt, while having a full line of products by the mid-1930s, was often identified with feminine-style dresses trimmed with lace. After the organization was formed, illustrations of her designs in publications tended to be more varied and often featured day dress or casual clothes. She might not have been manufacturing more of these more casual designs, but she was definitely receiving more coverage of them in the press. One example was a colorful trousered dinner outfit. The trousers were full and resembled a skirt when the wearer was standing. They were made of turquoise rayon jersey. The accompanying blouse was also rayon jersey, but coral. This outfit was featured in early 1940, with photographs, in newspapers as diverse as the *Billings Gazette* (February 11), *The Frederick Post* (February 3), and the *Fitchburg Herald* (February 6). While this outfit fits her reputation for using colorful fabrics, the use of trousers implies a more casual version of dinner attire than her more formal dresses.

Throughout her career, Dimmitt was always seeking ways to increase her business. After expanding nationwide, she explored other ways to increase her income. In 1938 she formed a short-lived partnership with Los Angeles designer Barney Max. Max kept a scrapbook of newspaper and magazine clippings chronicling his career; the scrapbook is now in the collections at the Fashion Institute of Design and Merchandising Museum in Los Angeles. Unfortunately, many of the clippings are uncited or undated, but they do provide information about this partnership. The two of them formed a new business to create casual clothes under the name Casa California. Other items retained the Viola Dimmitt label. An undated announcement in the scrapbook explains that Casa California Sportswear, designed by Barney Max, would be available, priced from $4.75 to $10.75. Dimmitt's usual line of sport, evening, and bridal clothes could be purchased from $12.75 to $39.75. The Viola S. Dimmitt label was more expensive. Just two years later, in 1940, they dissolved their partnership ("Coast" 1940); Barney Max had sold his interest in Casa California to Viola S. Dimmitt. The article further noted that Casa California would continue as a subsidiary of her dress manufacturing business. There is no evidence as to when she discontinued this line.

Not content with multiple labels, she also added manufacturing facilities to make other designers' clothing. The most widely publicized was her manufacturing Howard Greer's Venetian Blind dress in 1941 ("Los Angeles" 1941). This unusual dress had a device inside the waistband that reversed the pleats in the skirt, changing the dominant color when pulled. Greer had been running a strictly custom business in Los Angeles since he left Paramount Studios in 1927, and his salon did not have the capacity to manufacture garments in large quantities. Dimmitt did so, and the dress was sold throughout the United States, including at Lord and Taylor in New York City. She continued this practice throughout the 1940s, and some advertisements feature the words "Made by Viola S. Dimmitt" (Advertisement 1948).

By the end of the 1930s, Dimmit was firmly established as an American designer and manufacturer. In 1939 the world was at war and it was not long before the United States entered the conflict. Soon after the bombing of Pearl Harbor in 1941 Dimmitt was asked to comment about anticipated shortages and changes in American fashions (Hampton 1942). Her advice was to buy colorful spring styles as they were already in production. She believed that color might be a casualty of war. She went on to explain that chemicals were needed to produce dyes and chemicals were going to be needed by the military. She further stated that while the range of colors might be limited, those colors remaining might be available in various hues to satisfy customers. Her concern with color is apparent during the war years, as color was an integral and important part of her designs.

At the beginning of the war, the daytime designs she advertised did not differ greatly from her earlier work. But her styles changed dramatically by 1943. While laces and fabrics appropriate for evening and wedding dresses were not restricted by the War Production Board, many textile factories were switching to fabrics needed by the military. Dimmit, instead of altering her designs to meet the circumstances, concentrated on more practical garments. She was quoted as saying that instead of producing fifty designs four times a year, she was now producing only six but that they were "indestructible" (Andreeva 1943). The columnist noted that "They are created for the times in which they are to be worn—times for thrift, practicality, strength and versatility. One such number is her raincoat dress, known to buyers the country over, which does double duty both in and out of doors." It is this raincoat, first manufactured in 1942, that formed the bulk of her production during the Second World War and for several years afterward.

Her raincoats were actually coat dresses—garments that could do double duty, worn either as a dress or as a coat over other garments; they were rain- and wind-resistant. Coat dresses were not new to her designs as she had shown them as early as 1933 at the fashion show at Robinson's. Her new coat dresses were colorful. They were available in the traditional beige and also royal blue, Kelly green, yellow, and red. Although these raincoats had small variations in design, they all buttoned down the front with a concealed placket and had a removable hood for rainwear. Most had patch pockets, a buttoned flap over the shoulder, and a cinch belt. They were priced competitively at about $20—far below the cost of her 1930s evening dresses. An existing example in the collections of The Los Angeles County Museum of Art, in Kelly green, shows that the fabric, while sturdy, is not stiff so it would drape better on the body than many of the fabrics used in rainwear. From a comparison of the garment with advertisements in the *California Stylist*, it is clear that this particular coat is made of Cohama Elkskin, a combination of cotton and rayon.

American stores promoted these raincoats as practical. One such advertisement in the *San Antonio Express* (March 1, 1943) featured the heading "Attention War Workers." The text explains that a woman could wear the raincoat as a dress to the office or factory where she could then change into a uniform, thus saving the wear and tear on her wardrobe. Dimmitt's name is featured prominently below the illustration of the raincoat. This design for a convertible dress/raincoat won a Blue Ribbon award at the fashion showings at Market Week in Los Angeles in January of 1943 (Weaver 1943).

Near the end of the Second World War, fashion designers were considering their postwar offerings. Dimmitt and other California designers were no different. In January 1945, for the first time since she introduced her raincoat, she featured a dress, a full-length printed one, in her advertising (*California Stylist*, January 1945). In May of that year, Filene's department store in Boston sponsored a trip by the California manufacturers to unveil a "Sunrama" collection. ("Designers" 1945; "Californian Designers" 1945; Arndt 1945). The group included notables such as Louis Tabak, Louella Ballerino, and Viola Dimmitt. The newspaper columnist noted that the designs they presented were not startlingly different from earlier designs but that many could serve more than one function. Since the exhibition was in Boston the writer noted that many of the clothes had "come home" because many of the fabrics used to make them were produced in New England.

With the war's end, Dimmitt did not abandon her raincoats. Instead, she changed the design slightly and included different fabrics. The newer designs also

FIGURE 13.2 Dimmitt's Rain or Shine Coat dress was rain repellent and came in a variety of bright colors. *California Stylist*, August 1945. Courtesy FIDM Museum Special Collections.

required more fabric. One style had a large cape collar (*Syracuse Post Standard*, September 5, 1946) and other advertisements featured a fuller, monastic style hood (*Los Angeles Times*, September 16, 1948; *California Stylist*, January 1947). One of her new featured fabrics was a 100 percent rayon. She created an evening version of her raincoat, one in emerald green water-resistant rayon with a wide, full-length sweeping skirt (*Los Angeles Times*, February 18, 1947). The *Los Angeles Times* also reported (Hammond 1946) that her raincoats were now available in plaid taffeta. She incorporated other fabrics, including corduroy in this expanded line of coat dresses for all seasons and times of day.

Although Dimmitt was returning to a postwar environment, she did not immediately return to those cocktail and evening clothes that had originally cemented her reputation. Instead, her designs were tailored and lacked ornamentation. These garments also featured some of the newer fabrics available, especially plisse nylon, more commonly known as puckered nylon. As the *New York Times* stated in 1949 ("Television Frocks"), "Viola Dimmitt placed greatest stress on nylon plisse with which she has been so successful this spring. This fabric is washable, needs no ironing and is practically wrinkle-proof. Miss Dimmitt uses it in street, daytime and cocktail styles." She also made day dresses in knit jersey.

But she did return a few years later "to pretty, feminine sheer dresses, full-skirted, detailed with tucks, unpressed pleats and touches of lace" ("Shoulders Bared" 1950). One of the rare Dimmitt evening dresses in a museum collection is an example at the Henry Art Gallery in Seattle, Washington, from around this date. The dress is made of pastel chiffon, having a fitted bodice with spaghetti straps and a very full skirt. There is a large dark green bow with streamers and artificial flowers attached to the waist at the back. From the front this dress appears very demure and feminine. From the back it is dramatic.

In 1951 or early 1952, Dimmitt suddenly closed her business; there are no published notices of the closure. In 1950 she was widely covered in the press. In 1951 her collections were covered but her name disappeared from the list of the members of the Associated Apparel Manufacturers of Los Angeles at the end of the year and never reappeared. The reason for the closure is unclear. It is easy to speculate on the reasons, but without documentation it is impossible to ascertain exactly what happened. To begin with, although she was only 57 at the time, she had been in business for almost thirty years. She had other business interests, including investments in restaurants and real estate in Los Angeles (author's personal email with her grandnephew, Mark Dimmitt). But the postwar California fashion industry was different than it had been before the war. The industry had expanded rapidly and competition was rampant. The tenor of the promotions and advertising also changed. In the 1930s she had been closely identified with Hollywood and the glamour of that business. As the California industry matured, she was just one of many California designers whose collections were covered in the press as part of regular fashion features. Store advertisements paralleled this change and no longer promoted her as a Hollywood designer. Whatever the reasons, once she closed her clothing business, the only references to her in newspapers are in the social columns of the Los Angeles newspapers as a patron of charity events, not as a fashion designer. She died in 1978.

FIGURE 13.3 Coulter's, a Los Angeles specialty store, featured this nylon plisse dress in an advertisement they placed in the playbill for a local theater, 1949. Image out of copyright/author's collection.

Viola S. Dimmitt is one of those little known but important figures in the formative years of the California fashion industry. Her involvement with the movie industry points out the complicated relationship between the Los Angeles clothing and film industries between and during the wars. Further research into other Los Angeles designing manufacturers will shed additional light on this relationship. Dimmitt herself was a savvy businesswoman; she used that association and her hard work to parley a small business into a nationally recognized label. She knew that fashion is a business and used innovations and marketing to expand her operations. She had nationwide label recognition long before that became common. Initially, she was something of an anomaly in California as her ready-to-wear business was built upon elaborate dinner and evening dresses, not the casual clothes for which the California industry was known. With the United States entering the Second World War, she completely changed directions and focused on her rain-resistant coat dress. Her lifelong willingness to experiment is evident in her postwar designs incorporating newly available fabrics. Her work is representative of the colorful and innovative designs emerging from the California fashion industry.

Bibliography

Advertisement (1935), *San Antonio Light*, July 29, 1935.
Advertisement: J.W. Robinson Co. Golden Anniversary (1933a), *Los Angeles Times*, March 12: B8.
Advertisement: J.W. Robinson Exhibition of American Designers' Models (1933b), *Los Angeles Times*, September 26: 9.
Advertisement: Viola Dimmitt (1948), *California Stylist*, May: 200.
Alden, Alice. "Dress Designer Gives Inside Facts on Clothes Worn by Movie Stars," The Clearfield Progress, Clearfield, PA, July 16, 1930, p. 7.
Alden, Alice (1930), "Dress Designer Gives Inside Facts on Clothes Worn by Movie Stars," *The Clearfield Progress*, Clearfield, PA, July 16, 1930: 7.
Andreeva, Tamara (1943), "Top Artists Make 'Indestructible' Designs: Hollywood Designers—No. 2," *Christian Science Monitor*, October 26: 8.
Arndt, J.A. (1945), "East Greets West at Filene's—California Designers Visit Hub," *The Christian Science Monitor*, May 23: 13.
Bailey, M.J. (1982), *Those Glorious Glamour Years: Classic Hollywood Costume Design of the 1930s*, New York: Citadel Press Book.
"Beverly Hills Girl Marries" (1933), *Los Angeles Times*, October 1: B2.
Bureau of the Census, *Census of the United States*, 1900, 1910, 1920, 1930.
"Californian Designers Gather in Boston" (1945), *The Christian Science Monitor*, May 22: 5.
"Coast Coat Mfr. Adds Sportswear Dept" (1940) *Women's Wear Daily*, April 19: 32.
"The Complete Costume Appears in Market Week Fashion Show" (1939), *California Stylist*, January: 12–13.
"Designers in Movies Reach Boston for 'Sunorama' Show" (1945), *The Christian Science Monitor*, May 21: 2.

"The Dream and the Dress" (1945), *California Stylist*, August: 74–75.

"'Dressy Dress Coming Back Designer Says" (1936), *El Paso Herald-Post*, March 18: 8.

Gray. O. (1933), "Revue Emphasizes Los Angeles Designs: Extreme Features of Screen and Stage Gowns Made Practical," *Los Angeles Times*, September 26: A6.

Hall, M., Carne, M. and Sheppard, S. (2002), *California Fashion: From the Old West to New Hollywood*, New York: Harry N. Abrams.

Hammond, F. (1946), "Fashion Affiliates Feature Joint Styles Showing," *Los Angeles Times*, June 5: A5.

Hampton, M. (1942), "Women Are Advised to Buy Colorful Clothes This Year in Face of Future Dye Restrictions," *Fresno Bee*, January 24: 4A.

Kidwell, C. and Christman, M. (1974), *Suiting Everyone: The Democratization of Clothing in America*, Washington, DC: Smithsonian Institution Press.

"Lace Coat Over Satin—Worn by Queen of the Tournament of Roses" (1937), *Women's Wear Daily*, January 8: 15.

Landis, D.N. (2012), "Setting the Scene; A Short History of Hollywood Costume Design 1912-2012," in *Hollywood Costume*, 12–47, Richmond, VA: The Virginia Museum of Fine Arts in Association with the Victoria and Albert Museum.

Leventon, M. (2011), *Modernism in Textiles and Fashion Living in a Modern Way: California Design 1930–1965*, Los Angeles: Los Angeles County Museum of Art. 233–261.

"Los Angeles Market Section: Viola S. Dimmitt Takes Added Plant" (1941), *Women's Wear Daily*, March 7: 32.

Max, B., Scrapbook at The Fashion Institute of Design and Merchandising Museum, Los Angeles, CA.

NEA Service (1930a), "She Studies the Stars—to Design Their Clothes," *Ogden Standard*, June 22, 1930: B12.

NEA Service (1930b), "She Studies the Stars—to Design Their Clothes," *Ventura County Star*, June 20, 1930: 31.

Parsons, L.O. (1944), *The Gay Illiterate*, Garden City, NY: Doubleday, Doran and Co., Inc.

"Shoulders Bared In Coast Fashions" (1950), *The New York Times*, January 19: 32.

"Style Leader to Visit Frost's" (1936), *San Antonio Express*, February 16: 4A.

"Television Frocks Among New Styles: California Group Displays Fall Lines—Wearability and Femininity Stressed" (1949), *The New York Times*, May 20: 31.

Untitled Photo Feature (1945), *California Stylist*, January 1945.

"Valley Girl Weds Sunday" (1930), *Brownsville Herald*, April 16: 8.

"Velvet and Moire for Evening" (1938), *Women's Wear Daily*, July 8: 12L.

"Vera Field Becomes Bride of Dr. Ivan Gessler" (1938), *Delta Star*, June 22: 3.

"Viola Dimmitt Started a New Style on the Sunny Side of the Rain" (1948), *California Stylist*, January: 135, 151.

Weaver, S. (1943), "Style Show Sign Says 'Sold Out,'" *Los Angeles Times*, January 15: A6.

"Who Are the Real Designers???" (1941), *California Stylist*, March: 35.

14 KIVIETTE: STAR PERFORMER

DILIA LÓPEZ-GYDOSH

A "star performer" in *Vogue*'s February 1, 1940, Americana issue (148), Yeda Kiviette (1893–1978), designer of theatrical costumes and high-end ready-to-wear, is virtually unknown in the history of American fashion. With a career spanning almost half a century, Kiviette, as she would be known professionally, left her mark both as a designer of theatrical costumes on Broadway and as one of the top American wholesale designers. It is a career that took her through two world wars, the Great Depression, the rise of Hollywood, and the establishment of America's fashion leadership in the world stage.

Born on Staten Island, Yetta Schimansky (aka Yetta Kiviat, Yvette Kiviat, Kiviat, Kiviette, and many other variations) was the oldest of five children, and "always wanted to be in a creative field" (Kiviette 1942: 2). Married thrice and divorced twice, she had one son. Her passion for the arts led her to pursue studies at the New York School of Applied Design for Women (NYSADW) and the Art Students League of New York. In 1909 as a student at the NYSADW, Kiviette received a $10 award for second place in the category of Composition in the school's annual exhibition ("In the Art Schools" 1909). Her natural artistic talent, in combination with her academic work, laid the foundation for very successful careers in theater and fashion design.

"Costumes by Kiviette"

In 1912, as a freelance sketch artist, Kiviette entered into a partnership with Katherine M. Hubbard as Hubbard & Schimansky. As fashions in America were strongly influenced by France, a woman's choice for fashionable wear came down to four options: acquiring an imported French model, obtaining an American-made identical copy, purchasing a lower-quality copy, or buying an adaptation (Milbank 1989). Accordingly, Hubbard and Schimansky's work centered on creating and selling sketches of French imports/models to the clothing trade. The second half of the 1910s brought about the end of Hubbard & Schimansky and the establishment of Mignonette. A registered trade name, Mignonette was the partnership between Kiviette and Maurice M. Berger; it evolved from a focus on fashion to theatrical costumes, coinciding with the height of vaudeville and burlesque. In 1917 Kiviette received her first credit as costume designer, for the Broadway production of *Odds & Ends*, followed by the 1919 Shubert production of *Monte Cristo, Jr.* No longer associated with Mignonette, and with a belief that "you are always as good as your last show" (Paterek 1961: 122), the following year Kiviette took the unusual step of creating her own vaudeville revue. Titled *Vanity Fair*, an advertisement described the fashion revue as "A Dazzling display of Frocks, Frills and Fascinating Femininity" and touted its "New Genius Designer" (Advertisement 1920). This latest hit brought the Mahieu Costume Company knocking on Kiviette's door with an offer to join their firm.

This launched Kiviette's ascendancy as one of Broadway's top costume designers. Her career spanned five decades and a total of eighty-eight productions in which she was given program credits or acknowledgment in the media. Her first show with Mahieu was the 1920 *Silks and Satins*. Thirty years later, her last show was *Great to Be Alive!* The bulk of Kiviette's career as a costume designer was between 1928 and 1934, correlating with owning her own costume shop. Ownership came about after stints working for such costume companies as Mahieu, Brooks-Mahieu, and then just Brooks. The first half of the 1920s saw Kiviette receiving accolades for her work. For instance, *Women's Wear* remarked how, in *Helen of Troy, New York* "the costumes, especially the Russian ones, are gorgeous" ("Amusement Notes" 1923), and *Brooklyn Life* ("Plays and Players" 1926) reported on the "marvelous new wardrobe of wondrous frocks and gowns" in *The Tuneful Song Shop Revue*.

As her theatrical creations continued to gain praise and attention, from not only the theater community but also the audiences, Kiviette was presented with an offer from Starr & Herbert, manufacturers of dresses, to design women's apparel. On March 4, 1925, *Women's Wear* (21) informed their readers that

> Monday will see the opening of the showrooms of Kiviette, Inc., 347 West 37th street, a company recently formed to make dresses for the miss and small woman... The concern is named after its designer, Mme. Kiviette, formerly head of the designing staff of the Brooks-Mahieu Costume Co. The company will specialize in dance and evening frocks.

While designing ready-to-wear dresses, Kiviette continued to design for the theater. Her work in *Captain Jinks*, seen on Broadway in 1925, was commercially

FIGURE 14.1 Publicity portrait of Kiviette, 1933. Courtesy of Vandamm/©New York Public Library.

tied to Kiviette, Inc. with the creation of the "Captain Jinks!' Dance Frocks" (Advertisement 1925). A standout from the collection was her handling of color, a design element she became known for. Her collection sold and made it to retail stores as far West as Joske Bros. Co. in San Antonio. Still, within a year Kiviette, Inc. closed. Alice Alden, in her story on Kiviette, may have shed some light on the cause, when she mentions that "the commercial atmosphere and routine irked her and suddenly she resigned" (1932). However, Kiviette's term in fashion was not over, as she continued to work for Starr and Herbert designing dresses for their label and then later with the E. Davis Co., manufacturers of misses and junior dresses. As a designer, Kiviette traveled to Europe for the fashion collections, bringing back original imports and her own adaptations. Just as with Kiviette, Inc., her time with E. Davis Co., which filed for bankruptcy in 1928, was short and she returned to theatrical costuming full time.

After her flirtation with commercial fashion design, instead of joining another costume company, Kiviette established the Kiviette Costume Co. at 37 West Forty-Seventh Street. Originally subsidized by Broadway producers Laurence Schwab and Frank Mandel, the studio designed and manufactured their costumes. But, as its own incorporated business, the company also created and/or produced wardrobes for such producers as Aarons and Freedley, Sam H. Harris, and Max Gordon. Most of the productions that Kiviette was associated with were musicals, comedies, and revues, including *Good News*, *Girl Crazy*, *The Band Wagon*, *Strike Me Pink*, and *Jackpot*, to name just a few. Her costume design credits ranged from dressing the entire show to just costuming one principal.

Kiviette's costume design style evolved from novelty or fantasy costumes to more sophisticated fashions. In the early twentieth century, costuming of musical shows had no relevance to the numbers as most featured an overabundance of ostrich feathers, spangles, and tulle, along with exaggerated or exotic dresses. Her early work followed the recipe of such over-the-top imagery, but by the mid-1920s, Kiviette was introducing the use of modern fashionable clothes for modern settings, while asserting the needs of a show. As she said in 1942, "the success of a play … depends on continuity. The costumes must adhere to the time, place and character of the play as much as do the lines, the cast and the setting" (McCullough). Reviewers took note of the change and welcomed it. For *Ups-A-Daisy*, *Women's Wear Daily* (*WWD*) commented on the "great relief to see a musical comedy where the costumes aren't all spangles and gewgaws. The costumes … of principals and chorus … illustrate a distinctly wearable quality" ("Yellow Greens" 1928).

In the first decades of the twentieth century, original American fashion design was establishing its identity. Within the industry and theater community, voices such as *Vanity Fair* magazine and Cecil Cunningham of the Winter Garden, promoted the idea of real American style already existing on the Broadway stage. And the *New York Times* in 1928 commented on the difficulty for theatrical costume designers to rely on the latest Paris fashions, as by the time their show opens, the costumes will be off mode to the detriment of "the most rabid theatre goers … to musical shows"—women ("That Costume Problem"). In their view, the costume designer is not an imitator, but is a creator of fashion. Herein lies the legacy of Kiviette, who stated in a 1942 Brooklyn Museum of Art Library questionnaire that one of her outstanding achievements was "revolutionizing the costuming of musical plays from the tinsel era to the fashion-conscious" (2). Her stage costumes proved to have a notable effect upon the general fashion and her career. As *Theatre Magazine* noted in 1929, "Many women reading the tiny credit note have visited Kiviette's shop wanting a dress just like the one she made for Gertrude Lawrence or Zelma O'Neil" (38). If they could not afford a custom model from Kiviette, they had another option: to duplicate a Kiviette theater costume. With an extensive resume of shows, Kiviette provided plenty of opportunities for women to admire her designs. So popular was her work that a fan club of more than 300 hopeful fashion designers existed. From show to show, they kept track of any new theatrical creations by their "designing idol" Kiviette (James 1932).

Follow Thru, a musical comedy looking at Country Club life and golf, introduced some noteworthy creations. Kiviette dressed Madeleine Cameron and the chorus in side pleated white flannel and checkered shorts, respectively. As *WWD* ("Sports Costume" 1929) pointed out regarding resort wear, shorts were being considered for tennis or the beach. However, Kiviette presented shorts as sportswear, coordinating them with fashionable separates for Cameron's overall look. The following year, Kiviette introduced sunburst/fan pleated crepe pajamas in *Three's a Crowd*, a musical revue. Worn by the Albertina Rasch dancers in a ballet routine, she matched them with little velvet Zouave jackets. It is said to have stimulated a general demand for sunburst pleated pajamas (Cotier 1935: 3). In 1933 Kiviette costumed what could be considered her dream production, the musical comedy *Roberta*. The story is set in a fashion house in Paris, giving her the opportunity to design clothing in the height of fashion, and this she did. The fashions created by Kiviette were such a success that the press could not stop commenting. A review of the show, published in the *San Antonio Express* (Associated Press 1933: 2), points out that

> Quite apart from the plot, the parade of striking, extraordinary gowns is an entertainment in itself. As one critic put it, the designer, Kiviette, should have equal billing with the author ... the feminine members of the audience depart happily, planning to wheedle the price of a new gown from friend husband.

Among all the fabulous frocks and gowns in *Roberta*, one in particular was quite innovative. Featured in the bar scene and worn by Lyda Roberti, the black sheer, lustrous striped gown with full skirt and jacket was made out of a woven cellulose acetate material called Sylph-Sheen by the Sylvania Industrial Corporation. The ad by Sylvania in *WWD* (1933: 5) pronounced Kiviette's creation "The Gown of Tomorrow," describing the fabric as "brilliant, lustrous ... [with the] illusion of rich beading ... indestructible." Jean Pearson (1940: 18), the fashion editor for the *Detroit Free Press*, in discussing Kiviette, refers to the success of the fabric and its appearance in the French collections the following season, albeit in different styles.

The popularity of *Roberta* had fashionable women, "repeat" ticket buyers, requesting that their dressmakers copy some of the wardrobe. The interest in her

FIGURE 14.2 Lyda Roberti wearing Sylph-Sheen gown in *Roberta*, 1933. Courtesy of Vandamm/©New York Public Library/Museum of the City of New York. 68.80.2479.

theatrical costumes provided the opportunity early on for Kiviette's side business creating custom fashions. Her private clientele consisted mainly of actresses and society women, such as Adele Astaire, Beatrice Lillie, Fanny Brice, and Ginger Rogers, for whom she created a dress of pale green Chantilly lace for her wedding in 1934 ("Green Lace"). Earlier, Kiviette designed Dorothea Scudder's wedding dress for her marriage to John Hope Doeg, national singles tennis champion. Such was the social importance of this, and other weddings, that sketches of the dresses were featured in *WWD* ("Dresses: A Bridal" 1931). *Roberta* firmly cemented Kiviette's reputation as one of the top costume designers of the stage and provided the affirmation for her to revisit designing "smart" clothes for the American woman.

Kiviette, Inc.

The years preceding the Occupation of Paris in 1940 are often considered the most significant period in the formation of an important and respected American fashion industry. This was the time when American designers came into their own, began to be more accepted by the American consumer, and started the separation process from the French fashion industry. Recognized factors influencing change involved the economic depression, the challenging fit of the new formfitting bias silhouette, and the efforts by the American press and fashion industry to promote American style creators, as exemplified in Lord & Taylor's 1932 American designers campaign. The "talented native designers," (Milbank 1989: 98) at every price level, emerged from wholesale houses, custom design houses, specialty shops, and department stores all throughout New York City's fashion district.

One of the American wholesale houses with a "native designer" making a statement in 1930s was Kiviette, Inc. With a successful career in theatrical design and custom work, Kiviette jumped back into the commercial side of fashion. Unlike her first experience in 1925, this time the move toward wholesale was gradual. In 1932, Annette Simpson, an American fashion designer based in Paris, approached Kiviette and Charles LeMaire, a renowned costume designer, with a proposition: a special fashion showing of strictly American style featuring their creations. By now, LeMaire and Kiviette had "kissed and made up" from an old feud and were in business together in costume design. This was an opportunity for both to test the waters of fashion at a commercial level. This was an important event, not only for the three designers but also for American fashion. As Annette Simpson ("Annette Simpson" 1932: 1) said when asked about the showing,

> this event is to be, in a manner, a test as to whether or not there is a demand and appreciation of clothes designed from the American standpoint... The fashion revue is intended for the benefit of all those who are interested in clothes created here, whether manufacturers, designers or others interested in clothes design.

With the cooperation of American textile and lace houses, the showing in the studio of Kiviette was a success. The fall collection of Annette Simpson, Kiviette, and Charles LeMaire featured dresses, suits, coats, and eveningwear. A few months later, B. Altman & Company advertised four "after six" velvet dresses designed by "the great American designer..." Kiviette (Advertisement 1932: 9). Based on the positive reception and national exposure Kiviette received for her collection, she took the next step and trademarked the name "Kiviette, New York." This move at the end of 1932 also signified the end of the business relationship with Charles LeMarie.

Within two years Kiviette expanded the wholesale business, discontinued private dressmaking, hired new personnel, leased additional space, and in 1934 incorporated her company, once again, as Kiviette, Inc. This was all accomplished while continuing her theater costume business. As a firm focused on high volume, it seemed Kiviette not only marketed her original designs but also sold French adaptations. Her travels to Paris for the mid-season shows are documented in trade publications; while in France, she gathered ideas, noted potential trends, and acquired models to bring back. Her travels were indicative of an industry still looking at Paris for fashion direction, while concurrently, gradually promoting American design and designers. Kiviette struggled with this dichotomy. On one hand, she was one of those American fashion designers exemplifying the need for more recognition of all capable designers and what they stand for. She spoke about this to the members of the fashion press as a guest speaker at the November 7, 1934 meeting of the Fashion Group in New York (Fashion Group International 1934: 8). On the other hand, Kiviette wanted to succeed and be profitable as a business owner and, therefore, catered to an American public still interested in French design and marketed fashions across the country.

Kiviette, Inc., a high-style wholesale house, fashioned collections of sports, street, afternoon, and evening apparel for all seasons as well as resort and cruise wear. With offerings in a wide range of prices, from moderate to high, the firm was recognized for discreet daytime fashions and glamorous evening gowns with beaded embroidery in unique fabrics, marked by the designer's zest for color, while complementing the natural lines of the body to emphasize the best features of the individual form. Kiviette and her house stood for creating clothes that have subtle sex appeal paired with simplicity and good taste that "dramatize feminine charm with a new smartness" ("Fall, Winter" 1937: 11).

Kiviette's story and fashions were being promoted across the nation via radio appearances, special events, fashion shows, magazines, and especially newspapers. In 1935 she was featured in The Retail Research Bureau's *American Fashion Designers* publication. She was also a member of the Fashion Group, an organization of fashion professionals. Also in 1935 the firm joined the Fashion Originators Guild of America, whose aim was to prevent style piracy in the industry. With a high-volume business plan, Kiviette, Inc.'s products sometimes ended up saturating the market. For example, three different retailers in Cincinnati—The H.S. Pogue Company, Henry Harris, and Gidding's—all carried the brand simultaneously. Given the adverse economic times, did the plan fail? After what could be considered a successful run in fashion, Kiviette, Inc. went out of business. In 1938 *WWD* ("Corsets" 1938) first announced a change in name from Kiviette, Inc., New York, to the Sea Island Dress Co. Not long after that, Kiviette canceled the Kiviette, New York, trademark. This was followed by her joining Maurice Rentner's design business, who compared bringing Kiviette in to "acquiring an institution in itself" ("Dresses: Quality" 1938: 17).

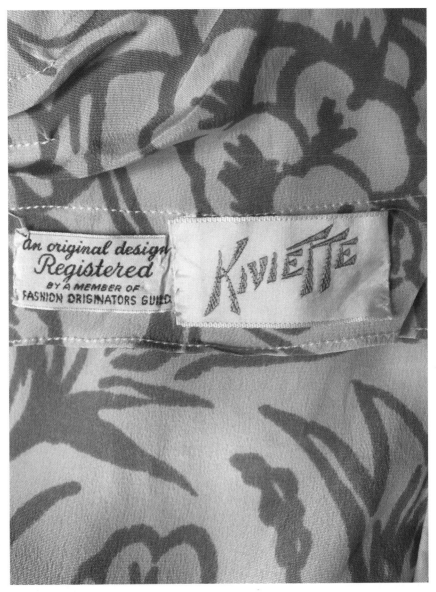

FIGURE 14.3 Kiviette, Inc. and Fashion Originators Guild of America labels, *c.* 1935–1937. Courtesy of Dilia López-Gydosh.

Kiviette Gowns, Inc.

The bump in the road was temporary. After less than a year with Maurice Rentner, Kiviette was back in business with a new partner. The May 9, 1939 issue of *WWD* ("Kiviette-Nabatoff": 1) announced that the

Formation of a new firm for the manufacture of high-style costumes was made known today. The name of the new firm is Kiviette-Nabatoff, and as this identifying title indicates, it includes Miss Kiviette, creator of dresses for the retail shops and for the stage, and Abraham L. Nabatoff.

After the fall showing, the partners split and Kiviette-Nabattoff, Inc. became Kiviette, Gowns, Inc. at 15 West Forty-Seventh Street. This new stage in Kiviette's fashion career would turn out to be her most successful, and her last.

The occupation of Paris during the Second World War, and the subsequent "pause" in Parisian fashion leadership, provided the needed jolt to the promotional campaigns on American style and their creators of the 1930s. As a result, Americans, and many around the world, looked to New York for direction, as reflected in editorials that appeared across the nation. The Director of the Chicago School of Costume Design wrote: "with Paris out of the picture, we must learn to design for ourselves and for the rest of the world as well" ("World Style" 1940: 4). In answer to questions about how women would respond to such designs, Jean Pearson of the *Detroit Free Press* declared "that American women have been wearing and accepting American designed fashions for years" (1940: 36). The American designers, including Kiviette, were ready for the challenge that found them defending their credentials as style creators of the new world's fashion center. In answering Schiaparelli's claim that neither New York nor any other city could become the world's fashion leader, Kiviette ("Designer Viewpoint" 1940: 2) said:

> There is absolutely nothing designers need that we can't get here—yarns, fabrics, dyes, trimmings—everything that is found in the world is here for us to use. But more vital than that is the fact that nowhere else in the world is there the inspiration for good design that there is right here in America.... The inspiration for good design is found in what is happening around us today. A designer must be vital, alert, aware of the world, its political, social, economic life—and a keen observer of human nature.

Kiviette practiced what she preached, as Latin America, fruit motifs, historical portraits, and her homeland inspired many of her collections. She was praised not only for the sources of inspirations but also the subtle manner in which she integrated characteristics of a source into the creation of a chic style. For example, Kiviette's American West collection featured cowboy gauntlet cuffs with gold and silver brandings on a black velvet cocktail dress. The inspiration also translated to the color palette with a Sierra blue daytime dress and evening ensembles in Coronado red and canyon blue ("American Design" 1940). Endorsing collaborations between American industries and fashion creators, Kiviette teamed with textile designers and producers as well as other fashion industry affiliates. She included in her designs Waldes Kover-Zip[pers] and, in another case, created a gown from DuPont's Cordura rayon for the inaugural "The Fashion of The Times" show staged by the *New York Times*. In addition, Kiviette collaborated with American textile designer Pola Stout to create an exclusive collection of fabrics for her designs.

In what may amount to lessons learned from the other business ventures, Kiviette Gowns, Inc. focused on high-end ready-to-wear to be sold by exclusive retailers throughout the country, such as New York's Bergdorf Goodman, J.L. Hudson (Detroit), Sanger Bros. (Dallas), and The Bon Marche (Seattle). The house first specialized in afternoon dresses and dinner and evening apparel, as well as tailored suits and coats. After the Second World War, American designers, including Kiviette, tuned in to a change in the *zeitgeist*, leading to an era of formality. The result was the re-introduction of apparel for occasion-wear, as in cocktail, theater, dinner, and dance ("Dress Occasion" 1946: 4). Influenced by this new category, by the 1950s Kiviette Gowns, Inc. specialized in fashions for weddings, debutante balls, parties, other formal events, and even beauty pageants. Throughout this period, the house presented ready-to-wear collections for every season, resort, holiday, and, later on, special occasions. What's more, Kiviette reinstated custom designs.

Kiviette once said, "It's the women of the country who are our inspiration" (Pearson 1940: 11). And it was the American woman who she considered when creating fashion. The Kiviette brand continued to stand for graceful simplicity for daytime and elegant glamour for evening. Her keen sense for line and color, developed from costuming Broadway, translated to an emphasis on the natural beauty of the woman wearing her clothes. In turn, Kiviette's designs provoked reactions of "what a stunning woman" not "what a stunning gown" (Pearson 1940: 11). The manner in which she incorporated color in her collections became a signature element of Kiviette's style. Her palette was a spectrum of color, from basic black to bright chrome yellow and every color in between, with pink being a favorite for evening. She was not afraid to experiment, combining unusual shades to create eye-catching effects. Her talent with color went well beyond her studio to her work as a consultant for television and Broadway productions. For daytime, her designs were based on the idea of timeless wearable beauty and functionality without losing style. This was very evident during the war years when working under the regulations of Government Order L-85. To eliminate the use of zippers, Kiviette introduced a dress with a wrapped skirt (Pearson 1941: 13). The Kiviette woman was well put together from head to toe, with coordinated accessories and jewelry designed by Kiviette. The legacy of the house is exquisite eveningwear, characterized by refined finishes, the finest fabrics, and the artistry of luxurious handwork embroidery and embellishments.

As one of the "nation's top-ranking fashion creators" ("Style Creators" 1943: 14), who helped establish American style and attained the admiration of the global fashion community, Kiviette's name appeared repeatedly in the list of designers

FIGURE 14.4 White crepe dinner suit, with all-over bugle beads by Kiviette, 1945. Courtesy of Bettman/Getty Images.

participating in a wide array of sponsored fashion events. One such event was the Museum of Costume Art exhibition in 1940, featuring modern creations by the invited designers displayed next to the historic source of inspiration from the museum. It was an event that proved the existence of American design inspiration. In 1942 the *New York Times* presented "Fashions of The Times," the first in a series of stage productions showcasing American fashion, in which Kiviette participated nine times. Then, in 1947 The New York Dress Institute (NYDI), an organization for the promotion of the New York fashion industry, presented Great Britain's Princess Elizabeth with an American-made trousseau. As a newcomer to the couture group of the NYDI, Kiviette created a pink English lace embellished formal gown as part of the twenty-five-piece wardrobe (Bundschu 1947).

As a designer of theatrical costumes and fashion, and a businesswoman, when opportunities came about to promote her brand, Kiviette took them. She was involved with a variety of commercial tie-ins, which provided great exposure and recognition. Her ventures included acquiring the rights to create a wardrobe in connection with the 1940 film *Rebecca*. A year later, at the request of Woodward & Lothrop, Kiviette produced an entire collection inspired by historical portraits to mark the opening of the newly formed National Gallery in Washington, DC. And, in what would become her last commercial tie-in, Kiviette worked with Joseph Bancroft & Sons, trademark owner of Everglaze, a cotton textile finishing process. As co-sponsor of the Miss America pageant, Bancroft & Sons furnished the winner with an extensive Everglaze designers' wardrobe for official use and its fashion advertising campaign. Kiviette's creations for Miss America, from 1951 to 1956, are representative of her brand's elegant eveningwear and the fundamentals of her signature style: graceful lines, marvelous color, and refined embellishments.

With little fanfare, on January 27, 1955 *WWD* ("Kiviette Retiring": 10) announced:

> Kiviette, custom designer, will close her salon at 15 West 47th Street and retire to private life, effective March 1.... Mme. Kiviette has been a leading designer for many years and was an early member of the Fashion Group. She has also costumed several Broadway shows.... Mme. Kiviette is credited with being one of the first major designers to recognize the high-fashion possibilities of cotton.

Conclusion

Yetta Kiviette: successful theatrical costume designer, fashion designer, artist, innovator, and businesswoman. Her theatrical creations introduced sophisticated modern fashions, revolutionizing attitudes toward contemporary clothing in costume design. Her costume design style bridged theater and fashion, shaping beautiful clothes with subtle dramatic appeal in custom apparel and ready-to-wear design. With a philosophy that fashion should flatter the woman, not vice versa, this high-end wholesale designer received accolades from *Vogue* to the *New York Times* and beyond. The list of her associates and collaborations reads as a "Who's who" of American fashion, among peers that included Jo Copeland, Nettie Rosenstein, Claire McCardell, Ceil Chapman, and Hattie Carnegie, to name a few.

Through it all, Kiviette was a champion of American style. Rising through the ranks in the 1930s, she was one of those original American designers trying to make a name in the shadow of French design. She called for more recognition of American creators and their work. And, when the lights went out in Paris and questions arose about New York's new role, she answered confidently with her voice and her designs, proving that under the spotlight, American style creators were ready to lead, establishing New York City as one of the fashion capitals of the world.

Bibliography

Advertisement: B. Altman & Co. (1932), *New York Times*, September 11: 9.

Advertisement: Kiviette Inc. (1925), *Women's Wear*, September 15: 39.

Advertisement: Sylvania Industrial Corporation (1933), *Women's Wear Daily*, November 20: 5.

Advertisement: Vanity Fair (1920), *Sun and New York Herald*, April 4: 48.

Alden, A. (1932), "Creates Beauty in Stage Costumes," *Evening News*, October 7: 19.

"American Design Fashion Show Coordinates Jewelry with Costume" (1940), *Women's Wear Daily*, September 3: 24.

"Amusement Notes" (1923), *Women's Wear*, June 20: 21.

"Annette Simpson in Cooperation with Other American Designers Plans Special Showings" (1932), *Women's Wear Daily*, May 27: 1.

Arnold, R. (2009), *The American Look*, London: I.B. Tauris.

Associated Press (1933), "Kern Writes New Broadway Hit," *San Antonio Express*, November 26: 2.

Bundschu, B. (1947), "N.Y. Dress Institute's Gift to Princess Valued at $10,000," *Evening Observer*, November 15: 12.

"Corsets & Brassieres: Change in Name" (1938), *Women's Wear Daily*, April 7: 12.

Cotier, V. (1935), "Designers of Today and Tomorrow," *Women's Wear Daily*, February 13: 3, 43.

"Designer Viewpoint Topic of Kiviette at Woodward & Lothrop" (1940), *Women's Wear Daily*, October 8: 2.

"Dress Occasion Clothes Bring Elegance to Outfits for Coming Fall Season" (1946), *Troy Record*, July 16: 4.

"Dresses: A Bridal Gown in the Moyenage Manner 'They Are Wearing' Reg. U. S. Pat. Off.," (1931), *Women's Wear Daily*, February 3: 1.

"Dresses: Kiviette, Inc., to Open Quarters Next Monday" (1925), *Women's Wear*, March 4: 21.

"Dresses: Quality Support Viewed Justified" (1938), *Women's Wear Daily*, July 7: 17.

Duncan, I. (1972), *The Complete Book of Needlecraft*, New York: Liveright.

Edwards, K. (2006), "Brand-Name Literature: Film Adaptation and Selznick International Pictures' Rebecca (1940)," *Cinema Journal*, 45(3): 32–58.

Ely, G. (1935), *American Fashion Designers*, New York: Personnel Group, National Retail Dry Goods Association.

"Fall, Winter Styles Viewed; Smart Frocks Are Displayed" (1937), *Cincinnati Enquirer*, May 21: 11.

"Fashion: Designers in America" (1940), *Vogue*, 3: 147–149.

Fashion Group International (1934), *The Fashion Group Bulletin*, New York: Fashion Group International: 8.

"Green Lace for Ginger Rogers' Bridal" (1934), *Women's Wear Daily*, November 20: 3.

"In the Art Schools" (1909), *American Art News*, 7(32): 2.

"Influence of Stage on Fashion of the Day" (1920), *Women's Wear*, July 20: 55.

James, R. (1932), "Reverting to Type," *Brooklyn Daily Eagle*, April 2: 9.

Katchen, A. (2009), *Abel Kiviat, National Champion*, Syracuse: Syracuse University Press.

"Kiviette Retiring; To Close 47th Street Design Salon March 1" (1955), *Women's Wear Daily*, January 27: 10.

Kiviette, Y. (1942), Questionnaire, Brooklyn Museum of Art, Library Collections, Fashion and Costume Sketch Collection, Designer Files.

"Kiviette-Nabatoff New Manufacturing High Style Firm" (1939), *Women's Wear Daily*, May 9: 1.

McCullough, T. (1942), "That's Kiviette's Idea and She's Clothed the Best of Them in the Show Business," *Asbury Park Press*, September 20: 10.

Milbank, C. (1989), *New York Fashion*, New York: Abrams.

New York City Telephone Directory (1917), New York: New York Telephone Company.

Owen, B. (2003), *The Broadway Design Roster*, Westport: Greenwood Press.

Paterek, J. (1961), "A Survey of Costuming on the New York Commercial Stage: 1914–1934," PhD thesis, University of Minnesota.

"Plays and Players" (1926), *Brooklyn Life*, January 23: 20.

Pearson, J. (1940), "Fashion Editor Views Kiviette Collection," *Detroit Free Press*, September 13: 18.

Pearson, J. (1941), "Clever Skirt Design Introduced by Kiviette," *Detroit Free Press*, December 8: 13.

R.L. Polk & Co. (1912), *Trow's General Directory of the Boroughs of Manhattan and Bronx*, New York: Trow Directory, Printing and Bookbinding Company.

R.L. Polk & Co. (1916), *Trow General Directory of New York City Embracing the Boroughs of Manhattan and The Bronx*, New York: R. L. Polk & Co. Inc., Publishers.

"See American Fashion First!" (1919), *Vanity Fair*, 2: 60.

Skolsky, S. (1929) "Heard on Broadway," *Theatre Magazine*, 49(2): 38.

"Sports Costume Comes into Its Own in Country Club Scenes of Musical Comedy" (1929), *Women's Wear Daily*, January 10: 19.

"Style Creators Preparing Entries for 'Fashions of The Times'" (1943), *New York Times*, October 4: 14.

"That Costume Problem" (1928), *New York Times*, May 20: 102.

Warburton, G. and Maxwell, J. (1939), *Fashion for a Living*, New York and London: McGraw-Hill Book Co.

Welters, L. and Cunningham, P. (eds.) (2005), *Twentieth-Century American Fashion*, Oxford: Berg.

"World Style Leadership by U. S. Urged" (1940), *Women's Wear Daily*, August 26: 4.

"Yellow Greens Register in Stage Frocks; Audience in Gay Hues at 'Ups-A-Daisy'" (1928), *Women's Wear Daily*, October 9: 2.

15 ZELDA WYNN VALDES: UPTOWN MODISTE

NANCY DEIHL

Zelda Wynn Valdes (1905–2001) has been the subject of numerous articles and online posts posthumously crediting her with the "invention" of the original Playboy Bunny costume. Although she did not invent the original Bunny costume, Zelda Wynn Valdes's long career—which began in the 1920s and ended in the 1990s—is worthy of attention for many other reasons, and it prompts a reconsideration of some generally held beliefs about the American fashion industry of the twentieth century.

During the course of her career, the designer used several different names, including Zelda Wynn, Zelda Valdes, and Zelda Wynn Valdes, and her business was identified at different times as Zelda, Inc., Zelda Modiste, and Chez Zelda.[1] Her roster of clients was filled with internationally known celebrities including Josephine Baker, Ella Fitzgerald, Mae West, Jessye Norman, Marian Anderson, Constance Bennett, Diahann Carroll, Dorothy Dandridge, Eartha Kitt, Ruby Dee, Gladys Knight, Aretha Franklin, and others. But she also outfitted private citizens, including the wives of male celebrities. Wynn's work resists categorization. Often the job descriptions of fashion designer and costume designer are quite distinct. But she moved easily between fashion design and costume design throughout her career. Wynn focused on the custom market—a market that is not widely discussed with regard to the American fashion industry. The importance of in-house salons in the great department and specialty stores of large cities—Sophie (Gimbel) of Saks, for example—is widely recognized. But very few other custom designers and dressmakers are acknowledged in the prevailing narrative, Charles James and Ann Lowe (another African American designer) being two notable exceptions.

Perhaps the most important aspect of Zelda Wynn's career is its alignment with the Civil Rights movement. Her professional life spanned more than sixty years—particularly significant years in the history of the United States, during which racial segregation was enforced and a fashion system created by and for black Americans existed alongside the mainstream fashion industry. Through her professional success, Wynn was able to use her reputation and achievements—and sometimes even fashion itself—to advance the efforts of African Americans to forge a positive black identity.

Born Zelda Christian Barbour on June 28, 1905, in Chambersburg, Pennsylvania, a small rural town near Harrisburg, she was the eldest of seven children. Her father, James W. Barbour, was a cook on the Pennsylvania railroad and her mother, Blanche M. (née Christian) Barbour, was a homemaker. Zelda had a public school education and graduated from Chambersburg High School in 1923. While at school, she was in the commercial course, a business track, and all through her school years she also attended a Catholic music school in Pennsylvania where she learned to play the piano. She learned sewing from her mother and grandmother and from a dressmaker who made many of the grandmother's clothes. Zelda's first job in fashion was in her uncle's tailoring shop in White Plains, New York, where she moved with most of her immediate family in 1923. She later recalled (Wynn 1995: 6) that her uncle's clientele was white, including women from the affluent suburbs of Scarsdale and Bronxville, and a significant part of the business was in alterations. Zelda was put in charge of ladies alterations—she later said she had "good ideas" (Wynn 1995: 9) about how to remodel clothes—and also had some private dressmaking clients.

While Zelda was establishing her fashion career, she also held other jobs including interior design. During her years in White Plains, she began what would be a lifetime of civic engagement; as part of a women's auxiliary, she was elected financial secretary of the Pride of Westchester county chapter of the Moose lodge, a fraternal and service organization, in 1927. The same year, she married her first husband, Charlie Wynn. In the early 1930s, she held a variety of tailoring and sales clerk positions in the New York City area.

By 1935, Zelda Wynn established a business on Martine Avenue in White Plains, and in 1937 she was advertising in the *New York Amsterdam News* as a "Colored Designer of Fashions for Women and Misses" (May 15: 8) at a new address, 28 William Street, White Plains. Her husband Charlie Wynn died in the mid-1930s, and her sister Mary helped run the shop. Throughout 1937 Wynn ran a series of advertisements in that same newspaper, which was geared toward the African American population. She advertised alterations, millinery, hosiery, lingerie, and accessories, with a specialty in "Evening Gowns, Afternoon and Sportwear." She also advertised her skill as a Stylist and Copyist. While remodeling clothing was an important part of many fashion businesses during the Depression years, Wynn's message to her customers was that this "colored designer" was also bringing current styles to the community. She was a member of the Colored Merchants Business League of White Plains and hers was reportedly the only black-owned dressmaking business despite the fact that there was a significant black population in that town (Westchesterite 1941). She also began to participate in fashion shows, an activity that became a mainstay of her career for the next twenty years. The first record of her involvement in a fashion show is a notice in the *New York Amsterdam Star-News* (November 29, 1941) of a November 1941 event that included "various fashions … from housecoats to bridal ensembles … with models from the junior deb to senior matron" (25). The show was a collaboration with Hazel Miller, principal of the local beauty school, who oversaw the innovative coiffures of the models; this overlap of fashion and hairstyling was typical of many events throughout Wynn's career. The *Star-News* sponsored a fashion show the following year, held at Harlem's Renaissance Ballroom. It was "the first to stress war-time fashions" and Wynn contributed "two stunning evening gowns" ("Town Still Talking" 1942: 12). During the war years, she continued to build her business and show her designs, often featured at luncheons or cocktail-hour benefits for various social and service organizations.

Smart fashions for uptown

In 1948, Wynn opened a store named "Zelda Wynn" in New York City, on Broadway at 158th Street. She made the move to better serve her growing clientele, saying later that "I was so busy and it took so much time by running back and forth to New York, I decided to just move" (Wynn 1995: 11). She was by then married to her second husband, Oscar Valdes, who helped manage her shop. The move into Manhattan was a major step; in addition to housing her design and dressmaking studio, the shop also had a display window on bustling upper Broadway. In several later interviews, Wynn claimed that it was the first black-owned business on Broadway (Wynn 1995: 11). At its height, her design and dressmaking business employed nine skilled seamstresses. While her dressmaking customers were mostly black, white women also patronized the shop, particularly for the jewelry and accessories sold in the front of the store.

Two events that year exemplify her growing reputation and the, perhaps unexpected, role of fashion in race relations in New York. The wedding of Maria Hawkins Ellington to Nat King Cole on March 28, 1948, Easter Sunday, was a major media event—one that momentarily seemed to suspend the barrier of racial segregation, even prompting a brief notice in the Amusements page of the *New York Times* ("Nat Cole" 1948) a newspaper that did not generally cover "uptown." At the time, Nat Cole was one of the most popular male vocalists in America and Maria had been a jazz singer, performing with Duke Ellington (to whom she was not related) and Count Basie among others. Wynn outfitted all the women in the bridal party, which included seven bridesmaids, in full-length ice-blue satin dresses. The bride's expensive beaded gown, with an off-the-shoulder neckline, was a gift from her aunt, a prominent educator in North Carolina. A description in the *New York Amsterdam News* conveys the excitement of the event:

> Abyssinian Baptist Church was jammed to the rafters and the street outside was equally filled with would-be crashers, but nary a soul got in without a precious invite or proper identification. Equal precaution against "crashers" was taken later at the swank Belmont-Plaza where guests were double-checked for invitations so that the Moderne Room wouldn't be over-crowded... Photographers practically swamped the place taking pictures from every conceivable angle. (Chase 1948: 12)

The columnist went on to note that the wedding party was interracial and "a generous assortment of white friends of the couple, a number of them famous in radio and the theatre" attended both the church and the reception. His comments underline how segregation was both a physical and psychological phenomenon, but also illuminate the importance of fashion within the black community:

> One thing that marked the affair was the elegance of the guests who "fell in" togged as one should be togged on Easter Sunday. People entering the ultra swank Waldorf Astoria across the street didn't look half as smart as the guests entering the Belmont-Plaza for the reception. It made you feel very proud, indeed, because it isn't often that the folks downtown get the opportunity to see Harlemites in a smart, social light. Every so often, uptowners have a tendency to overdress when attending functions below the park, but not this time. (Chase 1948: 12)

Later that year, Wynn played an important role in another integrated event: New York City's Golden Jubilee. The Jubilee celebrated the fiftieth anniversary of the consolidation of the city's five boroughs and included a parade, exhibitions, and several fashion shows highlighting New York's garment industry. A young African American woman, Mildred Joanne Smith, a Broadway actress who also did some modeling, was added to the list of models in a fashion show in a last-minute attempt by the organizers to silence accusations of racial discrimination. However, Miss Smith was not assigned any clothes to model. In response, Wynn quickly created a "stunning" white evening gown for her to wear, and leather goods designer Cornele (Nele) Cuyjet, also well known in the black fashion community, provided matching accessories, enabling Harlem to be beautifully represented in the city-wide celebration ("Jubilee" 1948: 23).

FIGURE 15.1 Nat King Cole and Maria Hawkins Ellington at their 1948 wedding. She wears a gown by Zelda Wynn. Photo by Lisa Larsen/The LIFE Images Collection/Getty Images.

Tight, tight gowns

By the 1940s, Wynn began to develop a loyal following among performers looking for glamorous outfits for onstage and for their personal wardrobes. Ella Fitzgerald was one of her earliest celebrity clients (Wynn 1995: 9). They met at the Apollo theatre during the 1940s when Fitzgerald was busy touring and recording. Wynn made numerous dresses for Fitzgerald over the years—but often long distance.[2] In an interview in the *New York Times* in 1994, she stated that Fitzgerald often ordered three gowns at a time, and she "only fit [Fitzgerald] once in 12 years... I had to do everything by imagination for her. She liked fancy clothes with beads and appliqués." And as for accommodating changes in

FIGURE 15.2 Zelda Wynn, beaded dress, made for Ella Fitzgerald, late 1940s. Collection of the Smithsonian National Museum of African American History and Culture, Gift of the Estate of Ella Fitzgerald.

the singer's figure, "I'd just look at the papers and say, 'Gee, she's gotten larger'" (Gonzalez 1994: B3).

Business came from all strata of the theater and performance world. In 1947, Wynn brought (and subsequently settled) a lawsuit against the nightclub singer known as Tondelayo (Wilhelmina Levy) who had refused to pay for several garments she ordered, and wore. The pieces in question were described as a dress in "shocking pink hammered satin," a second in "sequined trimmed green crepe," and the third, a suit, "damaged beyond repair, was of white suede with black trim" ("La Tondelayo" 1947: 1). Edna Mae Robinson, a dancer and the wife of boxer Sugar Ray Robinson, was a steady client. She had many pieces by Wynn in her own wardrobe and often modeled the designer's creations. She wore the "[m]ost fabulous gown ever seen in Alabama society" in a fashion show sponsored by Alpha Kappa Alpha (AKA)[3] at Alabama State College in Mobile in 1953. As described in the press, the "20-pound creation of white satin was completely covered with jewels ... [and it] took two people to put her in it" (Major 1953). The following year, Robinson again modeled lavish dresses by Wynn in an AKA benefit show, including "a striking royal sunset evening gown and a dramatic Ebony rose evening dress" ("New York Beauty" 1954: 14). In 1953, after a few years away from performing, Robinson starred in an all-black version of "Born Yesterday" on Broadway and Wynn made her costumes.

Wynn's work was consistently noted for high-quality embellishment and also high price tags. In 1954, *Hue* magazine pictured Wynn fitting actress Dorothy Dandridge under the heading "The High Price of Stardom" with text about the wardrobe expenses incurred by glamorous female vocalists. The same year, a profile of Joyce Bryant, a sultry cabaret singer, credited Wynn's "extremely fashionable gowns" with helping the chanteuse move into the national spotlight. Wynn claimed to have talked Bryant out of her previous "sweet" style into a more aggressively sexy look, with "tight, tight" gowns (Wynn 1995:12). "Some of them cost as much as $800 and feature solid gold, diamond and jewel trimmings. Many of Joyce's gowns are created so form-fitting that the singer cannot sit down in them," forcing her to "develop a glide to move about in her gowns" (Peters 1954: SM4). Wynn's association with Joyce Bryant was a great distinction and often referred to in the press: "The snappy convertible auto that Zelda Wynn, who designs Joyce Bryant's gowns, rides around in is a gift from her hubby, Oscar. She plans to have a midget sewing machine built into the glove compartment" (Robinson 1953: 64). As her business expanded, Wynn's client list grew: she created dresses for Marian Anderson for concert recitals, made Ruby Dee's wedding suit (Reed Miller 2006: 85), and claimed to have made a gown for Constance Bennett for her presentation to Queen Elizabeth (Wynn 1995: 12). Another important commission was publicized in 1957 as trumpeter and bandleader Louis Armstrong ordered "four new creations for his vocalist, Velma Middleton, at a cost of $4,250" (Young 1957: A3).

The busiest years of Wynn's career corresponded to a period in fashion that emphasized precise grooming and a mature, polished aesthetic. Even for her non-

FIGURE 15.3 Singer Joyce Bryant in 1953 in a form-fitting gown by Zelda Wynn. Carl Van Vechten photograph©Van Vechten Trust. Image courtesy Yale Collection of American Literature, Beinecke Rare Book and Manuscript Library, Yale University.

celebrity clients, Wynn was committed to enhancing their beauty and allure. While few extant garments attest to her aesthetic, descriptions in the press consistently emphasize form-fitting silhouettes, luxurious materials, and eye-catching color combinations and embellishments. Since many of her clients were socially prominent black Americans, Wynn's designs were frequently described in the society columns of newspapers and magazines targeted to a black readership. For example, in 1947 the social columnist of the *New York Amsterdam News* reported that a guest at a "swellegant" party at the Renaissance Ballroom wore a "flesh-colored net (torso) gown of white, with low-cut Grecian lines. A creation by Zelda Wynn and it was real mad" (Chase 1947: 8).

After her early years in White Plains she did not advertise, so such press exposure was vital for her business. Although she did not sell ready-to-wear, Wynn regularly showed one-of-a-kind pieces in fashion shows in a wide variety of venues for a wide range of causes. Fashion shows were a popular feature of meetings, luncheons, and galas presented by church, social, and civic groups, and they often focused on evening dresses and special-occasion outfits. Many were very festive events, complete with live entertainment, including big-band-style music and dancing. "Fashions of 1951" presented at the Renaissance Casino "had as its theme the transformation of a Cinderella or an ugly duckling into a beautiful and charming woman." Buddy Walker's Society Orchestra provided music for the show and for dancing afterward ("Coif-Style" 1950: 9). Through the years, she participated in benefit fashion shows for Abyssinian Baptist Church, the Salvation Army, New York Baptist Home for the Aged, Jack and Jill, and many other organizations. In 1961, she showed a "$1,500 beaded gown" in "Night of Fabulous Fashions" to benefit the campaign of Herb Evans (later a judge and one of the founders of 100 Black Men), who was running for New York City Council (Major 1961: 38). For a "Four Seasons" themed event in Chicago in 1962, Wynn showed ten ensembles, including "a Turkish lounging suit, a hostess gown of 10 yards of turquoise silk organza over silk shantung, a walking suit with a matching hat in Spring colors of royal blue, turquoise, kelly green and white plaid and an olive green Italian knit jersey stole dress with black wool tassels and huge pockets" ("Famed New Yorker" 1962: 14). Throughout her career, sophistication and drama characterized her designs. A 1965 AKA luncheon in Westchester County included an evening gown by Wynn with a high neck and slight sleeves that had "absolutely, and we do mean absolutely, no back (from the lower waist up)." Worn by professional model Marion Barker, "the gown looked absolutely fabulous and really stopped the show" (Henderson 1965: 5).

The "Nafads"

In the postwar period, Wynn was an important figure in organizing efforts within the black fashion industry. While successful, she, like other black designers, was conscious of limitations on her professional opportunities. She was one of the founders of the National Association of Fashion and Accessory Designers (NAFAD), an association of black designers established in 1949 with the sponsorship of the National Council of Negro Women. The organization was formed to provide opportunities for networking and professional development and to nurture young talent through mentoring and scholarships. One of NAFAD's first activities was a conference at the Hotel Theresa in New York City. NAFAD members were invited to submit designs that were judged by a panel of fashion industry experts that included publicist Eleanor Lambert, milliner Sally Victor, fashion designer Mollie Parnis, and Esther Lyman, the manager-editor of *Vogue* (Major 1949). This initial effort to connect with the larger American fashion industry was typical of NAFAD's priorities. As designers sought greater recognition for their work, the organization invited representatives from Seventh Avenue to serve as speakers, consultants, judges, and panelists at their events. Other projects focused on expanding business opportunities. Because their members were not represented in the mainstream fashion industry, NAFAD attempted to establish a New York office where designer members could show their one-of-a-kind garments for wholesale or retail. They also put forward a plan to grow their monthly newsletter "Fashion Cues" into a general interest women's magazine. In addition, the organization sought affiliation with the Costume Institute of the Metropolitan Museum of Art so that the members would have access to "one of the major sources of ideas on style creations in America" ("Dress Designers" 1951: 11).

The "Nafads," as they were referred to in the press, held annual conventions that rotated among major cities. At the 1950 convention in Philadelphia, Wynn, a member of the New York chapter, was elected parliamentarian. She was one of the chief organizers of the second annual convention that took place in 1951 in New York and maintained an active role within the organization. She served as president of the New York chapter for several years and was the General Chairman of the convention that celebrated NAFAD's tenth anniversary and was held at New York's Waldorf Astoria ("NAFAD Show" 1959). At their 1962 convention, the Nafads saluted "America's Best Dressed Negro Women," a list that included educators, businesswomen, and a member of the Maryland State Assembly, among others. In 1964 NAFAD honored Josephine Baker. The highlight of that convention was a particularly gala luncheon fashion show in the grand ballroom of the Waldorf Astoria featuring designs by members. Wynn's contribution to the affair was a gown dedicated to Baker entitled "J'ai Deux Amours," an homage to one of La Baker's most popular musical numbers. The gown was made of white silk peau d'ange with a turquoise border and featured rhinestone sprays. The established Seventh Avenue designer Norman Norell was scheduled to present a plaque to the guest of honor but was taken ill and replaced at the last minute by famed opera singer Leontyne Price.

The 1960s

In 1959, Wynn briefly resigned from her position in NAFAD as her career entered a new phase; she vacated her shop on upper Broadway and moved the business to 151 West 57th Street, a distinguished location near fashionable shops and department stores and the famous concert venue Carnegie Hall. Reflecting her more upscale surroundings, she renamed the business "Chez Zelda." Despite the move to midtown Wynn remained engaged with the uptown community. After more than thirty years in business, she was often called upon to advise young designers, speak on panels, and serve as an authority on fashion. She was honored at a "LKM Showcase" by members and friends of Lambda Kappa Mu sorority in 1960 ("Lambdas" 1960) and was featured on a "Careers" radio show in 1966 (Aldridge 1966). In 1968, she served on a panel for a new fashion trades group at the Harlem Institute of Fashion, where the theme was "Where Black Power Really Is—Doing Our Own Thing" ("Newly Formed" 1968: 18).

In the early 1960s, she also began working with Harlem Youth Opportunities Unlimited and Associated Community Teams (HARYOU-ACT), a social service organization that was part of a federally funded anti-poverty program. As director of the Fashion and Design Workshop, Wynn taught sewing and fashion and costume design. In addition to her expertise, she was able to use her contacts in the garment industry for the benefit of the program and, in 1967, arranged a donation from Burlington industries of 100 yards of expensive fabric to the student workshops ("Zulu" 1967). In collaboration with other divisions of the program, she and her students costumed music and dance performances and participated in arts festivals. HARYOU-ACT became a well-known organization and part of the Harlem arts scene and the activities of the workshops were enthusiastically covered in the press. In 1968, she was one of the founders of The Harlem Youth Symphony Orchestra, "in response to the need for a vehicle of classical music in the Black community" ("Harlem Youth" 1969: 21).

In addition to her teaching and consulting, she was still committed to producing chic fashions for her customers and was included in an eclectic list of designers and labels—Givenchy, Hattie Carnegie, Cardin, and Jablow, among others—whose clothes would be perfect for the 1963 Easter Parade (Norford 1963). During this period, Wynn developed a relationship with the Playboy Club of New York which opened at 5 East 59th Street on December 8, 1962. She and her workshop fabricated at least thirty-five of the costumes worn by the bunnies there (Wynn 1995: 15). On the basis of that job, she developed a good working relationship with Hugh Hefner and was the first to stage a fashion show at the NYC Playboy Club (in 1963). She presented many fashion shows there; her showings at the Club were often publicized as "Zelda at the Playboy" and proved to be a valuable promotional outlet for her business on 57th Street which remained open until about 1989.

Dance Theatre of Harlem

It was through her work with HARYOU that Wynn met Arthur Mitchell, the founder of Dance Theatre of Harlem (DTH), as Mitchell's nieces studied with Wynn. Her work with Arthur Mitchell began in 1970, when she was already 65 years old, and challenged her in a different way. While Wynn's earlier designs had imposed a fashionably restrictive silhouette on glamorous performers, her work for DTH celebrated freedom of movement, enabling the spectacular form for which the troupe's dancers were known. She was recruited by Mitchell based on what he later said was her "discipline, knowledge and strength... She takes the same kind of care and determination in sewing as I do in dancing" (Gonzalez 1994: B3). During almost thirty years with the ballet, she designed for many of their productions, and also fabricated costumes designed by others, including Karinska and Geoffrey Holder. Notable examples of her work included a "silvery leotard" for the Snake in *Manifestations*, DTH's retelling of the Garden of Eden (Kisselgoff 1999: E5), and "sheer black and white costumes ... (with noticeable string bikinis underneath)" for *South African Suite* (Bleigerg 2000: F05). She toured internationally with the troupe. Her reminiscences about the travels ranged from encountering racism in Italy to the pleasure of meeting Margaret Thatcher (Wynn 1995: 34). One of her costuming initiatives was tights dyed to match the skin tone of each dancer, an aesthetic departure from the standard pale pink of ballet, that respected the variety of skin colors of the DTH dancers. A short tribute to Wynn in *Pointe* magazine, marking her death in 2001, showed dancer China White in Wynn's filmy chiffon costume for *Holberg Suite*, the first production she costumed for Dance Theatre of Harlem (Photo 2001).

Conclusion

Zelda Wynn Valdes's career was full of accomplishments. Although she had no formal training in fashion, she created striking dresses and ensembles for celebrated, visible women. After building her business for twenty years, the dresses she designed for the 1948 Cole wedding placed her at the nexus of African American high society: with a celebrity couple, a notable officiant (who was also a U.S. congressman), and a ceremony held in Harlem's most famous church. Wynn remained friends with the Coles; she visited them in Los Angeles and was the godmother of their daughter, vocalist Natalie Cole (Wynn 1995: 23). Although described by Rosemary E. Reed Miller as "a quiet, calm person" (Reed Miller 2006: 79), Wynn was successful enough to please high-profile clients and maintain a shop in an expensive neighborhood of Manhattan. Her financial success enabled her to be a donor to Dance Theatre of Harlem, where she also contributed to the unique aesthetic of the dance troupe.

Accounts of her career were mainly restricted to the black press, newspapers that included *The New York Amsterdam News*, *Baltimore Afro-American*, and *Chicago Defender*, and magazines targeted to a black audience. But the frequency and detail of those accounts attest to her stature within the African American community. In these sources, the designer was often referred to as "our Zelda" or "one of our outstanding designers" conveying the sense of community and the consciousness that Black Fashion was its own world.

Her connection with Playboy Enterprises was particularly important because the Playboy Club in New York was not segregated. The clientele was mixed and the corps of Bunnies was integrated; African American women were known as Bronze Bunnies. In that context Wynn was able to leave the segregated space of Harlem and participate in a larger fashion world. Wynn herself never claimed to have "invented" the Bunny costume. In a 1995 interview she said she had been "recommended to make the bunny costumes"; the claim of "invention" has been applied to her (Wynn 1995: 15). However, the Playboy costume myth has contributed to a rediscovery of Zelda Wynn Valdes and a rationale to examine her long, rich career.

Notes

1   As the label on the one located extant garment reads "Zelda Wynn," the designer is referred to by that name in this chapter.

2   One of two known extant garments by Zelda Wynn is a dress made for Ella Fitzgerald, dated late 1940s, satin with beads and sequins, in the Collection of the National Museum of African American History and Culture. The other dress was designed for Eartha Kitt's 1955 cabaret season and is reportedly in the collection of the Black Fashion Museum founded by Lois Alexander-Lane in 1979. This collection was donated to the Smithsonian National Museum of African American History and Culture in 2007 and as of the date of this publication was still being catalogued ("Spotlight" 2001).

3   Alpha Kappa Alpha is an important African American sorority founded at Howard University in 1908.

Bibliography

Aldridge, C. (1966), "PS: Action on Harlem Scene," *New York Amsterdam News*, May 28: 18.

Alexander, L.K. (1982), *Blacks in the History of Fashion*, New York, NY: Harlem Institute of Fashion.

Bleigerg, L. (2000), "Strength Through Simple Storytelling: The Harlem Dancers Show the Other Side of Founder Arthur Mitchell's Talents," *Orange County Register*, February 21: F05.

Chase, B. (1947), "All Ears! The Secret's Out! Dr. Marshall Becomes Groom Again at Elkton," *New York Amsterdam News*, April 26: 8.

Chase, B. (1948), "All Ears!" *New York Amsterdam News*, April 3: 12.

"Coif-Style Revue Ultra in Chic, Unique in Entertainment Value" (1950), *Chicago Defender*, December 30: 9.

"Dress Designers Set to Study Plan for New York Office: NAFAD Plans Central Site" (1951), *Baltimore Afro-American*, April 28: 11.

"Famed New Yorker Designs for the 'Associates' Fashion Extravaganza" (1962), *Chicago Defender*, June 6: 14.

Fanger, I.M. (1983), "Keeping the Ballet in Stitches; Designer-Seamstress Zelda Wynn Has the Dance Theater of Harlem Leaping in Style," *Boston Globe*, November 3. Available online: http://ezproxy.library.nyu.edu:2048/login?url=http://search.proquest.com/docview/294193536?accountid=12768

Gonzalez, D. (1994), "Matriarch of Dancers Sews Clothing of Delight," *New York Times*, March 23: B3.

"Harlem Youth Symphony Giving Free Concert" (1969), *New York Amsterdam News*, March 29: 21.

Henderson, I. (1965), "Westchester Potpourri," *New Pittsburgh Courier*, October 2: 5.

"Jubilee Fashion Show Accepts Negro Girl" (1948), *New York Amsterdam News*, August 21: 1, 23.

Kisselgoff, A. (1999), "Dance: Adam, Eve and Snake Romp in That Garden Dance Theater of Harlem City Center," *New York Times*, October 4: E5.

"La Tondelayo Settles Suit Out of Court" (1947), *New York Amsterdam News*, January 11: 1.

"Lambdas Plan Regional Meet" (1960), *Baltimore Afro-American*, October 29: 14.

Major, G. (1949), "Around 'n' About," *New York Amsterdam News*, April 9: 12.

Major, G. (1953), "Society World," *Jet*, April 16: 46.

Major, G. (1961), "Society World," *Jet*, August 31: 38.

"NAFAD Show Set for Waldorf Astoria" (1959), *Atlanta Daily World*, April 28: 2.

"Nat Cole Marries in Harlem" (1948), *New York Times*, March 29: 18.

"New York Beauty Guest Model at Texas AKAs Gay Fashionetta" (1954), *Chicago Defender*, April 24: 14.

"Newly Formed N.Y. Trades Group Ends" (1968), *Philadelphia Tribune*, September 28: 18.

Norford, T. (1963), "Chic New Yorkers Ready with Smart Easter Styles," *New York Amsterdam News*, April 13: 13.

Peters, A. (1954), "Joyce Bryant Newest of the Red-Hot Mamas," *Pittsburgh Courier*, January 9: SM4.

Photograph of China White (2001), *Pointe*, November/December: 19.

Reed Miller, R.E. (2006), *Threads of Time, The Fabric of History: Profiles of African American Dressmakers and Designers, 1850-to the Present*, 3rd edition, Washington, DC: Toast and Strawberries Press.

Robinson, M. (1953), "New York Beat," *Jet*, September 10: 64.

"Society by Cynthia" (1963), *New Pittsburgh Courier*, October 5: 4.

"Spotlight on Black Design" (2001), *New York Times*, May 2: 2.

"Town Still Talking About Fashion Show" (1942), *New York Amsterdam Star-News*, May 2: 12–13.

"Westchesterite Designs Clothes" (1941), *New York Amsterdam Star-News*, November 15: 12.

Wynn, Z. (1995), Interview with Ed Schoelwer [Transcript of an Oral History Interview], May 4, New York, NY.

Young, M. (1957), "The Grapevine," *Pittsburgh Courier*, June 8: A3.

"Zulu, Swahili Songs Offered" (1967), *New York Amsterdam News*, January 14: 16.

16 VICKY TIEL: A COUTURIÈRE IN PARIS

LOURDES FONT

In 1963 Vicky Tiel was a 19-year-old student at New York's Parsons School of Design. Her outrageous personal style caused her to stand out among her classmates. A typical outfit was a leather mini-skirt and a see-through lace top. The head of the fashion design department threatened to expel her, saying that she had no future on Seventh Avenue and should consider Hollywood or Las Vegas. The young woman responded that she had no interest in Seventh Avenue: "I'm going to be a couturier in Paris" (Tiel 2011: 18). For over fifty years, Vicky Tiel has been exactly that—an American-born *couturière* in Paris. She first made her name as one-half of Fonssagrives-Tiel, Sixties "youthquake" designers and co-owners of the boutique Mia-Vicky. During the next three decades, she evolved into a *couturière* whose evening gowns give women hourglass curves and movie star glamour. In 1989, she introduced the first of her fragrances, and in 2011, she published a memoir, *It's All About the Dress,* that stands out in its genre for its candor and practical advice.

Vicky Tiel's career began when she was still in junior high school in Chevy Chase, Maryland. Her father was a building contractor and her mother a "frustrated artist" (Tiel 2011: 5) who divorced in her early childhood. In 1954, when Tiel was 11, her mother's remarriage to an official in the Internal Revenue Service took them to the Washington, DC, suburb, where most fathers worked for the federal government and most mothers were at home. The mother of Tiel's best friend, however, managed the couture salon of the local Saks Fifth Avenue and brought home fashion magazines that the two girls pored over. The glamour exuded by the model Dorian Leigh and the film star Elizabeth Taylor, whose hairstyle Tiel tried to imitate, made an indelible impression. At the age of 12, Tiel decided to become a fashion designer; she acquired a sewing machine and taught herself to make clothes. By the time she was in high school, she was selling her original designs to classmates, with labels reading "Vickie Tiel." In her school yearbook, a classmate wrote: "I'll see you in Paris where I'll buy your dresses" (Tiel 2011: 7). Her immediate destination, however, was New York.

In 1961 Tiel enrolled at the Pratt Institute in Brooklyn, where she spent the fall term before transferring to Parsons and her own apartment in Greenwich Village. She arrived in the Village at the height of the folk music scene (Hajdu 2001). Armed with a "fearless personality" (Tiel 2011: 88) and a confidence in her body that she attributed to ballet and cheerleading, she flourished in its atmosphere of social and sexual revolution. At first, she attended parties "filled with crazily dressed artists of all colors and shapes" (Tiel 2011: 12) dressed in black cocktail dresses, but she soon freed herself from conventional good taste. She frequented the Playhouse Café and the Café Wha?, hoping to be hired as a "pass-the-hat girl" for the performers. Though she saw Bob Dylan, Woody Allen, and Lenny Bruce perform, she was particularly interested in the singer Steve DeNaut, whose image in tight black leather had dominated the walls of her dorm at Pratt. Tiel began to dress in leather herself. Soon she was DeNaut's girlfriend and passed the hat at his performances, and he publicly christened her "Peaches LaTour." At her apartment, decorated with fashion sketches and mirrors, she held weekly costume parties where she might appear wearing a "G-string along with autumn leaves glued to my breasts" (Tiel 2011: 21). Semi-nude, she was photographed for *Show*, a new magazine covering the arts. Within two years, Tiel had become the Kiki de Montparnasse of Greenwich Village.

At the same time, she began to take her work more seriously. Her father told her that after graduation she would be on her own and advised her to always earn her own money and never be dependent on a man. She came to appreciate this advice as "revolutionary" and inspiring (Tiel 2011: 10). Peaches LaTour, the freewheeling, bohemian student, was also an entrepreneur. At her parties, the apartment became a boutique, with leather skirts and matching fringed, beaded vests hung on the brick walls. She sold the outfits for $175, the cost of her monthly rent, and they sold well because there was nothing like them in conventional stores. In 1962 Tiel made her shortest leather skirt yet; in an attempt to create an ensemble of skirt, vest, and matching bag, she ran out of material. The skirt was four inches above her knee, and she didn't think anyone would buy it, so she wore it herself. She remembered that "when I walked down the street, men's heads turned! What a feeling! I would make the next skirt shorter, then shorter" (2011: 16).

Vicky Tiel's student designs were some of the first mini-skirts seen on the streets of New York. By 1962, she was wearing see-through crochet mini-dresses and her first wrap dresses. Ironically, her innovations did not win her any praise at Parsons. In the early 1960s, the school's faculty and guest critics were mostly men with conservative tastes. They included James Galanos and Norman Norell, both

FIGURE 16.1 Mini-skirts, fringed leather, and crochet lace: Vicky Tiel's student designs, 1962. Sketch by Vicky Tiel. © Vicky Tiel, 2016.

renowned for ready-to-wear that rivaled the quality of Paris couture (Finger 1982; Bradley 1996). Tiel found them to be "shy and nervous. They seemed to fret and worry about where to place each button, and every decision prompted a major discussion. I found all this fussiness extremely tedious" (2011: 17). The greatest gift she got from Parsons, Tiel recalled, was "girlfriends. I sat in class with Mary Alice Orito, now the president of the National Association of Women Artists, on one side of me, and Mia on the other" (Tiel 2016a).

Mia Fonssagrives was the daughter of the Swedish model Lisa Fonssagrives (*née* Bernstone) and her first husband Fernand Fonssagrives, a photographer and sculptor, and the stepdaughter of Irving Penn. She too created all her own clothes, in simple but innovative shapes. Most of Mia's classmates were intimidated by her (Tiel 2011). The tall brunette was well on her way to becoming one of the "Beautiful People" in Diana Vreeland's *Vogue*. In the August 15, 1963 issue, she modeled her own black sweater dress for Penn's camera. To Tiel, Mia was "fashion royalty" (2011: 45), but she did not hesitate to approach her when fashion brought them together:

> One day I walked into our classroom at Parsons wearing a turquoise burlap wrap skirt with a black lace see-thru T-shirt. Mia was wearing a purple rectangle wrap skirt with two strings that crossed around her narrow hips. Wrap skirt meets wrap skirt... "Our skirts have to meet," I told her with a smile. (2011: 27)

During their final year at Parsons, their individual styles converged. As Tiel put it, "we were each other's favorite designer" (2011: 43). They decided to go into business together and move to Paris. Tiel had visited the city for the first time the previous summer during a Parsons course in Europe and fallen "madly in love with Paris" (Tiel 2011: 33).

They arrived in June 1964 with eighteen pieces of luggage and two sewing machines. Tiel had $2,000 saved from sales of her leather ensembles. Mia had an asset that proved to be more valuable: an introduction to her mother's friend Dorian Leigh (Tiel 2011). The former model had lived in Paris since the 1950s and founded the first professional modeling agency there (Gross 1995). Mia and Vicky went to see her, wearing "cut-velvet see-through lavender and peach minidresses with ostrich-feather boas" (Tiel 2011: 38). The following day, they were guests at Dorian Leigh's wedding to her fifth husband, where their dresses were six inches shorter than those of the other women. They made an impression on the couturier Louis Féraud, who invited them to contribute designs, which they would model themselves, to his next collection (Tiel 2011).

A former boutique owner from Cannes, Louis Féraud was himself a newcomer in Paris fashion. Propelled by the patronage of Brigitte Bardot, he presented his first haute couture collection in 1960 (Quintanilla 1999). The press (Brady 1964; Petersen 1964) associated him with the emerging "ye-ye" popular culture, influenced by American music and films. Working in their hotel room, Mia and Vicky sketched independently and edited their sketches together. Tiel remembered that "we knew the two designs we chose would make us or break us, as the world fashion press never missed a Louis Féraud fashion show" (2011: 43). The show took place on July 27, 1964 (Brady 1964). Mia wore a purple suede mini-dress cut to reveal her navel. Vicky wore a denim mini-coat lined in lime green *faux* fur (Petersen 1964; Tiel 2011). When they stepped onto the runway, they were launched on a magic carpet ride that lasted for the rest of the decade.

In the weeks that followed, Mia and Vicky became "It girls" at the center of a storm of publicity. They were photographed everywhere in Paris, in the streets, in nightclubs, at the apartment they rented near the Arc de Triomphe, and "wearing bikinis on swings in the Luxembourg Gardens" (Tiel 2011: 43). Since they were not just models and personalities, but also designers, they were offered contracts to design dresses, coats, swimwear, and hosiery. Between 1964 and 1967, they designed collections for two Paris boutiques, Snob and Madd, the British chain Wallis Shops, the New York department store Bloomingdale's, and the Seventh Avenue manufacturer Andrew Arkin ("Fashion" 1965; "Eye: MADD Clothes" 1966; Bender 1967; Sheppard 1967; Sweetinburgh 1966; Tiel 2011). For the American swimsuit brand Rose Marie Reid, they designed string bikinis (Tiel 2011). For a profile in *LIFE* magazine, they were photographed working at their Paris apartment—sketching on the roof, cutting out patterns on the living room floor, and dyeing fabric in their bathroom in their bikinis. Mia and Vicky, the reporter wrote, had "the city of Dior and Balenciaga at their feet" ("Fashion" 1965). In December 1964 they briefly returned to New York to appear on the *Tonight Show* with Johnny Carson, Vicky in a green mini-jumpsuit and Mia in a purple velvet coat (Tiel 2014).

The Mia and Vicky phenomenon can be seen as another example of the media's appetite for young and beautiful faces to spin stories around. Their instant success also demonstrates how much fashion had changed since the start of the 1960s. They favored metallic fabrics, bright colors, mini-dresses with cut-outs or girlish ruffles, skirt-and-bra ensembles, jumpsuits, tights in printed patterns or lace, feather boas, and floppy mobcaps. *LIFE* described their style as "wacky chic" and reported that they "frequently dash off outfits in late afternoon that they will wear out on dates that night" ("Fashion" 1965). By 1965, fashion had to be easy, fast, and fun, or it wasn't fashionable.

FIGURE 16.2 "Wacky Chic": Vicky Tiel and Mia Fonssagrives wearing their own designs in November 1967. Photo by Reg Lancaster/Daily Express/Getty Images.

When two Hollywood producers spotted Mia and Vicky dancing at Castel's nightclub, Mia in a navy and gold mini-dress with a triangle cut-out to show her navel, and Vicky in a gold lamé bra with a matching mini-skirt, they were hired to design their first film costumes ("Fashion" 1965; Tiel 2011). *What's New, Pussycat?* (1965) was a sex farce centering on the editor of a Paris fashion magazine, played by Peter O'Toole. It was also Woody Allen's screenwriting and feature film acting debut. "Fonssagrives-Tiel" were credited with Paula Prentiss's costumes, which included a printed lamé bra and matching mini-skirt much like Vicky's own Castel's outfit, and a polka-dot mini-dress trimmed with feathers. In honor of their coffeehouse days in Greenwich Village, Allen offered to write a small role for Tiel, but instead she asked that a look-alike actress appear in the opening scene (Tiel 2011). Allen's character is shown at a café with a young woman dressed in black leather and the same multicolored tights worn by both Vicky and Mia ("Fashion" 1965; Tiel 2011).

As new opportunities to work on films arose, Tiel took the lead. While Mia, who was romantically involved with Louis Féraud, remained in Paris, Tiel spent most of 1965 in Los Angeles working on film projects, including a screen adaptation of their own story, "two American girls who take on Paris couture" (Tiel 2011: 91). Although the script, titled *The Ye-Ye Girls* (Sweetinburgh 1966), was eventually shelved, Mia and Vicky were wealthier by $80,000, which they intended to finance their own boutique in the future (Tiel 2011).

In 1966 Edith Head sponsored Tiel's admission into the film costumers' union, and advised her not to try to do both costume and fashion design. That year she returned to Paris, but she and Mia continued to design for films (Tiel 2011). Their next was *Grand Prix* (1966), set in the world of Formula One racing. Françoise Hardy, the French pop star, played the girlfriend of a racecar driver. Mia and Vicky dressed her in simple separates in bright solid colors and stripes (Tiel 2011). It was a cleaner look than their "wacky chic" and in keeping with the film's sleek production design. The following year they dressed the teenage protagonist of *Candy* (1968) in "a mint green mini-wrap dress and white bunny fur minicoat" (Tiel 2011: 154) and also created the ruffled shirt and velvet jacket worn by Richard Burton. As a result of her relationship with Ron Berkeley, Burton's friend and makeup artist, Tiel joined the entourage of Burton and Elizabeth Taylor, then at the height of their fame (Tiel 2011).

In 1967, Mia and Vicky took steps to strike down roots in Paris. Mia married Louis Féraud (Emerson 1967) and she and Vicky announced that they would open their own boutique on the Left Bank, backed by Elizabeth Taylor (Bender 1967). They found a location off a courtyard at no. 21, rue Bonaparte. Mia described the boutique's first collection as "mad, crazy, sexy things" ranging widely in price. They wanted to dress the students at the nearby École des Beaux Arts and "very rich hippie people" (Bender 1967: 50), for whom they would make custom clothes in rare vintage fabrics they had been collecting. The sixty-piece collection was shown at a party at Elizabeth Taylor's favorite Paris restaurant, Maxim's, during the couture openings in January 1968. *The New York Times*'s Gloria Emerson described soft jerseys, satins and velvets, and hemlines ranging from "micro-mini" to "maxi." Luxury was emphasized with real diamonds, courtesy of Van Cleef & Arpels, decorating coats, dresses, and even swimsuits. One bikini had a semi-circular cut-out over the *derrière*, adorned with a diamond pin "just in case you didn't notice" (Emerson 1968: 36).

The day "Mia-Vicky" opened its doors, May 3, 1968, was also the first day of clashes between student demonstrators and police in the streets surrounding the Sorbonne, inaugurating the "events of May" that threatened to topple the French government (Lichfield 2008). That evening the festivities at the boutique were dampened only by rain, leaving the overflow crowd of "flower people … in the courtyard under umbrellas in drooping velvet and feathers" ("WWDeadline" 1968: 19). Over the next few weeks, as street battles escalated, tear gas reached the boutique and they were forced to close the door to the courtyard. Tiel remembered that "our beautiful new shop was filled with wounded students" (Tiel 2011: 121). In June, President De Gaulle's party won a decisive election victory, and by July revolutionary fervor had subsided. Historians believe that the legacy of May 1968 was cultural rather than political, and see it as the manifestation in France of an international "youthquake" (Lichfield 2008).

The Mia-Vicky boutique, with its sunken "conversation pit," attracted young "rich hippies" like Bianca Jagger, as anticipated (Tiel 2011: 130–131). Tiel fueled their taste for the exotic with Bedouin caftans that she bought in Israel while working on the film *Bloomfield* (1971). The shop's collections were made by couture-trained workers, led by a master tailor and a dressmaker hired from Féraud's atelier (Tiel 2016a). The designs were reproduced in America by the Youthquake division of Puritan Fashions, owners of the Paraphernalia boutiques. Tiel traveled to New York to select American fabrics for the line, and she told the press that "when we create for Paris, we'll be creating exactly the same clothes for the American market." She said their fall 1969 collection would be "simple—not wild or way out. There are too many freakish clothes around today" (McDermott 1969: 67).

Striking a balance between youthful and "freakish" in 1969, however, proved difficult. The fall collection they showed in July featured "hot pants," the abbreviated shorts they had worn themselves for years, jumpsuits, and a long crochet sweater with *trompe-l'oeil* hands reaching up to cover the breasts. As Tiel later acknowledged, "nothing sold," and "the photo shoots stopped" (2011: 174–175). She sensed that their magic carpet ride was coming to an end: "Mia and I had had almost six years of glory—of being photographed and adored everywhere we went while we were young and beautiful—and now it was time to move on" (2011: 175). By 1970, Mia had moved on, withdrawing from the boutique and ending her marriage to Féraud. She returned to the United States and became a sculptor and jewelry designer (Tiel 2011; Havens 2009).

In the early 1970s, Tiel met the challenge of establishing herself in Paris as a solo designer. She renamed the boutique "Vicky Tiel" and changed the décor, creating a setting "like a garden in a Cecil Beaton picture" (De Leusse 1972: 26). Staying true to her preference for flattering, feminine clothes in soft fabrics, she never again strayed into "freakish" territory. "I've gotten away from ugly or costumy fashion," she told a journalist in March 1971. "Now I'm concentrating on romantic, pretty clothes" (McL 1971). Some of her designs were reminiscent of Vionnet, such as the "Bra Dress," a slender, bias-cut dress with a draped bodice ("French Ready-to-Wear" 1972). She benefited from the boom in European ready-to-wear, establishing ties to American retailers who wanted made-in-Paris labels. In 1972, she envisioned that "the boutique will become a sort of junior couture, in between boutique and couture" (De Leusse 1972: 26). The shop attracted the sophisticated "It girls" of the era, such as Jacqueline Bisset and Marisa Berenson ("Eye: In Paris" 1974; "Eye: Budding Artist" 1974). In 1973 Tiel toured the United States and Canada in support of her spring collection ("Eye: On The Road" 1973). In France, her hard work began to pay off as well. She told *Women's Wear* that "even the French are now accepting me as a designer and not just 'the American girl' or 'Elizabeth Taylor's friend'" (Grassi 1973). She continued to design for films, dressing Faye Dunaway in *La maison sous les arbres* (1971) and Racquel Welch, Virna Lisi, and Nathalie Delon, Richard Burton's co-stars in *Bluebeard* (1972). In February 1971, the Burtons attended her wedding to Ron Berkeley, and until her first son, Rex, was born in January 1975, Tiel often traveled with them from luxury hotel to yacht to rented villa. By the time her younger son, Richard, was born three years later, her way of life had dramatically changed (Tiel 2011).

In the late 1970s and early 1980s, Tiel and her family lived surrounded by fashion in a sprawling apartment on the Boulevard Saint-Germain. She moved her design staff into the front rooms so she could work at home (Tiel 2011). In 1978, she welcomed the *New York Times*'s Bernadine Morris with "one child in her arms, the other clinging to her skirts" (Morris 1978: C1). There were also "dogs, cats, … two nannies…, a Portuguese driver, and Tunisian-Italian seamstresses" (Tiel 2011: 192). Many of Tiel's workers worked in their own homes, in close-knit immigrant communities in the suburbs of Paris. A van emblazoned "Vicky Tiel" shuttled back and forth among the workforce. As her designs grew more structured and ornamented, she drew upon Portuguese women's embroidery skills, and the Tunisians' experience with corsetry techniques. Some workers would be with her for thirty or forty years (Tiel 2016a). In 1978, her ready-to-wear collections were carried in forty-five American stores (Morris 1978). At Henri Bendel, the New York store known for its "street of shops," she had her own boutique from 1976. In 1980, Dawn Mello, fashion director of Bergdorf Goodman, encouraged her move to Bergdorf's (Tiel 2016a). On the West Coast, in stores such as Giorgio's Beverly Hills, her dresses were often selected by film costumers, who instead of creating original designs, now increasingly shopped for their costumes (Stroud 1974; LaVine 1980).

During these years, Tiel began to concentrate on her couture evening dresses:

> I enjoyed being a hands-on designer like Coco Chanel, measuring and designing gowns for each individual woman, entering their lives with a special dress for a special moment. (Tiel 2011: 193)

This shift was also timely, since Paris couture was enjoying a revival as fashion's "laboratory of ideas" (Jacobs 1995: 27). Yves Saint Laurent, the living designer Tiel most admired (Tiel 2016a), had demonstrated that a single dazzling haute couture collection could still change the course of fashion. From his "Ballets Russes" collection in July 1976 to the July 1987 opening of Christian Lacroix, haute couture attracted a new generation of clients. Nonetheless, most couture houses operated at a significant loss (George 1987). Vicky Tiel, on the other hand, built a profitable couture business on a smaller scale, by personally catering to her clients.

One such client was Anne Parillaud, a young French actress who needed a dress for the Cannes Film Festival in 1979. Tiel designed a dress in lime green chiffon, with drapery around the neckline and hips and a scarf falling to the floor. It appeared to be very light and ethereal, but inside was an armature of twenty-four metal bones, giving the body an hourglass shape. This was the first "Torrid" dress (Tiel 2011). It came out of Tiel's study of corsets made by Poupie Cadolle, whose family firm had been making custom lingerie in Paris since 1889. The metal bones, arranged in pairs and shaped to fit the individual woman, were available only from a French supplier. The fact that she worked in Paris and had access to such resources thus made a difference in Tiel's evolution as a designer. As she expressed it, "Paris is the place where the body comes first" (Tiel 2016a).

Tiel's impulse toward corsetry was driven by a 1950s inspiration, common to many designers in the 1980s. She later wrote that "Torrid" was inspired by a sculpture of Ava Gardner seen in the 1954 film *The Barefoot Contessa* (Tiel 2011). She also remembered the elegance of Lisa Fonssagrives and the allure of Dorian Leigh in the fashion magazines she had grown up with. In the 1980s her evening dresses recaptured that glamour for her clients, who included Farrah Fawcett, Goldie Hawn, Anjelica Huston, Princess Stephanie of Monaco, and the stars of the television series *Dynasty* (Johnson 1986). The strapless, figure-hugging "Mummy" and the "Pouf" dress with a bubbly puffed skirt were designs that, like "Torrid," became Vicky Tiel classics. In 1986, Tiel was photographed wearing a "Mummy" dress, surrounded by models, for *People* magazine (Johnson 1986). Her appearances in full-page advertisements in *Vogue* also raised her profile in the United States. In her early forties, Vicky looked like the ultimate woman of the 1980s, in "power suits" with padded shoulders and fitted waistlines (Advertisement 1986a) or in sensuous evening dresses (Advertisement 1986b). She considered her strapless red

FIGURE 16.3 Designs of the 1970s, culminating in "Torrid." Sketch by Vicky Tiel. © Vicky Tiel, 2016.

leather gown "the perfect outfit for seduction" (2011: 248), and she put her theory into practice in the mid-1980s, as her marriage to Ron Berkeley broke down and she rejoined the dating scene. In 1987, Tiel met her second husband, Mike Hamilton, while visiting friends in Key West, Florida. Tiel felt the same way about Florida as she did about Paris: "love at first sight" (Tiel 2011: 263). She began to divide her time between Paris, New York, and Key West, later moving to a farm in northern Florida. At the end of the 1980s, she prepared to take on a new challenge.

One of the highlights of Tiel's life, when she was first establishing her solo career in Paris, was meeting Gabrielle "Coco" Chanel shortly before she died. In the fall of 1970, Elizabeth Taylor and Richard Burton threw a dinner party at the home of the hairdresser Alexandre to give Tiel the opportunity to meet her "idol" (Tiel 2011: 313). Chanel advised the young fashion designer to launch her own fragrance. Success in fashion was ephemeral, Chanel said. Only a great fragrance lasted. Tiel acted on this advice with her first fragrance, "Vicky Tiel," launched in America in 1990 ("Tiel's Saks Act" 1990; Collier 1990). In that year she also opened new couture salons at Bergdorf Goodman and Neiman-Marcus (Tiel 2011) and had a hand in one of the most successful films. A red silk jersey version of her "Torrid" dress, a perennial favorite at Giorgio's Beverly Hills, was spotted in the store's windows by the costume designer for *Pretty Woman*. It was then made for Julia Roberts to wear in the film's climactic scenes. In the 1990s, Tiel continued to travel throughout the United States to attend to clients, telling a journalist that she had personally hemmed a client's dress that day ("Tiel's Seduction" 1990). In 1992, she told *Women's Wear Daily* she was making 5,000 dresses a year, "handmade, one by one, in Paris" that sold for up to $5,000 (Haber 1992: 12). Although she never gave celebrities free dresses, they were seen on red carpets from London to Los Angeles.

FIGURE 16.4 Vicky Tiel's "Torrid" evening dress in ivory lace, at the Academy of Motion Picture Arts and Sciences Oscar Fashion Preview, March 1999. REUTERS/Alamy Stock Photo.

In 1994, for John Lennon's induction into the Rock n' Roll Hall of Fame, Yoko Ono wore a black Vicky Tiel dress with a corseted, beaded bodice. A year earlier, two of her designs had entered the Metropolitan Museum of Art (MMA).

As the new century began, Tiel "woke up and realized I was about to have a forty-year career without a break! Collection after collection, season after season" (2011: 313). She had created a repertory of designs and a style that was recognizably hers. By the time her memoir appeared in 2011, she was venturing into new fields, selling fragrances and a ready-to-wear line on the Home Shopping Network, writing for the *Huffington Post*, and lecturing to fashion design students in New York. Believing that women designers have a greater understanding of women's needs and desires, Vicky Tiel has sought to "simply make flattering dresses for women to wear for personal empowerment" (Tiel 2013). She is now the longest-surviving woman designer in Paris and still going strong.

Bibliography

Advertisement: Vicky Tiel, Photograph by Ron Berkeley (1986a), *Vogue* [U.S.], 176(4) April 1: 141.

Advertisement: Vicky Tiel, Photograph by Ron Berkeley (1986b), *Vogue* [U.S.], 176(1) January 1: 52.

Bender, M. (1967), "The Burtons Buy a Share in Mia-Vicky: An Instant Success Here on Business," *New York Times*, October 25: 50.

Bradley, B.W. (1996), *Galanos*, Cleveland: The Western Reserve Historical Society.

Brady, J.W. (1964), "The Main Event: Paris Opens Today," *Women's Wear Daily*, 109(18) July 27: 1, 20.

Collier, E. (1990), "Beauty & Health: Scent and Sensibility: More Designer Fragrances are Competing to Seduce the Woman of Style," *Vogue*, 180 (5) May 1: 278–279.

De Leusse, C. (1972), "Vicky Tiel: Gentleness on Her Mind," *Women's Wear Daily*, 124(24) February 3: 26.

Emerson, G. (1967), "A Fashion Wedding in Paris," *New York Times*, March 27: 28.

Emerson, G. (1968), "Boutique with New Label: Liz Taylor," *New York Times*, January 22: 36.

"Eye: Budding Artist" (1974), *Women's Wear Daily*, 129 (112) December 5: 6.

"Eye: MADD Clothes" (1966), *Women's Wear Daily*, 112 (81) April 25: 2.

"Eye: In Paris" (1974), *Women's Wear Daily*, 128(66) April 4: 7.

"Eye: On The Road" (1973), *Women's Wear Daily*, 126(5) January 8: 16.

"Fashion: Two American Girls Show Paris" (1965), *LIFE*, 58(5) February 5: 94–99.

"Fashions in Living: Irving Penn's Love Letter to a Farm" (1963) *Vogue* [U.S.], 142(3) August 15: 120–129.

Finger, M. (1982), *Memoirs of Norman Norell: Six People Interviewed by Mildred Finger*. [Typescript of sound recording]. At: New York: Fashion Institute of Technology Library, Special Collections, TT139.O73.v45.

"French Ready-to-Wear: A Special WWD Feature" (1972), *Women's Wear Daily*, 124(53) March 16: 21–28.

George, L. (1987), "Paris Couture: Alive and Well," *Women's Wear Daily*, 153(41) March 3: 1, 4.

Grassi, A. (1973), "Eye: Monte Carlo Opening," *Women's Wear Daily*, 126(110) June 5: 18.

Gross, M. (1995), *Model: The Ugly Business of Beautiful Women*, New York: William Morrow.

Haber, H. (1992), "Costa to Produce Line of Bridge-Price Evening Wear by Tiel," *Women's Wear Daily*, 163(37) February 24: 11.

Hajdu, D. (2001), *Positively 4th Street*, New York: Farrar, Straus and Giroux.

Havens, L. (2009), Mia Fonssagrives Solow. Available online: http://www .miafonssagrivessolow.com/bio.html

Jacobs, L. (1995), *The Art of Haute Couture*, New York: Abbeville.

Johnson, B. (1986), "American in Paris Vicky Tiel Has Built Her Reputation on Gowns a Cut Below the Rest," *People*, 26(9) September 1: 119ff.

LaVine, W. R. (1980), *In a Glamorous Fashion: The Fabulous Years of Hollywood Costume Design*, New York: Charles Scribner's Sons.

Lichfield, J. (2008), "Egalité! Liberté, Sexualité!: Paris, May 1968," *The Independent*, February 22. Available online: http://www.independent.co.uk/news/world/europe /egalit-libert-sexualit-paris-may-1968-784703.html

McDermott, T. (1969), "Fashion RTW: Confirm Mia-Vicky Sign Puritan Fashions Pact," *Women's Wear Daily*, 118(64) April 1: 37.

McL [*sic*], B. (1971), "Boutique Row: On Her Own," *Women's Wear Daily*, 122(43) March 4: 12.

Metropolitan Museum of Art [MMA]. Available online: http://www.metmuseum.org/art /collection#!?q=Vicky%20Tiel&sortBy=Relevance&sortOrder=asc&offset=0&pageSi ze=20

Morris, B. (1978), "An American in Paris: The Eclectic Spirit," *New York Times*, May 18: C1.

Petersen, P. (1964), "Newcomer a Hit as Paris Shows Open," *New York Times*, July 28: 21.

Quintanilla, M. (1999), "Master of French Fashion: Louis Feraud," *Los Angeles Times*, December 29. Available online: http://articles.latimes.com/1999/dec/29/news/mn -48557

Sheppard, E. (1967), "Inside Fashion: The Fashion Show Was on the Guests," *Women's Wear Daily*, 115(207), October 25: 8.

Stroud, K. (1974), "Eye: Top Tiels," *Women's Wear Daily*, 129(122) December 19: 8.

Sweetinburgh, T. (1966), "The Knack of Two Darlings," *Women's Wear Daily*, 112(37), February 22: 10.

Tiel, V. (2011), *It's All About the Dress: What I Learned in Forty Years About Men, Women, Sex, and Fashion*, New York: St. Martin's Press.

Tiel, V. (2013), "Fashion Historians and Fashionistas Take Note," *The Huffington Post*, July 26. Available online: http://www.huffingtonpost.com/vicky-tiel/fashion-historians-fashio_b_3654566.html

Tiel, V. (2014), "Artists, Assume the World is Waiting for You," *The Huffington Post*, July 23. Available online: http://www.huffingtonpost.com/vicky-tiel/artists-assume-the -world-_b_5609600.html

Tiel, V. (2016a), Telephone interviews with the author, July 25–26, 2016.

Tiel, V. (2016b), Vicky Tiel's website: Celebrity Sketches. Available online: http://vickytiel .com/celebrity-sketches/ Vicky Tiel.com

"Tiel's Saks Act" (1990), *Women's Wear Daily*, 159(78) April 20: 12.

"Tiel's Seduction" (1990), *Women's Wear Daily*, 159(14) January 19: 12.

"WWDeadline: Swinging in the Rain" (1968), *Women's Wear Daily*, 116(90) May 7: 19.

INDEX